DEDUCTION

Deduction

P.N. Johnson-Laird

Department of Psychology
Princeton University
Green Hall
Princeton
NJ 08544, USA.

Ruth M.J. Byrne

Department of Psychology
Trinity College
University of Dublin
Dublin 2, Ireland

LAWRENCE ERLBAUM ASSOCIATES, PUBLISHERS
Hove (UK)   Hillsdale (USA)

Reprinted 1992

Lawrence Erlbaum Associates Ltd., Publishers
27 Palmeira Mansions
Church Road
Hove
East Sussex, BN3 2FA
U.K.

British Library Cataloguing in Publication Data

Johnson-Laird, P.N. (Philip Nicholas)
   I. Title II. Byrne, Ruth M.J.
   162

Librarians please shelve under subject classification:
Psychology. Human Deduction

   ISBN 0-86377-148-3 (Hbk)√
   ISBN 0-86377-149-1 (Pbk)
   ISSN 0959-4779 (Essays in Cognitive Psychology)

Printed and bound in the United Kingdom by BPCC Wheatons Ltd., Exeter

Contents

I'm thirsty, he said. I have sevenpence. Therefore I buy a pint. ...
The conclusion of your syllogism, I said lightly, is fallacious, being based
on licensed premises.

Flann O'Brien. At Swim-two-Birds. (1939, p. 20)

Prologue

In 1983, Phil Johnson-Laird published *Mental Models*, a book in which he argued that when people understand discourse they construct an internal representation—a mental model—of the state of affairs that it describes. These models are akin to those that are constructed when people perceive the world, though discourse models are rudimentary and incomplete. He also proposed that deduction depends, not on formal rules of inference, but on a search for alternative models of the premises that would refute a putative conclusion. Perhaps the most important models, however, are those that individuals have of themselves because these models lie at the heart of consciousness and intentional behaviour.

With one exception, *Mental Models* was well-received by cognitive scientists. The exception was the reaction of ardent advocates of rule theories—those who believe that reasoning depends on formal rules of inference. Johnson-Laird was surprised by the intensity of this small chorus of dissenters. He had imagined (in retrospect, naively) that the experimental evidence about various forms of reasoning ruled decisively in favour of mental models.

In 1983, Ruth Byrne started research on a novel way of studying reasoning. Even the simplest valid deductions could be suppressed, she showed, if the subjects' general knowledge conflicted with the conclusion. Other researchers had used the technique to suppress fallacious inferences, but she was the first to suppress valid deductions. And she used the theory of mental models to explain the phenomenon. This research was the foundation of her Ph.D., which was subsequently awarded by the University of Dublin, Trinity College.

In 1986, we began a joint investigation into the psychology of deduction. Our starting point was both the need to extend the mental model theory of reasoning to the full range of deductive inferences, and the need to strengthen the experimental evidence in favour of the theory. These goals have now been achieved. We have formulated the first comprehensive theory in psychology to explain all the main varieties of deduction—propositional reasoning, relational reasoning, and quantificational reasoning. The evidence from our experiments has enabled us to compare formal rules and mental models as theories of human reasoning. There will be no prize for guessing the outcome. Finally, we have implemented computer programs that model the theory, and, as an exercise in artificial intelligence, we have developed other programs that transcend the limitations of human reasoning.

The present monograph brings together the principal results of our research during the last three years. We hope that it will convince dispassionate readers that the mental model theory provides a powerful explanation of how logically-untutored individuals make deductions. We have striven to make our results accessible to anyone with an interest in how the mind works. No previous background in cognitive science is necessary. The research has been exciting and we aim to communicate some of the fun that it has given us.

Phil Johnson Laird
Ruth Byrne
January, 1990

Acknowledgements

Any book on research is a doubly collaborative effort. There are those who have helped to carry out the research and those who have helped in the preparation of the book. We have been fortunate: these two groups have far exceeded their duties, and some exceptional individuals have been members of both teams. Our long-standing research partners are: Mark Keane (University of Dublin, Trinity College, Ireland) on the psychology of argumentation; Jane Oakhill and Alan Garnham (University of Sussex, England) on the effects of beliefs on reasoning; Walter Schaeken (University of Leuven, Belgium) on propositional inference; and Patrizia Tabossi (University of Bologna, Italy) on multiply-quantified inference. In addition, our research on deduction has benefited from thought-provoking discussions with Tony Anderson, Bruno Bara, Martin Conway, John Darley, Rachel Falmagne, Ken Gilhooly, Sam Glucksberg, Thomas Green, Ben Johnson-Laird, Paolo and Maria Legrenzi, Christopher Longuet-Higgins, Juan Garcia Madruga, Tony Marcel, Jesus Martin Cordero, George Miller, Allen Newell, Ian Nimmo-Smith, Keith Oatley, Thad Polk, Steve Pulman, Stuart Sutherland, David Shanks, Paul Thagard, Eric Wanner, and, finally, the doyen of the psychology of deduction, Peter Wason. Many others, of course, have given us stimulating ideas and encouragement, and our ideas have been sharpened by comments from the referees of our papers, and from members of the audiences of talks that we have given. We thank all these individuals.

The research was carried out while we were both at the Medical Research Council's Applied Psychology Unit in Cambridge. We thank its Director, Alan Baddeley, for providing us with the facilities that we needed for our research, and we thank our colleagues there for the supportive ambiance they provided. We are also grateful to our new homes for accommodating us so swiftly, and enabling us to complete this book: The Department of Psychology, and the Program for Cognitive Studies, at Princeton University; and the Departments of Psychology, University of Dublin, and University of Wales, Cardiff.

Several people read the entire first draft of the book: Jonathan Evans, Alan Garnham, Mark Keane, Patrizia Tabossi, Paul Pollard, Stuart Sutherland. They made many helpful suggestions and saved us from many errors and infelicities. We are grateful for their efforts, but readers should not blame them for any errors that remain: we made them in trying to correct those that they discovered. Larry Erlbaum and Michael Forster have been all that publishers should be: generous, committed, and informed.

We are indebted to our families: to Mo, Ben, and Dorothy Johnson-Laird; and to Mark Keane, Mary and Paul Byrne, Mary Alicia Tracey, Linda, Noel, Paul and Laura Deighan, and Cathy, Tony, Lisa, Steven and Jenny Fitzgerald. We dedicate the book, with thanks, to them.

CHAPTER 1

The Logic of Deduction

INTRODUCTION AND PLAN OF THE BOOK

Sherlock Holmes popularized a profound misconception about deduction. At their first meeting, the great detective surprised Dr. Watson by remarking: "you have been in Afghanistan". Later he explained his methods:

> From long habit the train of thoughts ran so swiftly through my mind that I arrived at the conclusion without being conscious of intermediate steps. There were such steps, however. The train of reasoning ran, "Here is a gentleman of a medical type, but with the air of a military man. Clearly, an army doctor, then. He has just come from the tropics, for his face is dark, and that is not the natural tint of his skin for his wrists are fair. He has undergone hardship and sickness, as his haggard face says clearly. His left arm has been injured. He holds it in a stiff and unnatural manner. Where in the tropics could an English army doctor have seen much hardship and got his arm wounded? Clearly in Afghanistan." The whole train of thought did not occupy a second. I then remarked that you came from Afghanistan, and you were astonished.

(Conan Doyle, 1892, p.24)

Holmes is undoubtedly reasoning, but is he making deductions? Granted that his perceptions and background knowledge are accurate, does it follow that his conclusion must be true? Of course, not. He could have blundered, and Watson might have replied:

1

I am an army doctor, but I have *not* been in Afghanistan. I have been in a Swiss Sanatorium recovering from TB. The sun is responsible for my tan, and my arm was injured in a climbing accident.

Holmes reached a plausible conclusion but he did not make a valid deduction. By definition, a *valid* deduction yields a conclusion that must be true given that its premises are true. The great detective did not always succeed in his cases, but remarkably he seems never to have drawn a conclusion that turned out to be false.

Our topic is deduction, but the case of Sherlock Holmes forces us to consider other sorts of thinking if only to put deduction in its proper place. Plausible inference is different from deduction; daydreaming is different from problem solving; mental arithmetic is different from making a decision. But intuition soon ceases to be a reliable guide to the varieties of thought. A more systematic taxonomy can be based on a computational analysis, and it yields several main sorts of thought (see Johnson-Laird, 1988a). A process of thought can be directed by a goal or it may flow undirected in a "stream of consciousness" in which each idea suggests another. Hobbes (1651) drew the same distinction:

> This Trayne of Thoughts, or Mentall Discourse, is of two sorts. The first is *Unguided, without Designe*, and inconstant .... In which case the thoughts are said to wander, and seem impertinent one to another, as in a Dream.... The second is more constant; as being *regulated* by some desire, and designe. (p. 95)

Among goal-directed thinking, reasoning begins with a definite starting point—a set of observations or premises, and so it can be distinguished from creative processes, which can occur with no clear starting point beyond, say, a blank canvas or an empty sheet of paper. There are three main varieties of reasoning: calculation, deduction, and induction. Calculation is the routine application of a procedure known by heart, as in mental arithmetic. Deduction is a less systematic process in which the goal is to draw a valid consequence from premises. Induction sacrifices validity for plausibility. Like Sherlock Holmes, one often does not have sufficient information to be able to draw a valid inference.

Association, creation, induction, deduction, and calculation, underlie all forms of thought, and so a complete theory of thinking has to explain each of them. In this monograph, we have set ourselves a more modest goal: to explain the nature of deduction and to characterize its underlying mental processes.

Why deduction? One reason is because of its intrinsic importance: it plays a crucial role in many tasks. You need to make deductions in order to formulate plans and to evaluate actions; to determine the consequences of assumptions and hypotheses; to interpret and to formulate instructions, rules, and general principles; to pursue arguments and negotiations; to weigh evidence and to assess data; to decide between competing theories; and to solve problems. A world without deduction would be a world without science, technology, laws, social conventions, and culture. And if you want to dispute this claim, we shall need to assess the validity of your arguments. Another reason for studying deduction is that it is ripe for solution. Unlike the other processes of thought, deduction has been studied sufficiently to be within our grasp. Psychologists have accumulated 80 years' worth of experiments on deductive reasoning (for reviews, see e.g. Wason and Johnson-Laird, 1972; Evans, 1982); they have proposed explicit information-processing theories of its mechanism (see e.g., Erickson, 1974; Braine, 1978; Johnson-Laird, 1983); and workers in artificial intelligence have developed many computer programs that carry out deduction (see e.g. Reiter, 1973; Doyle, 1979; Robinson, 1979; McDermott, 1987).

The present book focuses on our own research, and its plan is simple. In this chapter, we provide a brief but necessary background in logic. We then plunge into the murkier problems of psychology, beginning with the theories of reasoning that were current when we started our research in October 1986. The major part of the book is devoted to our own studies. We start with deductions that depend on propositions that have been formed using such connectives as "and", "or", and "not". We then spend an entire chapter on the notorious problems of "if"—problems that have led some philosophers to abandon hope of a semantic analysis of conditional assertions. Next, we consider deductions that depend on relations between entities, such as "Lisa is taller than Jenny", "Steven is in the same place as Paul", or "Cathy is related to Linda". Relations can hold between sets of individuals and, hence deductions about them often hinge on such words as "any", and "some", and so we consider these quantifiers. We deal with arguments in which each premise contains only a single quantifier (i.e. "syllogisms"), before we turn to premises containing more than one quantifier, such as, "none of the children is in the same place as any of the adults". The three domains of propositional, relational, and quantificational reasoning exhaust the main sorts of deduction. But, an important higher-order sort of thinking is *meta-deduction*, in which deductions concern other deductions or statements explicitly assigning truth or falsity to propositions. Meta-deduction is an important ability because without it human beings are unlikely to have invented formal logic as a discipline. We therefore devote a chapter to the topic. In developing our theory, we have written computer programs that model it. In the penultimate chapter, we describe how to build programs that make deductions from models. We address a problem that workers in artificial intelligence have often confronted: "non-monotonic" reasoning, which is the withdrawal of a conclusion in the light of subsequent information. We also address a problem that they have often evaded: how to draw conclusions that are maximally parsimonious. This work solves a major problem in the design of electronic circuits: how to find the simplest possible circuit for carrying out a particular Boolean operation. Finally, we recapitulate our theory of human reasoning, explore its consequences for cognitive science, and attempt to answer our critics.

We begin with logic because it is the true science of deduction (*pace* Holmes), which arose from a need to determine whether or not inferences are valid. We give a brief introduction to the subject in order to establish the distinction between formal and semantic methods. Readers should proceed at once to the next chapter if they understand why there are direct semantic methods for testing validity in the propositional calculus, but *not* in the predicate calculus.

THE CONCEPT OF LOGICAL FORM

Aristotle, who by his own account was the first logician, noted that certain inferences are valid in virtue of their *form* (see e.g. Kneale and Kneale, 1962). Thus, the valid argument:

All cows are mammals.
All mammals are warm-blooded.
Therefore, all cows are warm-blooded.

has the form:

All A are B.
All B are C.
Therefore, All A are C.

No matter what terms we substitute for A, B, and C, the result is a valid deduction, e.g:

All politicians are authoritarians.
All authoritarians are virtuous.
Therefore, all politicians are virtuous.

You may object that this last conclusion is patently false. And so it is, but remember that a valid conclusion is one that must be true *if* its premises are true. In this case, the premises are false; had they been true, the conclusion would have been true too. Aristotle based his logic on arguments of this sort, which are known as *syllogisms*, and which were long thought to be the centre of the subject; we now know that they are one of its minor suburbs. Nevertheless, the notion of the *form* of a deduction has been central to the development of logic.

Form is a matter of syntax: it depends on the position of certain words, such as "all" and "some", and of other terms within the premises and conclusion. Hence, formal logic is in essence a syntactic device for testing whether the form of an argument is a valid one. Indeed, Leibniz (1666) dreamt of a universal system that would enable all disputes to be resolved by such dispassionate calculations. A step towards the realization of this dream was the invention of the propositional calculus in the nineteenth century.

THE PROPOSITIONAL CALCULUS

The propositional calculus deals with arguments that depend on sentences containing such connectives as "not", "if", "and", and "or". It can be set up in many different, though equivalent, ways. One way, the method of "natural deduction", uses formal rules of inference for each of the different connectives (see e.g. Gentzen, 1935; Prawitz, 1965). A typical example of a formal rule is the following one, which is known as the rule of *modus ponens*:

If p then q
p
Therefore, q.

where p and q are variables that can denote any propositions, no matter how complex. The rule can be used to make the deduction:

If Arthur is in Edinburgh, then Carol is in Glasgow.
Arthur is in Edinburgh.
Therefore, Carol is in Glasgow.

The premises have a logical form that matches the rule, where p equals "Arthur is in Edinburgh" and q equals "Carol is in Glasgow", and so it yields the conclusion. In general, a conclusion can be derived from premises provided that it has a proof in which each step can be made by applying a formal rule of inference to one or more of the earlier assertions in the derivation. Logicians refer to this formal method as "proof-theoretic".

What about the meanings of the connectives? In fact, they can be given an explicit account that motivates the choice of formal rules. Each proposition is assumed to be either true or false. Strictly speaking, it is a mistake to assign truth or falsity to *sentences* in a natural language, because a sentence can be used to assert many different propositions, e.g. "I am here" asserts different propositions depending on who asserts it and where they are. Hence, it is propositions, not sentences, that are true or false (see Strawson, 1950). The meaning of a connective, such as "and", can then be defined solely as a function of the truth values of the propositions that it interconnects. Thus, the conjunction of any two propositions:

p and q

is itself true provided that both of its two constituent propositions are true, and it is false only if one or both of them are false. This definition can be stated in a truth table:

p	q	p and q
True	True	True
True	False	False
False	True	False
False	False	False

where each row represents a separate possible combination of truth values. Because by assumption any proposition is either true or false, there are only four rows in a truth table based on two propositions. The truth value of the conjunction depends solely on the truth values of p and q, and, as the table shows, it is true only if both of them are true.

The meaning of "or" is defined analogously. An *inclusive* disjunction of any two propositions:

p or q, or both

is true provided that at least one of its two constituent propositions is true, and it is false only if they are both false. This definition can also be stated in a truth table:

p	q	p or q (or both)
True	True	True
True	False	True
False	True	True
False	False	False

An *exclusive* disjunction:

p or q, but not both

in contrast, is true only when one of the two propositions is true.

In ordinary discourse, a connective such as "and" may transcend a truth-table definition. The assertion:

He fell off his bicycle and broke his leg.

is usually taken to mean that the first event occurred before the second. Hence, the following conjunction has a different meaning:

He broke his leg and fell off his bicycle.

The two assertions are synonymous according to the truth table definition. This divergence has led some philosophers to argue that the meaning of "and" in certain of its uses does not correspond to any truth table: it can express a temporal or causal relation. Others, notably Grice (1975), have defended the truth table, and argued that it is merely overlaid by pragmatic factors that depend on general knowledge and the conventions of discourse.

The most puzzling case is that of conditional assertions, such as:

If Arthur is in Edinburgh, then Carol is in Glasgow.

This proposition is true when its antecedent ("Arthur is in Edinburgh") and consequent ("Carol is in Glasgow") are both true, and false when its antecedent is true and its consequent false. But, suppose that its antecedent is false, i.e. Arthur is *not* in Edinburgh, is the conditional then true or false? It can hardly be false, and so, since the propositional calculus allows only truth or falsity, it must be true. This treatment yields the following truth table, and the corresponding connective in the calculus is known as *material implication*:

p	q	if p then q
T	T	T
T	F	F
F	T	T
F	F	T

where we have abbreviated "True" as "T" and "False" as "F".

In everyday language, conditional assertions often suggest a relation between antecedent and consequent (see Fillenbaum, 1977). The relation may be a cause or a reason, e.g. "If you tidy your room, then I will take you to the cinema", conveys an implicit negative relation, "if you don't tidy your room, then I won't take you to the cinema". The positive and negative relations taken together are equivalent to the bi-conditional:

If *and only if* you tidy your room, then I will take you to the cinema.

This connective has the following truth table, and it is known as *material equivalence*:

p	q	if and only if p then q
T	T	T
T	F	F
F	T	F
F	F	T

The meaning of "not" concerns only a single proposition, and it reverses its truth value:

p	not p
T	F
F	T

Logicians have considered the equivalences between different combinations of connectives, and they have shown that any truth table can be expressed in terms of negation and inclusive disjunction. For example, the truth table for material implication corresponds to the inclusive disjunction, not-p or q. This construal rather than the conditional, if p then q, perhaps yields a better correspondence between language and logic.

We have shown how to derive conclusions from premises using formal rules, which are sensitive only to the syntactic form of expressions. The reader may be wondering whether there is a way to make deductions that depends, not on the form of expressions, but on their meaning. There is a way that we will now illustrate using the following premises:

Arthur is in Edinburgh or Betty is in Dundee, or both.
Betty is not in Dundee.
If Arthur is in Edinburgh, then Carol is in Glasgow.

We abbreviate the individual atomic propositions as follows: a for "Arthur is in Edinburgh", b for "Betty is in Dundee", and c for "Carol is in Glasgow". The set of possibilities for these three propositions is:

a	b	c
T	T	T
T	T	F
T	F	T
T	F	F
F	T	T
F	T	F
F	F	T
F	F	F

What we want to discover is which of these possibilities, if any, must be true given the truth of the premises. The first premise, a or b (or both), rules out two possibilities, i.e. those in which a and b are both false:

a	b	c	a or b, or both
T	T	T	
T	T	F	
T	F	T	
T	F	F	
F	T	T	
F	T	F	
F	F	T	F
F	F	F	F

The second premise, not-b, rules out four further possibilities, i.e. those in which b is true:

a	b	c	not-b
T	T	T	F
T	T	F	F
T	F	T	
T	F	F	
F	T	T	F
F	T	F	F

The third premise, if a then c, eliminates the case in which a is true and c is false:

a	b	c	if a then c
T	F	T	
T	F	F	F

As Sherlock Holmes remarked, when you have eliminated the impossible then whatever remains, however improbable, must be the case. There remains only a single possibility, in which c is true, and so the corresponding proposition:

Carol is in Glasgow.

is a valid conclusion. In general, a conclusion can be derived from premises provided that the premises eliminate all but the contingencies in which it is true. Logicians refer to this semantic method as "model-theoretic".

We have demonstrated two distinct ways of making deductions in the propositional calculus. The "proof-theoretic" way is syntactic and depends on formal rules of inference. The "model-theoretic" way is semantic and depends on eliminating those states of affairs that are false given the truth of the premises.

In the case of the propositional calculus, it can be proved that if a conclusion is valid using the semantic method then it can be derived using the syntactic method, and the calculus is therefore said to be "complete". Conversely, if a conclusion can be derived using the syntactic method, then it is valid using the semantic method, and the calculus is therefore said to be "sound". You might therefore imagine that the two methods are merely trivial variants of one another. You would be wrong. The higher-order predicate calculus (to be described presently) is not complete: no consistent formalization of it can capture all valid conclusions. What is valid cannot always be established by syntactic derivations from the logical form of premises. This mismatch drives a wedge between syntax and semantics. They are not trivial variants of one another.

THE PREDICATE CALCULUS

Many deductions in daily life hinge on matters internal to propositions rather than on the external connections between them. For instance, the *relational* deduction:

Anna is in the same place as Ben.
Ben is in the same place as Con.
Therefore, Anna is in the same place as Con.

is intuitively valid, yet its validity cannot be accounted for in the propositional calculus, for which the argument has the form:

p
q
Therefore, r.

What we need is the predicate calculus, which includes the propositional calculus as a proper part, but which goes beyond it by introducing machinery for dealing with the internal structure of propositions. Each of the premises in the example contains the relation, "is in the same place as", which for convenience we will abbreviate as follows:

Anna in-same-place Ben.
Ben in-same-place Con.

Before the deduction can proceed using formal rules, we have to introduce a further premise that expresses the fact that the relation is transitive, which we can express in "Loglish", a language that closely resembles the predicate calculus, as:

For any x, any y, any z, if x in-same-place y, and y in-same-place
z, then x in-same-place z.

Here, "any" corresponds to one of the two quantifiers that are used in the predicate calculus, the so-called "universal quantifier", which is sometimes symbolized as "∀". The variables x, y, and z, can have as values any individuals in the domain under discussion. Because this premise expresses a consequence of the meaning of "is in the same place as", it is known as a *meaning postulate*. Other postulates can express matters of fact, e.g. "if x is a dog, then x needs a license".

The formal derivation of a conclusion in the predicate calculus depends on three stages:

1. eliminating the quantifiers from the premises;
2. reasoning with the propositional connectives;
3. re-introducing, if necessary, appropriate quantifiers.

Only one premise in our example (the meaning postulate) contains quantifiers, and they are all universal, i.e. "any". According to the rule of inference for eliminating a universal quantifier, if a predicate applies to any individual in the domain of discourse, then one can freely substitute the name of any specific individual in the domain in place of the quantified variable. Using this rule, we can replace the variables in the meaning postulate by a convenient choice of names:

∴ If Anna in-same-place Ben and Ben in-same-place Con then
  Anna in-same-place Con.

We now proceed to the propositional stage of inference:

∴ Anna in-same-place Ben and Ben in-same-place Con.
  (A conjunction of the two premises.)
∴ Anna in-same-place Con.
  (Modus ponens from the previous two assertions.)

This conclusion is the one that we need: Anna is in the same place as Con, and so the third stage—the restoration of quantifiers—is unnecessary.

Many deductions depend on the other quantifier used in the predicate calculus, the so-called "existential quantifier" which logicians define as meaning, "at least some", and which they often symbolize as "∃". Thus, the premises:

Some Avon letters are in the same place as all Bury letters.
All Bury letters are in the same place as all Caton letters.

validly imply the conclusion:

Some Avon letters are in the same place as all Caton letters.

If a predicate applies to at least *some* individual in the domain under discussion, then there is a formal rule that permits the name of an individual to be substituted in place of the quantified variable. But, because the individual stands in for an existentially quantified variable, the name must not have occurred already in the argument, or else one may be led to a fallacious conclusion. Consider, for example, the premises:

Someone is tall.
(In Loglish: for at least some x, x is a person and x is tall.)
Someone is not tall.
(For at least some x, x is a person and x is not tall.)

"Anna" can be substituted for x in the first premise, but if the same name were then substituted in the second premise, there would be a contradiction: Anna cannot be both tall and not tall. In the third stage of deduction, when a quantifier is re-introduced in place of a name, one must use the rule that restores an existential quantifier for those names that have been introduced by the existential rule. Readers who wish to see a complete formal derivation in the predicate calculus should consult Tables 7.1 and 7.2 in Chapter 7.

The specification of a semantics for the predicate calculus is a more complicated business than the use of truth tables. It depends, as Tarski (1956) established, on characterizing *models*, which can concern either the real world or more abstract mathematical realms. The procedure is complicated because a model may contain an infinitude of different individuals (as in arithmetic where there are infinitely many numbers). For the sake of illustration, we will consider a finite model in which there are just three individuals: Arthur, Betty, and Carol, and one relation: x is in the same place as y, where x and y take individuals as their values. We stipulate that in our model:

Arthur is in the same place as Betty.

and, of course, that everyone is in the same place as themselves:

Arthur is in the same place as Arthur.
Betty is in the same place as Betty.
Carol is in the same place as Carol.

Logicians use two sorts of semantic rules for the interpretation of sentences. The first sort assign interpretations to basic terms, e.g. "Arthur" refers to the individual, Arthur, in the model; and "is in the same place as" refers to the set of pairs of individuals in the model who satisfy the relation, namely, Arthur and Betty, Arthur and Arthur, Betty and Betty, and Carol and Carol. The second sort of semantic rules work in parallel to the syntactic rules defining the well-formed expressions in the calculus. These semantic rules build up the interpretation of a sentence in a way that depends on both the interpretation of its parts and the syntactic relations amongst those parts. Logicians refer to this system as a "compositional" semantics.

A key role is played by the semantic rules for quantified sentences. The syntax of a universally quantified sentence, such as:

For any x, Arthur is in the same place as x

can be analyzed as having two constituents:

For any x, S

where S equals "Arthur is in the same place as x". S is the *scope* of the quantifier and it binds any occurrence of x within its scope. Hence, the semantic rule for a universally quantified assertion states that the assertion is true if and only if replacing the occurrences of x in S by the name of *any* individual in the model results in a true sentence. Thus, the assertion is true provided that each of the following sentences is true in the model:

Arthur is in the same place as Arthur.
Arthur is in the same place as Betty.
Arthur is in the same place as Carol.

The first two sentences are true in our model, and the third is false. Hence, the quantified assertion is false.

There is an analogous semantic rule for existential quantification. An existentially quantified assertion:

For some x, S

is true if and only if replacing the occurrences of x in S by the name of *at least one* individual in the model results in a true sentence. Thus, the assertion:

For some x, Arthur is in the same place as x

is true provided that at least *one* of the above triplet of sentences is true. In this case, the quantified assertion is true, because Arthur is in the same place as Betty (and himself).

The interpretation of assertions with two quantifiers, such as:

For some x, for any y, x is in the same place as y
(i.e. Someone is in the same place as everyone.)

or:

For any y, for some x, x is in the same place as y
(i.e. For everyone, someone in the same place as them.)

calls for a double application of the rules. At its highest level, the first of these sentences has the syntactic analysis:

For some x, S

and so it is true provided that S itself is true, i.e. provided that:

For any y, x is in the same place as y

is true. In short, we can interpret a sentence containing several quantifiers by, in effect, peeling them off one at a time, and looping through the substitutions within their respective scopes. When we get to the "bottom line", i.e. an assertion that does not contain variables, e.g.:

Arthur is in the same place as Betty.

its truth value is given by the basic semantics—the particular relations among the individuals in the model. The order of the quantifiers can obviously affect the interpretation of a sentence, because the quantifier with the larger scope is interpreted before the quantifier with the smaller scope. Hence, there is a difference in meaning between the two examples above.

Formal rules for the first-order predicate calculus, which we have now outlined, can be framed in a way that is complete, i.e. all valid deductions are derivable using them. This condition is not true, however, for the "second-order" predicate calculus in which properties can be quantified as well as individuals. This calculus is needed in order to give a full analysis of such assertions as, "Some sergeants have all the qualities of a great general", or of such unorthodox quantifiers as, "More than half" (see Barwise and Cooper, 1981). This logic is not complete: it cannot be formalized in a consistent way that guarantees that all valid deductions can be derived. Syntax is not equivalent to semantics.

One final point is vital before we can turn to the psychology of deduction. The alert reader will have noticed that we have described a semantic method for deduction in the propositional calculus (truth tables), but *not* one for deduction in the predicate calculus. Logicians have not proposed any deductive system that works directly with models of quantified sentences. A valid deduction must have a conclusion that is true in any possible model of the premises, and even a simple assertion about the real world, such as, "The cat sat on the mat", has infinitely many models. (Think of all the different possible configurations of cat and mat.) No practical procedure can examine infinitely many models in searching for a possible counterexample to a conclusion. Hence, what logicians have proposed are systems of *formal rules* based on the idea of such a search for counterexamples (see Beth, 1955; Hintikka, 1955; Smullyan, 1968). The method is simple, and has largely replaced "natural deduction" in textbooks. Each connective and quantifier has formal rules of inference that build up a search tree and that enable an avenue of exploration to be closed off whenever an inconsistency is encountered (see Jeffrey, 1981, for an excellent introduction, and Oppacher and Suen, 1985, for a computer implementation). But, the rules operate at one remove from models: they manipulate logical forms as do the rules of a natural deduction system.

What we aim to show in this monograph is: 1. that in everyday reasoning the search for counterexamples can be conducted directly by constructing alternative models; 2. that the psychological evidence implies that this procedure is used by human reasoners; and 3. that its simplicity and capacity to cope with certain finite domains make it an excellent method for the maintenance of systems representing knowledge in computers.

CHAPTER 2

The Cognitive Science of Deduction

The late Lord Adrian, the distinguished physiologist, once remarked that if you want to understand *how* the mind works then you had better first ask *what* it is doing. This distinction has become familiar in cognitive science as one that Marr (1982) drew between a theory at the "computational level" and a theory at the "algorithmic level". A theory at the computational level characterizes what is being computed, why it is being computed, and what constraints may assist the process. Such a theory, to borrow from Chomsky (1965), is an account of human competence. And, as he emphasizes, it should also explain how that competence is acquired. A theory at the algorithmic level specifies how the computation is carried out, and ideally it should be precise enough for a computer program to simulate the process. The algorithmic theory, to borrow again from Chomsky, should explain the characteristics of human performance—where it breaks down and leads to error, where it runs smoothly, and how it is integrated with other mental abilities.

We have two goals in this chapter. Our first goal is to characterize deduction at the computational level. Marr criticized researchers for trying to erect theories about mental processes without having stopped to think about what the processes were supposed to compute. The same criticism can be levelled against many accounts of deduction, and so we shall take pains to think about its function: what the mind computes, what purpose is served, and what constraints there are on the process. Our second goal is to examine existing algorithmic theories. Here, experts in several domains of enquiry have something to say. Linguists have considered the logical form of sentences in natural language.

Computer scientists have devised programs that make deductions, and, like philosophers, they have confronted discrepancies between everyday inference and formal logic. Psychologists have proposed algorithmic theories based on their experimental investigations. We will review work from these disciplines in order to establish a preliminary account of deduction—to show what it is, and to outline theories of how it might be carried out by the mind.

DEDUCTION: A THEORY AT THE COMPUTATIONAL LEVEL

What happens when people make a deduction? The short answer is that they start with some information—perceptual observations, memories, statements, beliefs, or imagined states of affairs—and produce a novel conclusion that follows from them. Typically, they argue from some initial propositions to a single conclusion, though sometimes merely from one proposition to another. In many practical inferences, their starting point is a perceived state of affairs and their conclusion is a course of action. Their aim is to arrive at a valid conclusion, which is bound to be true given that their starting point is true.

One long-standing controversy concerns the extent to which people are logical. Some say that logical error is impossible: deduction depends on a set of universal principles applying to any content, and everyone exercises these principles infallibly. This idea seems so contrary to common sense that, as you might suspect, it has been advocated by philosophers (and psychologists). What seems to be an invalid inference is nothing more than a valid inference from other premises (see Spinoza, 1677; Kant, 1800). In recent years, Henle (1962) has defended a similar view. Mistakes in reasoning, she claims, occur because people forget the premises, re-interpret them, or import extraneous material. "I have never found errors," she asserts, "which could unambiguously be attributed to faulty reasoning" (Henle, 1978). In all such cases, the philosopher L. J. Cohen (1981) has concurred, there is some malfunction of an information-processing mechanism. The underlying competence cannot be at fault. This doctrine leads naturally to the view that the mind is furnished with an inborn logic (Leibniz, 1765; Boole, 1854). These authors, impressed by the human invention of logic and mathematics, argue that people must think rationally. The laws of thought are the laws of logic.

Psychologism is a related nineteenth century view. John Stuart Mill (1843) believed that logic is a generalization of those inferences that people judge to be valid. Frege (1884) attacked this idea: logic may ultimately depend on the human mind for its discovery, but it is not a subjective matter; it concerns objective relations between propositions. Other commentators take a much darker view about logical competence. Indeed, when one contemplates the follies and foibles of humanity, it seems hard to disagree with Dostoyevsky, Nietzsche, Freud, and those who have stressed the irrationality of the human mind. Yet this view is reconcilable with logical competence. Human beings may desire the impossible, or behave in ways that do not optimally serve their best interests. It does not follow that they are incapable of rational thought, but merely that their behaviour is not invariably guided by it.

Some psychologists have proposed theories of reasoning that render people inherently irrational (e.g. Erickson, 1974; Revlis, 1975; Evans, 1977a). They may draw a valid conclusion, but their thinking is not properly rational because it never makes a full examination of the consequences of premises. The authors of these theories, however, provide no separate account of deduction at the computational level, and so they might repudiate any attempt to ally them with Dostoyevsky, Nietzsche, and Freud.

Our view of logical competence is that people are rational in principle, but fallible in practice. They are able to make valid deductions, and moreover they sometimes *know* that they have made a valid deduction. They also make invalid deductions in certain circumstances. Of course, theorists can explain away these errors as a result of misunderstanding the premises or forgetting them. The problem with this manoeuvre is that it can be pushed to the point where no possible observation could refute it. People not only make logical mistakes, they are even prepared to concede that they have done so (see e.g. Wason and Johnson-Laird, 1972; Evans, 1982). These meta-logical intuitions are important because they prepare the way for the invention of self-conscious methods for checking validity. Thus, the development of logic as an intellectual discipline requires logicians to be capable of sound pre-theoretical intuitions. Yet, logic would hardly have been invented if there were never occasions where people were uncertain about the status of an inference. Individuals do sometimes formulate their own principles of reasoning, and they also refer to deductions in a meta-logical way. They say, for example: "It seems to follow that Arthur is in Edinburgh, but he isn't, and so I must have argued wrongly." These phenomena merit study like other forms of meta-cognition (see e.g. Flavell, 1979; Brown, 1987). Once the meta-cognitive step is made, it becomes possible to reason at the meta-meta-level, and so on to an arbitrary degree. Thus, cognitive psychologists and devotees of logical puzzles (e.g. Smullyan, 1978; Dewdney, 1989) can in turn make inferences about meta-cognition. A psychological theory of deduction therefore needs to accommodate deductive competence, errors in performance, and meta-logical intuitions (cf. Simon, 1982; Johnson-Laird, 1983; Rips, 1989).

Several ways exist to characterize deductive competence at the computational level. Many theorists—from Boole (1847) to Macnamara (1986)—have supposed that logic itself is the best medium. Others, however, have argued that logic and thought differ. Logic is *monotonic*, i.e. if a conclusion follows from some premises, then no subsequent premise can invalidate it. Further premises lead monotonically to further conclusions, and nothing ever subtracts from them. Thought in daily life appears not to have this property. Given the premises:

Alicia has a bacterial infection.
If a patient has a bacterial infection, then the preferred
treatment for the patient is penicillin.

it follows validly:

Therefore, the preferred treatment for Alicia is penicillin.

But, if it is the case that:

Alicia is allergic to penicillin.

then common-sense dictates that the conclusion should be withdrawn. But it still follows validly in logic. This problem suggests that some inferences in daily life are "non-monotonic" rather than logically valid, i.e. their conclusions can be withdrawn in the light of subsequent information. There have even been attempts to develop *formal* systems of reasoning that are non-monotonic (see e.g. McDermott and Doyle, 1980). We will show later in the book that they are unnecessary. Nevertheless, logic cannot tell the whole story about deductive competence.

A theory at the computational level must specify what is computed, and so it must account for what deductions people actually make. Any set of premises yields an infinite number of valid conclusions. Most of them are banal. Given the premises:

Ann is clever.
Snow is white.

the following conclusions are all valid:

Ann is clever and snow is white.
Snow is white and Ann is clever and snow is white.

They must be true given that the premises are true. Yet no sane individual, apart from a logician, would dream of drawing them. Hence, when reasoners make a deduction in daily life, they must be guided by more than logic. The evidence suggests that at least three extra-logical constraints govern their conclusions.

The first constraint is *not* to throw semantic information away. The concept of semantic information, which can be traced back to medieval philosophy, depends on the proportion of possible states of affairs that an assertion rules out as false (see Bar-Hillel and Carnap, 1964; Johnson-Laird, 1983). Thus, a conjunction, such as:

Joe is at home and Mary is at her office.

conveys more semantic information (i.e. rules out more states of affairs) than only one of its constituents:

Joe is at home.

which, in turn, conveys more semantic information than the inclusive disjunction:

Joe is at home or Mary is at her office, or both.

A valid deduction cannot increase semantic information, but it can decrease it. One datum in support of the constraint is that valid deductions that do decrease semantic information, such as:

Joe is at home.
Therefore, Joe is at home or Mary is at her office, or both.

seem odd or even improper (see Rips, 1983).

A second constraint is that conclusions should be more parsimonious than premises. The following argument violates this constraint:

Ann is clever.
Snow is white.
Therefore, Ann is clever and snow is white.

In fact, logically untutored individuals declare that there is no valid conclusion from these premises. A special case of parsimony is not to draw a conclusion that asserts something that has just been asserted. Hence, given the premises:

If James is at school then Agnes is at work.
James is at school.

the conclusion:

James is at school and Agnes is at work.

is valid, but violates this principle, because it repeats the categorical premise. This information can be taken for granted and, as Grice (1975) argued, there is no need to state the obvious. The development of procedures for drawing parsimonious conclusions is a challenging technical problem in logic. We present a solution to it, which is based on our psychological theory, in Chapter 9.

A third constraint is that a conclusion should, if possible, assert something new, i.e., something that was not explicitly stated in the premises. Given the premise:

Mark is over six feet tall and Karl is taller than him.

the conclusion:

Karl is taller than Mark, who is over six feet tall.

is valid but it violates this constraint because it asserts nothing new. In fact, ordinary reasoners spontaneously draw conclusions that establish relations that are not explicit in the premises.

When there is no valid conclusion that meets the three constraints, then logically naive individuals say, "nothing follows" (see e.g. Johnson-Laird and Bara, 1984). Logically speaking, the response is wrong. There are always conclusions that follow from any premises. The point is that there is no valid conclusion that meets the three constraints. We do not claim that people are aware of the constraints or that they are mentally represented in any way. They may play no direct part in the process of deduction, which for quite independent reasons yields deductions that conform to them (Johnson-Laird , 1983, Ch. 3).

In summary, our theory of deductive competence posits rationality, an awareness of rationality, and a set of constraints on the conclusions that people draw for themselves. *To deduce is to maintain semantic information, to simplify, and to reach a new conclusion.*

FORMAL RULES: A THEORY AT THE ALGORITHMIC LEVEL

Three main classes of theory about the process of deduction have been proposed by cognitive scientists:

1. Formal rules of inference.
2. Content-specific rules of inference.
3. Semantic procedures that search for interpretations (or mental models) of the premises that are counterexamples to conclusions.

Formal theories have long been dominant. Theorists originally assumed without question that there is a mental logic containing formal rules of inference, such as the rule for modus ponens, which are used to derive conclusions. The first psychologist to emphasize the role of logic was the late Jean Piaget (see e.g. Piaget, 1953). He argued that children internalize their own actions and reflect on them. This process ultimately yields a set of "formal operations", which children are supposed to develop by their early teens. Inhelder and Piaget (1958, p.305) are unequivocal about the nature of formal operations. They write:

> No further operations need be introduced since these operations correspond to the calculus inherent to the algebra of propositional logic. In short, reasoning is nothing more than the propositional calculus itself.

There are grounds for rejecting this account: we have already demonstrated that deductive competence must depend on more than pure logic in order to rule out banal, though valid, conclusions. Moreover, Piaget's logic was idiosyncratic (see Parsons, 1960; Ennis, 1975; Braine and Rumain, 1983), and he failed to describe his theory in sufficient detail for it to be modelled in a computer program. He had a genius for asking the right questions and for inventing experiments to answer them, but the vagueness of his theory masked its inadequacy perhaps even from Piaget himself. The effort to understand it is so great that readers often have no energy left to detect its flaws.

Logical Form in Linguistics

A more orthodox guide to logical analysis can be found in linguistics. Many linguists have proposed analyses of the logical form of sentences, and often presupposed the existence of formal rules of inference that enable deductions to be derived from them. Such analyses were originally inspired by transformational grammar (see e.g. Leech, 1969; Seuren, 1969; Johnson-Laird, 1970; Lakoff, 1970; Keenan, 1971; Harman, 1972; Jackendoff, 1972). What these accounts had in common is the notion that English quantifiers conform to the behaviour of logical quantifiers only indirectly. As in logic, a universal quantifier within the scope of a negation:

Not all of his films are admired.

is equivalent to an existential quantifier outside the scope of negation:

Some of his films are not admired.

But, unlike logic, natural language has no clear-cut devices for indicating scope. A sentence, such as:

Everybody is loved by somebody.

has two different interpretations depending on the relative scopes of the two quantifiers. It can mean:

Everybody is loved by somebody or other.

which we can paraphrase in "Loglish" (the language that resembles the predicate calculus) as:

For any x, there is some y, such that if x is a person then y is a person, and x is loved by y.

It can also mean:

There is somebody whom everybody is loved by.
(There is some y, for any x, such that y is a person and if x is a person, then x is loved by y.)

Often, the order of the quantifiers in a sentence corresponds to their relative scopes, but sometimes it does not, e.g.:

No-one likes some politicians.
(For some y, such that y is a politician, no x is a person and x likes y.)

where the first quantifier in the sentence is within the scope of the second.

Theories of logical form have more recently emerged within many different linguistic frameworks, including Chomsky's (1981) "government and binding" theory, Montague grammar (Cooper, 1983), and Kamp's (1981) theory of discourse representations. The Chomskyan theory postulates a separate mental representation of logical form (LF), which makes explicit such matters as the scope of the quantifiers, and which is transformationally derived from a representation of the superficial structure of the sentence (S-structure). The sentence, "Everybody is loved by somebody", has two distinct logical forms analogous to those above. The first corresponds closely to the superficial order of the quantifiers, and the second is derived by a transformation that moves the existential quantifier, "somebody", to the front—akin to the sentence:

Somebody, everybody is loved by.

This conception of logical form is motivated by linguistic considerations (see Chomsky, 1981; Hornstein, 1984; May, 1985). Its existence as a level of syntactic representation, however, is not incontrovertible. The phenomena that it accounts for might be explicable, as Chomsky has suggested (personal communication, 1989), by enriching the representation of the superficial structure of sentences.

Logical form is, of course, a necessity for any theory of deduction that depends on formal rules of inference. Kempson (1988) argues that the mind's inferential machinery is formal, and that logical form is therefore the interface between grammar and cognition. Its structures correspond to those of the deductive system, but, contrary to Chomskyan theory, she claims that it is not part of grammar, because general knowledge can play a role in determining the relations it represents. For example, the natural interpretation of the sentence:

Everyone got into a taxi and chatted to the driver.

is that each individual chatted to the driver of his or her taxi. This interpretation, however, depends on general knowledge, and so logical form is not purely a matter of grammar. Kempson links it to the psychological theory of deduction advocated by Sperber and Wilson (1986). This theory depends on formal rules of inference, and its authors have sketched some of them within the framework of a "natural deduction" system.

One linguist, Cooper (1983), treats scope as a semantic matter, i.e. within the semantic component of an analysis based on Montague grammar, which is an application of model-theoretic semantics to language in general. A different model-theoretic approach, "situation semantics", is even hostile to the whole notion of reasoning as the formal manipulation of formal representations (Barwise, 1989; Barwise and Etchemendy, 1989a,b).

Formal Logic in Artificial Intelligence

Many researchers in artificial intelligence have argued that the predicate calculus is an ideal language for representing knowledge (e.g. Hayes, 1977). A major discovery of this century, however, is that there cannot be a full decision procedure for the predicate calculus. In theory, a proof for any valid argument can always be found, but no procedure can be guaranteed to demonstate that an argument is invalid. The procedure may, in effect, become lost in the space of possible derivations. Hence, as it grinds away, there is no way of knowing if, and when, it will stop. One palliative is to try to minimize the search problem for valid deductions by reducing the number of formal rules of inference. In fact, one needs only a single rule to make any deduction, the so-called "resolution rule" (Robinson, 1965):

A or B, or both
C or not-B, or both
∴ A or C, or both.

The rule is not intuitively obvious, but consider the following example:

Mary is a linguist or Mary is a psychologist.
Mary is an experimenter or Mary is not a psychologist.
Therefore, Mary is a linguist or Mary is an experimenter.

Suppose that Mary is not a psychologist, then it follows from the first premise that she is a linguist; now, suppose that Mary is a psychologist, then it follows from the second premise that she is an experimenter. Mary must be either a psychologist or not a psychologist, and so she must be either a linguist or an experimenter.

Table 2.1 summarizes the main steps of resolution theorem-proving, which relies on the method of *reductio ad absurdum*, i.e. showing that the negation of the desired conclusion leads to a contradiction. Unfortunately, despite the use of various heuristics to speed up the search, the method still remains intractable: the search space tends to

Table 2.1
A simple example of "resolution" theorem-proving

The deduction to be evaluated:
1. Mary is a psychologist.
2. All psychologists have read some books.
3. ∴ Mary has read some books.

Step 1: Translate the deduction into a *reductio ad absurdum*, i.e. negate the conclusion with the aim of showing that the resultant set of propositions is inconsistent:
1. (Psychologist Mary)
2. (For any x)(for some y)
          ((Psychologist x) → ((Book y) & (Read x y)))
3. (Not (For some z) (Book z & (Read Mary z)))

Step 2: Translate all the connectives into disjunctions, and eliminate the quantifiers. "Any" can be deleted: its work is done by the presence of variables. "Some" is replaced by a function (the so-called Skolem function), e.g. "all psychologists have read some books" requires a function, f, which, given a psychologist as its argument, returns a value consisting of some books:
1. (Psychologist Mary)
2. (Not (Psychologist x)) or (Read x (f x))
3. (Not (Read Mary (f Mary))

Step 3: Apply the resolution rule to any premises containing inconsistent clauses: it is not necessary for both assertions to be disjunctions. Assertion 3 thus cancels out the second disjunct in assertion 2 to leave:
1. (Psychologist Mary)
2. (not (Psychologist Mary))
These two assertions cancel out by a further application of the resolution rule. Whenever a set of assertions is reduced to the empty set in this way, they are inconsistent. The desired conclusion follows at once because its negation has led to a *reductio ad absurdum*.

---

grow exponentially with the number of clauses in the premises (Moore, 1982). The resolution method, however, has become part of "logic programming"—the formulation of high level programming languages in which programs consist of assertions in a formalism closely resembling the predicate calculus (Kowalski, 1979). Thus, the language PROLOG is based on resolution (see e.g. Clocksin and Mellish, 1981).

No psychologist would suppose that human reasoners are equipped with the resolution rule (see also our studies of "double disjunctions" in the next chapter). But, a psychologically more plausible form of deduction has been implemented in computer programs. It relies on the method of "natural deduction", which we described in Chapter 1, and which provides separate rules of inference for each connective. The programs maintain a clear distinction between what has been proved and what their goals are, and so they are able to construct chains of inference working forwards from the premises and working backwards from the conclusion to be proved (see e.g. Reiter, 1973; Bledsoe, 1977; Pollock, 1989). The use of forward and backward chains was pioneered in modern times by Polya (1957) and by Newell, Shaw, and Simon (1963); as we will see, it is part of the programming language, PLANNER.

Formal Rules in Psychological Theories

Natural deduction has been advocated as the most plausible account of mental logic by many psychologists (e.g. Braine, 1978; Osherson, 1975; Johnson-Laird, 1975; Macnamara, 1986), and at least one simulation program uses it for both forward- and backward-chaining (Rips, 1983). All of these theories posit an initial process of recovering the logical form of the premises. Indeed, what they have in common outweighs their differences, but we will outline three of them to enable readers to make up their own minds.

Johnson-Laird (1975) proposed a theory of propositional reasoning partly based on natural deduction. Its rules are summarized in Table 2.2 along with those of the two other theories. The rule introducing disjunctive conclusions:

A

∴ A or B (or both)

leads to deductions that, as we have remarked, throw semantic information away and thus seem unacceptable to many people. Yet, without this rule, it would be difficult to make the inference:

If it is frosty or it is foggy, then the game won't be played.
It is frosty.
Therefore, the game won't be played.

Johnson-Laird therefore proposed that the rule (and others like it) is an auxiliary one that can be used only to prepare the way for a primary rule, such as modus ponens. Where the procedures for exploiting rules fail, then the next step, according to his theory, is to make a hypothetical assumption and to follow up its consequences.

Braine and his colleagues have described a series of formal theories based on natural deduction (see e.g. Braine, 1978; Braine and Rumain, 1983). At the heart of their approach are the formal rules presented in Table 2.2. They differ in format from Johnson-Laird's in two ways. First, "and" and "or" can connect any number of propositions, and so, for example, the first rule in Table 2.2 has the following form in their theory:

$P_1, P_2, \ldots P_n$
Therefore, P_1 and P_2 and $\ldots P_n$.

Second, Braine avoids the need for some auxiliary rules, such as the disjunctive rule above, by building their effects directly into the main rules. He includes, for example, the rule:

If A or B then C
A
Therefore C

again allowing for any number of propositions in the disjunctive antecedent. This idea is also adopted by Sperber and Wilson (1986).

Braine, Reiser, and Rumain (1984) tested the theory by asking subjects to evaluate given deductions. The problems concerned the presence or absence of letters on an imaginary blackboard, e.g.:

If there is either a C or an H, then there is a P.
There is a C.
Therefore, there is a P.

The subjects' task was to judge the truth of the conclusion given the premises. The study examined two potential indices of difficulty—the number of steps in a deduction according to the theory, and the "difficulty weights" of these steps as estimated from the data. Both measures predicted certain results: the rated difficulty of a problem, the latency of response (adjusted for the time it took to read the problem), and the percentage of errors. Likewise, the number of words in a problem correlated with its rated difficulty and the latency of response.

Rips (1983) has proposed a theory of propositional reasoning, which he has simulated in a program called ANDS (A Natural Deduction System). The rules used by the program—in the form of procedures—are summarized in Table 2.2. The program evaluates given conclusions and it builds both forward-chains and backward-chains of deduction, and therefore maintains a set of goals separate from the assertions that it

Table 2.2
The principal formal rules of inference proposed by
three psychological theories of deduction

	Johnson-Laird	Braine	Rips
Conjunctions			
A, B ∴ A & B	+	+	+
A & B ∴ A	+	+	+
Disjunctions			
A or B, not-A ∴ B	+	+	+
A ∴ A or B	+		+
Conditionals			
If A then B, A ∴ B	+	+	+
If A or B then C, A ∴ C		+	+
A ⊢ B ∴ If A then B	+	+	+
Negated conjunctions			
not (A & B), A ∴ ¬B	+	+	
not (A & B) ∴ not-A or not-B			+
A & not-B .. not (A & B)	+		
Double negations			
not not-A ∴ A	+	+	
De Morgan's laws			
A & (B or C) ∴ (A & B) or (A & C)		+	
Reductio ad absurdum			
A ⊢ B & not-B ∴ not-A	+	+	+
Dilemmas			
A or B, A ⊢ C, B ⊢ C ∴ C		+	+
A or B, A ⊢ C, B ⊢ D ∴ C or D		+	
Introduction of tautologies			
∴ A or not-A		+	+

Notes
"+" indicates that a rule is postulated by the relevant theory.
"A ⊢ B" means that a deduction from A to B is possible. Braine's rules interconnect any number of propositions, as we explain in the text. He postulates four separate rules that together enable a *reductio ad absurdum* to be made. Johnson-Laird relies on procedures that follow up the separate consequences of constituents in order to carry out dilemmas.

has derived. Certain rules are treated as auxiliaries that can be used only when they are triggered by a goal, e.g.:

A, B

Therefore, A and B

which otherwise could be used *ad infinitum* at any point in the proof. If the program can find no rule to apply during a proof, then it declares that the argument is invalid. Rips assumes that rules of inference are available to human reasoners on a probabilistic basis. His main method of testing the theory has been to fit it to data obtained from subjects who assessed the validity of arguments. The resulting estimates of the availability of rules yielded a reasonable fit for the data as a whole. One surprise, however, was that the rule:

If A or B then C

A

Therefore, C

had a higher availability than the simple rule of modus ponens. It is worth noting that half of the valid deductions in his experiment called for semantic information to be thrown away. Only one out of these 16 problems was evaluated better than chance. Conversely, 14 of the other 16 problems, which maintained semantic information, were evaluated better than chance.

A major difficulty for performance theories based on formal logic is that people are affected by the content of a deductive problem. We will discuss a celebrated demonstration of this phenomenon—Wason's selection task—in Chapter 4. Yet, formal rules ought to apply regardless of content. That is what they are: rules that apply to the logical form of assertions, once it has been abstracted from their content. The proponents of formal rules argue that content exerts its influence only during the interpretation of premises. It leads reasoners to import additional information, or to assign a different logical form to a premise. A radical alternative, however, is that reasoners make use of rules of inference that have a specific content.

CONTENT-SPECIFIC RULES: A SECOND THEORY AT THE ALGORITHMIC LEVEL

Content-specific rules of inference were pioneered by workers in artificial intelligence. They were originally implemented in the programming language PLANNER (Hewitt, 1971). It and its many descendants rely on the resemblance between proofs and plans. A proof is a series of assertions, each following from what has gone before, that leads to a conclusion. A plan is a series of hypothetical actions, each made possible by what has gone before, and leading to a goal. Hence, a plan can be derived in much the same way as a proof. A program written in a PLANNER-like language has a data-base consisting of a set of simple assertions, such as:

Mary is a psychologist.
Paul is a linguist.
Mark is a programmer.

which can be represented in the following notation:

(Psychologist Mary)
(Linguist Paul)
(Programmer Mark)

The assertion, "Mary is a psychologist", is obviously true with respect to this data base. General assertions, such as:

All psychologists are experimenters.

are expressed, not as assertions, but as rules of inference. One way to formulate such a rule is by a procedure:

(Consequent (x) (Experimenter x)
(Goal (Psychologist x)))

which enables the program to infer the consequent that x is an experimenter if it can satisfy the goal that x is a psychologist. If the program has to evaluate the truth of:

Mary is an experimenter

it first searches its data base for a specific assertion to that effect. It fails to find such an assertion in the data base above, and so it looks for a rule with a consequent that matches with the sentence to be evaluated. The rule above matches and sets up the following goal:

(Goal (Psychologist Mary))

This goal *is* satisfied by an assertion in the data base, and so the sentence, "Mary is an experimenter" is satisfied too. The program constructs backward-chains of inference using such rules, which can even be supplemented with specific heuristic advice about how to derive certain conclusions.

Another way in which to formulate a content-specific rule is as follows:

(Antecedent (x) (Psychologist x)
(Assert (x)(Experimenter x)))

Whenever its antecedent is satisfied by an input assertion, such as:

Mary is a psychologist.

the procedure springs to life and asserts that x is an experimenter:

Mary is an experimenter.

This response has the effect of adding the further assertion to the data base. The program can construct forward-chains of inference using such rules.

Content-specific rules are the basis of most expert systems, which are computer programs that give advice on such matters as medical diagnosis, the structure of molecules, and where to drill for minerals. They contain a large number of conditional rules that have been culled from human experts. From a logical standpoint, these rules are postulates that capture a body of knowledge. The expert systems, however, use them as rules of inference (see e.g. Michie, 1979; Duda, Gaschnig, and Hart, 1979; Feigenbaum and McCorduck, 1984). The rules are highly specific. For example, DENDRAL, which analyzes mass spectrograms (Lindsay, Buchanan, Feigenbaum, and Lederberg, 1980), includes this conditional rule:

If there is a high peak at 71 atomic mass units
    and there is a high peak at 43 atomic mass units
    and there is a high peak at 86 atomic mass units
    and there is any peak at 58 atomic mass units
    then there must be an N-PROPYL-KETONE3 substructure.

(see Winston, 1984, p.196). Most current systems have an inferential "engine" which, by interrogating a user about a particular problem, navigates its way through the rules to yield a conclusion. The conditional rules may be definitive or else have probabilities associated with them, and the system may even use Bayes theorem from the probability calculus. It may build forward chains (Feigenbaum, Buchanan, and Lederberg, 1979), backward chains (Shortliffe, 1976), or a mixture of both (Waterman and Hayes-Roth, 1978).

Psychologists have also proposed that the mind uses content-specific conditional rules to represent general knowledge (e.g. Anderson, 1983). They are a plausible way of drawing inferences that depend on background assumptions. The proposal is even part of a seminal theory of cognitive architecture in which the rules (or "productions" as they are known) are triggered by the current contents of working memory (see Newell and Simon, 1972, and Newell, 1990). When a production is triggered it may, in turn, add new information to working memory, and in this way a chain of inferences can ensue.

A variant on content-specific rules has been proposed by Cheng and Holyoak (1985), who argue that people are guided by "pragmatic reasoning schemas." These are general principles that apply to a particular domain. For example, there is supposedly a permission schema that includes rules of the following sort:

If action A is to be taken then precondition B must be satisfied.

The schema is intended to govern actions that occur within a framework of moral conventions, and Cheng and Holyoak argue that it and other similar schemas account for certain aspects of deductive performance (see Chapter 4).

Content plays its most specific role in the hypothesis that reasoning is based on memories of particular experiences (Stanfill and Waltz, 1986). Indeed, according to Riesbeck and Schank's (1989) theory of "case-based" reasoning, human thinking has nothing to do with logic. What happens is that a problem reminds you of a previous case, and you decide what to do on the basis of this case. These theorists allow, however, that when an activity has been repeated often enough, it begins to function like a content-specific rule. The only difficulty with this theory is that it fails to explain how people are able to make valid deductions that do not depend on their specific experiences.

General knowledge certainly enters into everyday deductions, but whether it is represented by schemas or productions or specific cases is an open question. It might, after all, be represented by *assertions* in a mental language. It might even have a distributed representation that has no explicit symbolic structure (Rumelhart, 1989). Structured representations, however, do appear to be needed in order to account for reasoning about reasoning (see Chapter 9, and Johnson-Laird, 1988b, Chapter 19).

MENTAL MODELS: A THIRD THEORY AT THE ALGORITHMIC LEVEL

Neither formal rules nor content-specific rules appear to give complete explanations of the mechanism underlying deduction. On the one hand, the content of premises can exert a profound effect on the conclusions that people draw, and so a uniform procedure for extracting logical form and applying formal rules to it may not account for all aspects of performance. On the other hand, ordinary individuals are able to make valid deductions that depend solely on connectives and quantifiers, and so rules with a specific content would have to rely on some (yet to be formulated) account of purely logical competence. One way out of this dilemma is provided by a third sort of algorithmic theory, which depends on semantic procedures.

Consider this inference:

The black ball is directly behind the cue ball. The green ball is on the right of the cue ball, and there is a red ball between them.
Therefore, if I move so that the red ball is between me and the black ball, the cue ball is to the left of my line of sight.

It is possible to frame rules that capture this inference (from Johnson-Laird, 1975), but it seems likely that people will make it by imagining the layout of the balls. This idea lies at the heart of the theory of mental models. According to this theory, the process of deduction depends on three stages of thought, which are summarized in Figure 2.1. In the first stage, comprehension, reasoners use their knowledge of the language and their general knowledge to understand the premises: they construct an internal model of the state of affairs that the premises describe. A deduction may also depend on perception, and thus on a perceptually-based model of the world (see Marr, 1982). In the second stage, reasoners try to formulate a parsimonious description of the models they have constructed. This description should assert something that is not explicitly stated in the premises. Where there is no such conclusion, then they respond that nothing follows from the premises. In the third stage, reasoners search for alternative models of the premises in which their putative conclusion is false. If there is no such model, then the conclusion is valid. If there is such a model, then prudent reasoners will return to the second stage to try to discover whether there is any conclusion true in all the models that they have so far constructed. If so, then it is necessary to search for counterexamples to it, and so on, until the set of possible models has been exhausted. Because the number

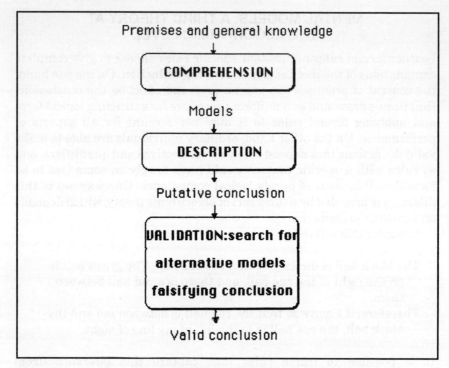

Figure 2.1.   The three stages of deduction according to the model theory.

of possible mental models is finite for deductions that depend on quantifiers and connectives, the search can in principle be exhaustive. If it is uncertain whether there is an alternative model of the premises, then the conclusion can be drawn in a tentative or probabilistic way. Only in the third stage is any essential deductive work carried out: the first two stages are merely normal processes of comprehension and description.

The theory is compatible with the way in which logicians formulate a semantics for a calculus (see Chapter 1). But, logical accounts depend on assigning an infinite number of models to each proposition, and an infinite set is far too big to fit inside anyone's head (Partee, 1979). The psychological theory therefore assumes that people construct a minimum of models: they try to work with just a single representative sample from the set of possible models, until they are forced to consider alternatives.

Models form the basis of various theories of reasoning. An early program for proving geometric theorems used diagrams of figures in order to rule out subgoals that were false (Gelernter, 1963). Although

The Euler circle representation of a syllogism

Premise 1: All psychologists are experimenters
Premise 2: All experimenters are sceptics

Each set of individuals is represented by a separate circle in the Euclidean plane

Premise 1 requires two diagrams

(p) e   p e

Premise 2 requires two diagrams

(e) s   e s

There are four ways of combining the sets of diagrams

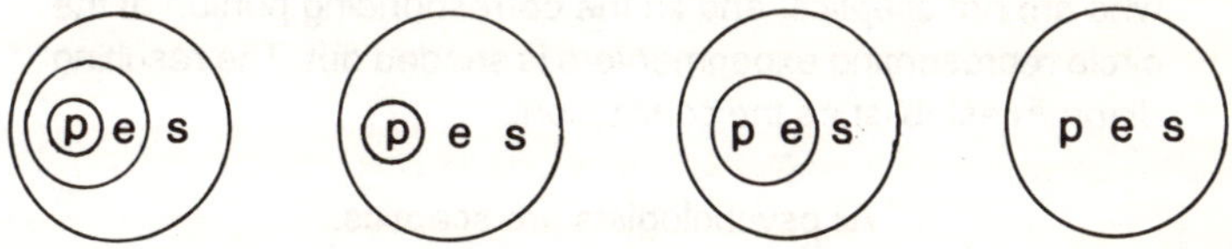

(p)e s   (p) e s   p e s   p e s

It follows from all the combinations:

All psychologists are sceptics

Figure 2.2. The Euler circle representation of a syllogism.

this idea could be used in other domains (see Bundy, 1983), there have been few such applications in artificial intelligence. Charniak and McDermott (1985, p.363) speculate that the reason might be because few domains have counterexamples in the form of diagrams. Yet, as we will see, analogous structures are available for all sorts of deduction.

Deductions from singly-quantified premises, such as "All psychologists are experimenters", can be modelled using Euler circles (see Figure 2.2). Psychological theories have postulated such representations (Erickson, 1974) or equivalent strings of symbols

---

The Venn diagram representation of a syllogism

Premise 1:   All psychologists are experimenters
Premise 2:   All experimenters are sceptics

Each of the three sets is initially represented by one of three overlapping circles within a rectangle that represents the universe of discourse.

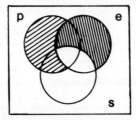

Premise 1 rules out the possibility of psychologists who are not experimenters, and so the corresponding portion of the circle representing psychologists is shaded out.
Premise 2 likewise rules out the possibility of experimenters who are not sceptics, and so the corresponding portion of the circle representing experimenters is shaded out. The resulting diagram establishes the conclusion:

All psychologists are sceptics.

Figure 2.3.   The Venn diagram representation of a syllogism.

(Guyote and Sternberg, 1981). These deductions can also be modelled using Venn diagrams (see Figure 2.3) or equivalent strings of symbols, and they too have been proposed as mental representations (Newell, 1981). A uniform and more powerful principle, however, is that *mental models have the same structure as human conceptions of the situations they represent* (Johnson-Laird, 1983). Hence, a finite set of individuals is represented, not by a circle inscribed in Euclidean space, but by a finite set of mental tokens. A similar notion of a "vivid" representation has been proposed by Levesque (1986) from the standpoint of developing efficient computer programs for reasoning. But, there are distinctions between the two sorts of representation, e.g. vivid representations cannot represent directly either negatives or disjunctions (see also

Etherington, Borgida, Brachman, and Kautz, 1989). The tokens of mental models may occur in a visual image, or they may not be directly accessible to consciousness. What matters is, not the phenomenal experience, but the structure of the models. This structure, which we will examine in detail in the following chapters, often transcends the perceptible. It can represent negation and disjunction.

The general theory of mental models has been successful in accounting for patterns of performance in various sorts of reasoning (Johnson-Laird, 1983). Errors occur, according to the theory, because people fail to consider all possible models of the premises. They therefore fail to find counterexamples to the conclusions that they derive from their initial models, perhaps because of the limited processing capacity of working memory (Baddeley, 1986).

The model theory has attracted considerable criticism from adherents of formal rules. It has been accused of being unclear, unworkable, and unnecessary. We will defer our main reply to critics until the final chapter, but we will make a preliminary response here to the three main charges that the theory is empirically inadequate:

1. Mental models do not explain propositional reasoning: "No clear mental model theory of propositional reasoning has yet been proposed" (Braine et al., 1984; see also Evans, 1984, 1987; and Rips, 1986). The next chapter renders this criticism obsolete.

2. Mental models cannot account for performance in Wason's selection task. The theory implies that people search for counterexamples, yet they conspicuously fail to do so in the selection task (Evans, 1987). The criticism is based on a false assumption. The theory does not postulate that the search for counterexamples is invariably complete—far from it, as such an impeccable performance would be incompatible with observed errors. In Chapter 4, we will show how the theory explains performance in the selection task.

3. Contrary to the previous criticism, Rips (1986) asserts: "Deduction-as-simulation explains content effects, but unfortunately it does so at the cost of being unable to explain the generality of inference". He argues that a modus ponens deduction is not affected by the complexity of its content, and is readily carried out in domains for which the reasoner has had no previous exposure and thus no model to employ. However, the notion that reasoners cannot construct models for unfamiliar domains is false: all they need is a knowledge of the meaning of the connectives and other logical terms that occur in the premises. Conversely, modus ponens can be affected by its content as we will show in Chapter 4.

CONCLUSION

We have completed our survey of where things stood at the start of our research. There were—and remain—three algorithmic theories of deduction. Despite many empirical findings, it had proved impossible to make a definitive choice among the theories. We now turn to the studies that will enable us to reach an informed decision about their adequacy as accounts of human deductive performance.

CHAPTER 3

Reasoning with Propositions

Deductions based on propositional connectives, such as "not", "if", "and", and "or", are one of the main domains of human deductive competence, playing a part in many of the inferences in the other two main domains (relational and quantificational deductions). In this chapter, we will examine a number of clues from the psychological laboratory, and try to solve the mystery of how people reason propositionally. Because they can make deductions that do not depend on general knowledge, we can set aside theories based on content-specific rules. They are chiefly pertinent to the effects of content to be described in the next chapter. We are left with a choice between formal rules and mental models.

When people reason from conditionals, they are readily able to make a modus ponens deduction:

If there is a circle then there is a triangle.
There is a circle.
Therefore, there is a triangle.

They are less able to make the modus tollens deduction:

If there is a circle then there is a triangle.
There is not a triangle.
Therefore, there is not a circle.

Indeed, many intelligent individuals say that nothing follows in this case (see Wason and Johnson-Laird, 1972; Evans, 1982). The difference in difficulty between the two sorts of deduction is so robust that it demands explanation. Rule theorists have two ways of explaining phenomena: the choice of rules that they postulate as part of mental logic, and the relative availability or ease of use of these rules. In the present case, theorists assume that mental logic contains a rule for modus ponens:

If A then B

A

Therefore, B

but does not contain a rule for modus tollens (see e.g. the theories summarized in Table 2.2). In order to make the modus tollens deduction, it is therefore necessary to make a series of deductions. Given premises of the form:

If p then q

not-q

reasoners can hypothesise p:

p
   (by hypothesis)

from which they can derive:

q
   (by modus ponens from hypothesis and first premise)

This conclusion, together with the second premise, yields a self-contradiction:

q and not-q
   (by conjuntion)

The rule of *reductio ad absurdum* entitles reasoners to derive the negation of any hypothesis that leads to a self-contradiction:

not-p
   (by *reductio*)

This chain of deductions is complicated, and so modus tollens should be harder than modus ponens.

The meaning of propositional connectives can be defined by truth tables, and, as we showed in Chapter 1, valid deductions can be made by using the meanings of premises to eliminate contingencies from truth tables. But, logically-untutored individuals are unlikely to use this method. It calls for too many contingencies to be kept in mind, as theorists of all persuasions are agreed (Wason and Johnson-Laird, 1972; Osherson, 1975; Braine and Rumain, 1983). Indeed, people are notoriously bad at manipulating truth tables, they have difficulty in describing them, and they often fail to consider all possibilities in tasks analogous to the assessment of truth tables (Byrne and Johnson-Laird, 1990a). To abandon truth tables, however, is not necessarily to abandon the semantic approach to propositional reasoning. What is needed is a theory that reconciles the semantics of truth tables with the constraints of mental processing, and that does so in a way that explains human performance.

MODELS FOR CONNECTIVES

Could there be a theory of propositional reasoning based on mental models? Because the approach was originally developed for spatial and quantificational reasoning, many critics have been skeptical (Braine et al, 1984; Rips, 1986; Evans, 1987). Happily, their skepticism has been overtaken by just such a theory. It assumes that people can form mental models of the states of affairs described in premises, but that they leave as much information as possible implicit in their models rather than spelling it out explicitly (Johnson-Laird, Byrne, and Schaeken, 1990). Given a conjunction describing what is on a blackboard, such as:

There is a circle and there is a triangle.

they build a single model of the following sort:

o   Δ

With a disjunctive premise, such as:

There is a circle or there is a triangle.

they build two alternative models to represent the possibilities:

o

    Δ

where we adopt the notational convention of putting separate models on separate lines. If, in addition to this disjunctive premise, someone asserts categorically:

There isn't a circle.

then reasoners can use this information to update the set of models. It eliminates the first model, which contains a circle. But it can be added to the second model:

¬○   △

where "¬" is a propositional-like tag representing negation. These tags may seem odd, particularly if one thinks of mental models as representing only physical or perceptible situations (Inder, 1987). In fact, propositional annotations are innocuous and easy to implement (see Polk and Newell, 1988; Newell, 1990), and they can be defended on psychological grounds (see Chapter 6).

The annotated model above corresponds to the description:

There is not a circle and there is a triangle.

One of the constraints on human deductive competence is parsimony, and so the procedure that formulates conclusions keeps track of categorical assertions and does not repeat them. It accordingly concludes:

There is a triangle.

which is valid because no other model of the premises falsifies it. Hence, a disjunctive deduction of the form:

p or q
not-p
Therefore, q

can be made by using the meanings of the premises to construct and to eliminate models. There is no need for formal rules of inference.

When psychologists test whether a disjunction, such as:

There is a circle or there is a triangle.

is interpreted inclusively or exclusively, they find that subjects do not respond in a uniform way. Typically, adults are biased towards an inclusive interpretation, but a sizeable minority prefer the exclusive interpretation (Evans and Newstead, 1980; Roberge, 1978). The results are not consistent from one experiment to another, though a semblance of consistency occurs if content (or context) suggests one or other of the two interpretations (see Newstead and Griggs, 1983). The lack of a consensus seems strange at first, as does the fact that people are normally aware neither of the two possible interpretations nor of settling on one of them as opposed to the other. The phenomena are still more puzzling viewed through the spectacles of rule theories, because these theories presuppose an initial recovery of the logical form of premises (see Braine, 1978; Rips, 1983), which makes explicit whether a disjunction is inclusive or exclusive.

The puzzle is resolved by the model theory. The initial representation of a disjunction by the models above is consistent with an inclusive or with an exclusive interpretation. The models can be fleshed out explicitly to represent either sort of disjunction. The distinction depends on making explicit that all instances of a particular contingency, e.g. those in which there are circles, have been exhaustively represented in the set of models. In other words, reasoners may know that there could be circles in other models, which they have yet to make explicit, or they may know that they have represented all circles explicitly. The contrast is a binary one, and we will use square brackets as our notation for the conceptual element corresponding to an exhaustive representation. Thus, the exclusive disjunction:

Either there is a circle or else there is a triangle, but not both.

has the following models:

[o]
    [△]

which represent explicitly all the contingencies containing circles and all the contingencies containing triangles. Hence, the further assertion:

There is a circle.

picks out the state of affairs in the first model. Because the triangles are exhausted in the second model, the first model can be "fleshed out" in only one way:

[o]   [¬△]

The procedure that formulates conclusions now yields:

There is not a triangle.

The explicit representation of the inclusive disjunction:

There is a circle or there is a triangle, or both.

allows for three alternative possibilities:

[o]   [Δ]
[o]
       [Δ]

including the joint contingency of circle and triangle. Where an item is not exhaustively represented—as shown in our notation by the absence of square brackets, then it is always possible to add further models containing that item. Hence, there is no need for the initial models of the disjunction:

o

Δ

to distinguish between inclusive and exclusive disjunction. One is at liberty to introduce or to exclude the joint contingency of circle and triangle.

A similar phenomenon occurs with conditionals. In a "binary" context, people interpret a conditional as implying its converse. Legrenzi (1970) demonstrated this point by using such conditionals as:

If the ball rolls to the left, then the red light comes on.

in a situation where the ball could roll either to the left or right, and the light was either red or green. But, when content and context are neutral, sometimes a conditional is taken to imply its converse, and sometimes not: people are neither consistent with one another nor from one occasion to another (see Wason and Johnson-Laird, 1972; Staudenmayer, 1975; Staudenmayer and Bourne, 1978; Evans, 1982). Again, it seems strange at first that there should be these vagaries in the interpretation of conditionals, and that one is not normally aware of them.

The model theory accounts for the phenomenon. A conditional, such as:

If there is a circle then there is a triangle.

calls for a model in which there is a circle (and thus a triangle), but the assertion is consistent with a state of affairs in which there isn't a circle. People do not initially make explicit the nature of this alternative, but merely represent its possibility in a second model that has no explicit content:

o   Δ
. . .

where the three dots denote a model with no explicit content. This second model allows for a subsequent explicit content, and it rules out a conjunctive description of the models. The categorical premise for modus ponens:

There is a circle.

is accommodated within the set of models by eliminating the second model, because a circle occurs in the first model:

o   Δ

The model supports the conclusion:

There is a triangle.

which is valid because no other model of the premises falsifies it. If the categorical premise is instead one for modus tollens:

There is not a triangle.

then it can be accommodated within the initial models for the conditional:

o   Δ
. . .

only by eliminating the first model which contains a triangle. This process leaves only the second model, which now incorporates the information from the categorical premise:

¬Δ

Because this model represents only the categorical premise, it seems that nothing follows. This response is the most frequent error that subjects make given these premises. In fact, a valid deduction can be made but it is necessary, as we will now show, to flesh out the models before eliminating anything.

In the initial models of "If there is a circle then there is a triangle" neither the circle nor the triangle is exhaustively represented. But, the models can be fleshed out explicitly either as a conditional (i.e., material implication) or as a bi-conditional (i.e., material equivalence). The bi-conditional interpretation, "if and only if there is a circle then there is a triangle" calls for both the antecedent and the consequent to be exhausted:

[o]   [Δ]
. . .

The first step towards the conditional interpretation is to represent the antecedent as exhausted:

[o]   Δ
. . .

These models can be further fleshed out to make explicit that a triangle can occur in the absence of a circle:

[o]   [Δ]
      [Δ]
. . .

The categorical premise:

There is not a triangle.

eliminates the first two models. Prior to this step, however, the models can be fleshed out completely:

[o]   [Δ]
[¬o]   [Δ]
[¬o]   [¬Δ]

Now the categorical premise eliminates the first two models and leaves behind only the third:

[¬o] [¬△]

This model supports the conclusion:

There is not a circle.

which is valid because no model of the premises falsifies it. The same procedure ensures that the same conclusion is drawn from the models of a bi-conditional. In both cases, modus tollens depends on fleshing out models and on detecting inconsistencies, and so it is a more complicated deduction than modus ponens.

Perhaps surprisingly, the difference in difficulty between modus ponens and modus tollens disappears when an implication is expressed by a statement using "only if" (see Evans, 1977b; Roberge, 1978), e.g.:

There is a circle only if there is a triangle.

This assertion has the same truth conditions as the conditional:

If there is a circle then there is a triangle.

because both are false only when there is a circle but no triangle. Evans and Beck (1981) suppose that the word "if" directs a reasoner's attention to the proposition that follows it, irrespective of the occurrence of "only". Hence, forward inferences from antecedent to consequent are easier with conditionals, whereas backwards inferences from consequent to antecedent are easier with "only if" assertions. Braine (1978, p.6) offers an alternative account:

> The behaviour of *p only if q* can be explained if we try to derive the meaning of *only if* as a compound of the meanings of *only* and *if*. In ordinary usage, *only* is equivalent to a double negative or *no ... other than* (e.g. *Only conservatives voted for Goldwater = No one other than conservatives voted for Goldwater*). We can use this equivalence to paraphrase *only* away from *p only if q*, for example, by the following steps: *p only if q = not p if other than q = if not q then not p*.

One trouble with both of these accounts is that they appear to predict a reversal in the difficulty of modus ponens and modus tollens rather than its disappearance. The model theory, however, offers a straightforward explanation. Following Braine's intuition and a linguistic analysis of "only" (Keenan, 1971), the theory assumes that an assertion, such as "there is a circle only if there is a triangle", leads to two explicit models right from the start. One represents the positive contingency: if there is a circle then there is a triangle; the other represents the negative contingency: if there isn't a triangle then there isn't a circle:

     [o]   Δ
     ¬o   [¬Δ]
        . . .

These initial models allow both modus ponens and modus tollens to be made without any further fleshing out. Because two explicit models are required, both deductions should be more difficult than modus ponens with a conditional. The data confirm this prediction.

Table 3.1 summarizes the models for the different connectives, both the initial models and the completely explicit ones.

The same interpretations can be used to build up models of premises containing more than one connective. Here, for example, is one of the problems that Braine et al. (1984) asked their subjects to rate for difficulty:

> If there is either a C or an H, then there is a P
> There is a C
> Therefore, there is a P.

Since there is no need for subjects to represent exhaustiveness for the problems used in this task, they are likely to have interpreted the first premise by building the following models:

     C   P
       H P
        . . .

The second premise then eliminates all but the first model:

     C   P

which supports the conclusion. This account is successful in explaining a number of aspects of the rating data that Braine et al.'s own theory leaves unexplained (see Johnson-Laird, Byrne and Schaeken, 1990).

Table 3.1
Models for the propositional connectives. Each line
represents an alternative model, and the square
brackets indicate that the set of contingencies
has been exhaustively represented

---

1. p and q
Initial model: p   q
Explicit model: [p] [q]

2. p or q
Initial models: p
                        q

Explicit models:	Inclusive	Exclusive
	[p] [¬q]	[p] [¬q]
	[¬p] [q]	[¬p] [q]
	[p] [q]	

3. If p then q
Initial models: p   q
                   . . .

Explicit models:	Conditional	Bi-conditional
	[p] [q]	[p] [q]
	[¬p] [q]	[¬p] [¬q]
	[¬p] [¬q]	

4. p only if q
Initial models: [p]   q
                ¬p [¬q]
                  . . .

Explicit models:	Conditional	Bi-conditional
	[p] [q]	[p] [q]
	[¬p] [¬q]	[¬p] [¬q]
	[¬p] [q]	

The relation between models and truth tables should now be evident.
Consider, for example, the truth table for an inclusive disjunction:

circle	triangle	circle or triangle, or both
T	T	T
T	F	T
F	T	T
F	F	F

An explicit set of models represents only those contingencies that are true:

[o]	[Δ]	–	the first line in the truth table
[o]	[¬Δ]	–	the second line in the truth table
[¬o]	[Δ]	–	the third line in the truth table

And with these contingencies only those elements that match the named constituents of the disjunction are represented at first:

        [o]   [Δ]
        [o]
                [Δ]

These models are precisely the ones for inclusive disjunction. The essence of the theory is accordingly that people use models that make explicit as little information as possible, and in this way, they overcome the unwieldy bulk of truth tables.

The theory makes three processing assumptions. The first is that the greater the number of *explicit* models that a reasoner has to keep in mind, the harder the task will be: it will take longer, and will be more likely to lead to errors. The second assumption is that a deduction that can be made from the initial models of the premises will be easier than one that can be made only by fleshing out the models with explicit information. This process also takes time and places a load on working memory. The third assumption is that it takes time to detect inconsistencies between elements of models (see e.g. Wason, 1959; Clark and Clark, 1977).

THREE PHENOMENA PREDICTED BY THE MODEL THEORY

1. Conditionals and Bi-conditionals

A new theory should lead to the discovery of new phenomena. The model theory does indeed make novel predictions, and so in this final part of the chapter we turn to them. We begin with a difference between conditionals and bi-conditionals. A conditional:

If Tony is in Kerry then Noel is in Dublin.

requires initially only one explicit model (and one implicit model), but when it is fleshed out to make a modus tollens deduction, it requires three explicit models. A bi-conditional:

If and only if Tony is in Kerry then Noel is in Dublin.

requires one explicit model for modus ponens, but only two for modus tollens. This difference leads to the prediction that modus tollens should be easier with a bi-conditional than with a conditional, but there should be no difference between the two for modus ponens, because both require only a single explicit model.

We tested this prediction in an experiment with sixteen adult subjects, who drew their own conclusions for two problems of each sort (see Johnson-Laird, Byrne, and Schaeken, 1990). The results confirmed the predictions. The percentages of correct conclusions were as follows:

Modus ponens with a conditional: 97%
Modus ponens with a bi-conditional: 97%
Modus tollens with a conditional: 38%
Modus tollens with a bi-conditional: 59%

Thus, modus tollens was easier with a bi-conditional than with a conditional, but there was no reliable difference between them for modus ponens.

Although a rule theory can accommodate these findings, it does so in an *ad hoc* way. The theory does not include a rule for modus tollens, and so the explanation cannot be based on the relative availability of such a rule for conditionals and bi-conditionals. Modus tollens depends on a chain of deductions. With our materials, the premises are of the form:

1. If p then q
2. q', where q is incompatible with q', i.e.:
3. If q then not-q'

and the chain of deductions is as follows:

4. Suppose: p
5. ∴ q
    (by modus ponens, from 1 and 4)
6. ∴ not-q'
    (by modus ponens, from 3 and 5)
7. ∴ q' and not-q'
    (by conjunction, of 2 and 6)
8. ∴ not-p
    (by *reductio ad absurdum*, from 4 and 7)

Why should this sequence of inferential steps be easier with a bi-conditional than with a conditional? The experiment did not detect any difference between the two sorts of conditional for modus ponens (the first two steps in the derivation after hypothesizing p). The only feasible explanation seems to be that it is easier to think of making a hypothetical argument with a bi-conditional than with a conditional. A rule theory has no machinery to explain why this difference should occur.

2. Conditionals and Exclusive Disjunctions

The model theory predicts that it should be easier to argue from a conditional, such as:

If Linda is in Amsterdam then Cathy is in Majorca.

than to argue from an exclusive disjunction, such as:

Linda is in Amsterdam or Cathy is in Majorca, but not both.

The conditional calls for the initial construction of only one explicit model, whereas the disjunction calls for the initial construction of two explicit models—one representing Linda in Amsterdam, and the other representing Cathy in Majorca. The theory therefore predicts that, in general, deductions based on conditionals should be easier to make than those based on exclusive disjunctions, because disjunctions from the outset place a greater load on working memory. Some corroboratory evidence exists in the literature. Roberge (1978), for example, obtained such an effect, but his study was limited to only one sort of deduction. Evans and Newstead (1980) similarly report that when one constituent of a conditional is negated, reasoners can still cope, but when one constituent of a disjunction is negated they become hopelessly lost.

We have also tested the prediction that modus ponens should be easier than the analogous affirmative deduction based on an exclusive disjunction:

Linda is in Amsterdam or Cathy is in Majorca, but not both.
Linda is in Amsterdam.
What follows?

In addition, we tested the prediction that modus tollens should be easier than the analogous negative deduction based on an exclusive disjunction:

Either Steven is in Donegal or Jenny is in Princeton, but not
    both.
Jenny is in London.
What follows?

The model theory also predicts that these negative deductions should
be harder than the affirmative deductions above, because the negative
deductions call for the detection of an inconsistency between elements
of models.

In principle, a negative deduction with a conditional calls for two or
three models to be made explicit whereas with the disjunction it calls
for only two explicit models, but the fleshing out of conditionals occurs
after their initial interpretation, whereas reasoners should already have
run into trouble with disjunctions. Will the two variables interact? The
theory predicts that they should, because the difference between the two
conditional deductions should be relatively large (one model versus two
or three models) whereas the only difference between the disjunctive
deductions is that the negative inference calls for detecting an
inconsistency.

In our experiment, fourteen adults drew their own conclusions for
four instances of each of the four sorts of problem (see Johnson-Laird,
Byrne, and Schaeken, 1990). The results were clear. The percentages of
correct conclusions were as follows:

Modus ponens:	91% correct.
Modus tollens:	64% correct.
Affirmative disjunction:	48% correct.
Negative disjunction:	30% correct.

As we had predicted, the conditional inferences were easier than the
disjunctive inferences, and the affirmative inferences were easier than
the negative inferences. Not a single subject violated either prediction.
There was also a trend towards the predicted interaction though it did
not reach significance.

Rule theorists can accommodate these observations by assuming that
the rule for modus ponens is easier to use than the disjunctive rule. Such
a hypothesis does not *explain* why the difference exists: it merely posits
it, or provides a parameter that can be estimated from data and used to
predict performance with other problems (e.g. Rips, 1983). In contrast,
the model theory explains why one sort of deduction is easier than the
other.

3. "Double Disjunctions"

A third group of phenomena is predicted by the model theory. If the number of alternative models to be kept in mind is large, then there should be a breakdown in deductive performance. In effect, the experimenter can overload working memory to the point where deduction ceases to be possible. The nature of the breakdown, however, should be revealing. The obvious way in which to increase alternative models is by introducing disjunctive premises; unlike conjunctions or conditionals, they immediately demand more than one explicit model.

Wason (1977) has devised a striking demonstration of the difficulty of keeping track of disjunctive alternatives. The subject is presented with four designs based on two shapes (diamond or circle) and two colours (black or white). The experimenter makes two assertions:

> First, there is a particular shape and a particular colour, such that any of the four designs which has one, and only one of these features is called a THOG.
> Second, the black diamond is a THOG.

The subjects' task is to classify as THOGs, or not THOGS, the three other shapes: the white circle, the black circle, and the white diamond. The experimenter's meta-assertion embraces four disjunctive possibilities:

1. If a design is a circle or else black, then it is a THOG.
2. If a design is a circle or else white, then it is a THOG.
3. If a design is a diamond or else white, then it is a THOG.
4. If a design is a diamond or else black, then it is a THOG.

The assertion that the black diamond is a THOG eliminates the fourth possibility because it refers to both properties, and it also eliminates the second one because it refers to neither property. Both of the remaining possibilities (1 and 3) yield the same classification: the white circle is a THOG, but neither the black circle nor the white diamond is a THOG. Few subjects solve the problem, and most decide that the white circle is *not* a THOG, and that the other two designs are either THOGs or of unknown status. The subjects fail to envisage the four disjunctive possibilities and attempt to make direct evaluations of the designs from the assertion about the black diamond. They appear to make the unwarranted inference:

If a black diamond is a THOG, then any design that is neither
black nor a diamond is not a THOG.

In studies where the four disjunctive possibilities are spelt out explicitly
for the subjects, their performance is reliably better (see Griggs and
Newstead, 1982, but cf. Girotto and Legrenzi, 1989).

We have devised an informative demonstration that we call the
"double disjunction" task, which the reader might like to attempt. It
concerns the locations of three people, Linda, Mary, and Cathy:

Linda is in Cannes or Mary is in Tripoli, or both.
Mary is in Havana or Cathy is in Sofia, or both.
What, if anything, follows?

The most frequent response is that nothing follows (see Johnson-Laird,
Byrne, and Schaeken, 1990). People indeed appear to be overwhelmed
by the possibilities. When they do draw a conclusion it is seldom correct.
In fact, the set of models for the first premise is:

[c]   [t]
[c]
       [t]

where c denotes Linda in Cannes and t denotes Mary in Tripoli. The set
of models for the second premise is:

[h]   [s]
[h]
       [s]

where h denotes Mary in Havana, and s denotes Cathy in Sofia. At least
one constituent proposition in each premise must be true, and so we can
multiply out all the possibilities excluding only those cases where Mary
is in Tripoli and Mary is in Havana, because one person cannot be in
two places at the same time:

[c]   [t]   [s]
[c]   [h]   [s]
[c]   [h]
[c]   [s]
       [t]   [s]

These models support the conclusion:

Linda is in Cannes or Cathy is in Sofia, or both.

or equivalently:

If Linda is not in Cannes then Cathy is in Sofia.

There is a simple way in which by giving subjects an *extra* premise the difficulty of a double disjunction is remarkably reduced. The phenomenon is predicted by the model theory. The reasoners are given a categorical premise such as:

Linda is not in Cannes.

in addition to the double disjunction above. They are then able to deduce that:

Mary is in Tripoli.

and that:

Cathy is in Sophia.

Why is the task so much easier? The answer is because it is no longer necessary to construct so many models. Given the models for Linda is in Cannes or Mary is in Tripoli:

[c]   [t]
[c]
        [t]

the categorical premise rules out the first two to leave only:

[t]

This model similarly eliminates all but one of the models for Mary is in Havana or Cathy is in Sofia.

[t]   [s]

Hence the deduction can be made without having to construct the full set of five models. Of course, knowledgeable subjects could carry out a double disjunction by spontaneously framing a hypothesis of their own in order to reduce the number of models they have to construct; the difficulty of the task implies that few logically-untrained individuals use this strategy.

When there is only one disjunction, deductions are more accurate from an exclusive disjunction than from an inclusive one. Newstead and Griggs (1983, p.97) argue that exclusive disjunctions are easier to grasp because the inferences are symmetrical: the truth of one constituent implies the falsity of the other, and *vice versa*. It is not clear, however, why this symmetry should make deduction easier. The model theory yields a simple alternative explanation: exclusive disjunctions call for a smaller number of explicit models than inclusive disjunctions. A double disjunction should therefore be reliably easier when the disjunctions are exclusive:

Linda is in Cannes or Mary is in Tripoli, but not both.
Mary is in Havana or Cathy is in Sophia, but not both.
What follows?

In this case, there are only three possible models:

```
        [t]    [s]
[c]            [s]
[c]     [h]
```

But, the same conclusion as before is valid:

Linda is in Cannes or Cathy is in Sophia, or both.

We tested 24 adult subjects with both sorts of double disjunction (see Johnson-Laird, Byrne, and Schaeken, 1990). They drew 15% correct conclusions with the exclusive disjunctions, but only 4% with the inclusive disjunctions. The overwhelming majority of their conclusions suggested that they could imagine some of the possible models but not all of them. The following conclusion from a double inclusive disjunction, for instance:

If Mary is in Tripoli, then Cathy is in Sofia and Linda may be in Cannes.

is entirely accurate as far as it goes, but suggests that the subjects who drew it considered only two of the models. Similarly, the conclusion:

Mary is in Tripoli and Cathy is in Sofia.

is invalid, but it is consistent with three of the models. Figure 3.1 shows the percentages of conclusions consistent with one model of the premises, with two models of the premises, and so on. There are two striking features. First, the most frequent conclusions are consistent with just one model of the premises. Second, few conclusions are not consistent with any of the models of the premises. In short, the subjects do seem to be reasoning by constructing models (or at least one model) of the premises.

Once again, theories based on formal rules cannot account either for the difficulty of the task or for the sorts of errors that occur. The inclusive double disjunction has the form:

1. p or q, or both
2. q' or r, or both, where q' is incompatible with q, i.e.:
3. If q then not q'

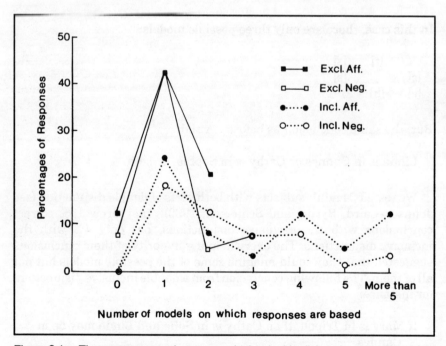

Figure 3.1. The percentages of responses in the double disjunction experiment that were consistent with one model of the premises, two models, and so on.

A formal derivation proceeds as follows:

4. Suppose: not p
5. ∴ q
   (disjunctive rule, from 1 and 4)
6. ∴ not q'
   (modus ponens, from 3 and 5)
7. ∴ r
   (disjunctive rule, from 2 and 6)
8. ∴ If not-p then r
   (conditional proof)

The derivation is no longer than the one above for modus tollens, and yet there is a massive difference in difficulty between the two deductions.

Perhaps the severest problem for theories based on formal rules is to account for the sorts of erroneous conclusions that are drawn. Psychiatrists and anthropologists have sometimes proposed invalid rules of inference in order to explain irrational thinking (see e.g. Levy-Bruhl, 1910; von Domarus, 1944; and see also Jackendoff, 1988, for a similar speculation), but this tactic sacrifices deductive competence for too slight a gain in explanatory power. Errors with a "double disjunction" clearly cannot be explained in terms of misunderstanding the premises. Yet, if errors are supposed to be the result of a "spanner in the inferential works", then why do they correspond so reliably to a subset of the models of the premises? The answer appears to be that people try to reason by manipulating models but often succeed in constructing only one or two of the possible models of the premises.

CONCLUSIONS

The model theory accounts for the existing phenomena of propositional reasoning and successfully predicts novel phenomena. It explains the following findings:

1. Disjunctions are interpreted in an indeterminate way if their content or context fails to elicit an inclusive or exclusive interpretation.
2. Conditionals are similarly interpreted in an indeterminate way.
3. Modus ponens is easier than modus tollens with conditional premises.

4. The difference disappears with "only if" premises, but both deductions are then slightly harder than modus ponens with a conditional premise.
5. Modus tollens is easier with a bi-conditional than with a conditional, but modus ponens is equally easy with both.
6. Deductions with conditionals are easier than deductions with exclusive disjunctions.
7. Double disjunctions are very difficult, but those with exclusive disjunctions are easier than those with inclusive disjunctions.

Different individuals reason in different ways. Some flesh out their models of a conditional in order to make a modus tollens deduction; others fail to do so. Some can construct several models of a "double disjunction"; others can construct only one model. The model theory predicts the general pattern of performance, and it could account for these individual differences in terms of such factors as the processing capacity of working memory. The theory has itself been modelled in two computer programs. Tho first implements our psychological assumptions: it uses implicit models until it is necessary to make them explicit, and it has a limited processing capacity. The second program, which we will describe in Chapter 9, is an exercise in artificial intelligence. It has no psychological constraints and so it draws a maximally parsimonious conclusion from any premises in the propositional calculus.

In this chapter, we have assumed an account of the meaning of connectives based on truth tables because our agenda has been dictated by theories based on formal rules. These theories are not intended to deal with *because* or *after* (or any connectives that lie outside truth tables). What is problematical is whether or not conditionals can be captured by truth tables. It is this and other puzzles of conditionals that we now take up.

CHAPTER 4

Conditionals

If there hadn't been guns I wouldn't have been shot.
If I hadn't been shot I wouldn't have been re-elected.
If I hadn't been re-elected, there wouldn't have been guns.
(Spitting Image's Ronald Reagan puppet)

If is problematical. Some connectives such as *and* and *or* have meanings that can be defined by truth tables, and apparent exceptions, such as the use of *and* to convey temporal sequence, can be explained as inferences based on general knowledge (Grice, 1975). Other connectives such as *because* and *when* cannot be defined by truth tables, because they invariably denote causal and temporal relations. But it is unclear whether *if* has a truth-table definition as we have provisionally assumed, or transcends such an analysis. The less that is known, the more that must be written; and the profundity of this puzzle is reflected in the number of books on conditionals (e.g. Harper, Stalnaker, and Pearce, 1981; Appiah, 1985; Traugott, ter Meulen, Reilly and Ferguson, 1986; Jackson, 1987). To explain reasoning with conditionals, however, we need to understand how they are understood. Our strategy will therefore be to outline a theory of the interpretation of "if", and then to show how this theory illuminates reasoning with conditionals. We begin with the meaning of neutral conditionals, which have no strong dependence on context or general knowledge for their interpretation, and then we consider other sorts of conditionals.

When people are asked to judge the truth or falsity of a neutral conditional, such as:

If there is a circle then there is a triangle.

they make the following characteristic judgements (see Johnson-Laird and Tagart, 1969; Evans, 1972):

Situation		Judgement
O	Δ	the conditional is true
O	*	the conditional is false
+	Δ	the conditional is irrelevant
+	*	the conditional is irrelevant

These judgements correspond to a "defective" truth table, and thus seem to bear out the view that a conditional makes an assertion conditional on the truth of its antecedent, and has no truth value when its antecedent is false (Quine, 1952; Wason, 1966). A related idea is that a conditional states a material implication, but a speaker who asserts a conditional knowing that its antecedent is false breaches the conventions of ordinary conversation (Grice, 1975; Lewis, 1976; Jackson, 1987).

Not all conditionals, however, have a defective truth table. A conditional with a negative antecedent:

If there isn't a circle then there is a triangle.

as even Stoic logicians noted, tends to be interpreted as equivalent to a disjunction:

There is a circle or there is a triangle.

A disjunction does have a complete truth table, and so these conditionals do too. A further class of conditionals lie outside truth tables altogether. They are counterfactuals, such as:

If there were a circle then there would be a triangle.

The truth or falsity of counterfactuals cannot depend merely on the truth or falsity of antecedent and consequent, because one normally takes for granted that these constituents are false, i.e. there isn't a circle, and there isn't a triangle. Although the linguistic distinction between indicative and counterfactual conditionals is not always clear cut (Dudman, 1988), theorists generally take counterfactuals to be true if, in any situation in which the antecedent is true, and which otherwise resembles the real world as closely as possible, the consequent is also true (see Stalnaker, 1968, 1981; Lewis, 1973; and Rips and Marcus, 1977).

In summary, some conditionals have a complete truth table, some have a defective truth table, and some seem to have no truth table at all. Not surprisingly, certain philosophers have abandoned the quest for their meaning. They do not have truth conditions, these skeptics claim, but only conditions in which it is justifiable to assert them, namely, provided that the consequent is highly probable given that the antecedent is true (see e.g. Adams, 1975; Appiah, 1985). Unfortunately for our purposes, if conditionals have no truth conditions then they cannot be true or false, and so they cannot occur in valid deductions, which by definition are truth preserving.

An ideal solution to the problem of "if" would be to establish a uniform semantics from which its chameleon-like interpretations would emerge. One distinguished proponent of formal rules, Braine (1979; Braine and O'Brien, 1989), has proposed such an account: a conditional is a rule of inference to the effect that its consequent can be inferred from its antecedent (see also Ryle, 1949, Chapter 5). The following cases, however, do not seem to warrant deductions from antecedent to consequent:

If you are interested then there is a Hitchcock movie on TV.
If you had needed some money then there was £10 in the desk.

but rather they are true or false merely in virtue of the truth values of their consequents. Similarly, one can judge the truth or falsity of a conditional, such as:

If there is a circle then there is a triangle.

by looking to see what is on the blackboard and without having to consider whether the consequent follows from the antecedent. Hence, we doubt the generality of Braine's thesis.

THE MODEL THEORY OF THE MEANING OF CONDITIONALS

Indicative Conditionals

The model theory provides an account of conditionals, but in order to establish it, we need to consider the metaphysics of everyday life, which distinguishes at least four sorts of situations: actual states of affairs, real possibilities, real impossibilities, and counterfactual situations. Actual states of affairs, such as:

Mrs. Thatcher won the 1979 election.

are what happened. Real possibilities, such as:

Mrs. Thatcher wins the next election.

could happen—no matter how remote their likelihood—given the actual state of the world. Real impossibilities could never happen, given the actual state of the world:

Mrs. Thatcher won the American presidential election.

They must be distinguished from counterfactual situations, which were once real possibilities, but are so no longer because they did not occur:

Mrs. Thatcher lost the 1979 election.

The ability to envisage counterfactual situations is an important part of how one evaluates what actually happens (Hofstadter, 1985, p.239; Kahneman and Miller, 1986). A situation represented in a model can thus be treated by the interpretative system as actual, possible, impossible, or counterfactual. These categories, in turn, apply to both factual and fictional discourse. Granted their existence, we can set out our theory (which is a development from Johnson-Laird, 1986).

The interpretation of a conditional's consequent is identical to its interpretation as an isolated main clause in a context that satisfies the conditional's antecedent. It follows that antecedents must describe states of affairs, whereas consequents can have any illocutionary force—they can make assertions, ask questions, or give commands. The function of an antecedent is to establish a context, i.e. a state of affairs to be presupposed in interpreting the consequent. Hence, when one asks logically-naive individuals to negate the conditional:

If there is a circle then there is a triangle.

their negation does not embrace the antecedent, and they assert instead:

If there is a circle then there is not a triangle.

The interpretation of an antecedent depends on its linguistic meaning and its context—in particular, the knowledge that is called to mind during the process of interpretation. An indicative antecedent, such as:

If there is a circle ....

calls for a model of a real possibility in relation to the current state of affairs, supplemented by an implicit model of an alternative, but real, possibility:

[o]

. . .

When these models have been established, the consequent can be interpreted in relation to the explicit antecedent model. Thus, the consequent:

. . .there is a triangle.

describes a state of affairs that obtains in the context described by the antecedent:

[o]   Δ

. . .

This interpretation is consistent with subsequently fleshing out the models explicitly as a conditional or a bi-conditional.

The conditional is true provided that its consequent is true in any situation that satisfies the explicit antecedent model. The consequent is interpreted in a context where the antecedent is presupposed, and so the conditional has nothing to say—at least initially—about any alternative where the antecedent fails to hold, that is, the implicit model does not specify anything about the situation in which there is no circle. When the truth of a conditional is assessed in a situation where its antecedent is false, it is judged to be "irrelevant", because the models:

[o]   Δ

. . .

do not specify anything explicitly about a situation in which there is no circle. This same lack of content, as we saw in the previous chapter, is responsible for the failure to make a modus tollens deduction.

Why should a negative antecedent, but not a negative consequent, lead to a disjunctive interpretation? A denial is plausibly used to correct a misconception, e.g. "A whale is not a fish" (see Wason, 1965), and so a negation is likely to call to mind the affirmative alternative.

Antecedents, unlike consequents, are exhaustively represented in models. Hence, a conditional with a negative antecedent:

If there isn't a circle then there is a triangle.

yields models in which the negative antecedent is exhaustively represented, and so models containing circles are the only alternative:

    [¬o] Δ
    [o]
    [o]

This set of models is equivalent to the set for the disjunction: circle or triangle. Indeed, some subjects may merely represent the two positive instances:

         Δ
    [o]

A conditional with a negated consequent:

If there is a circle then there isn't a triangle.

only has models in which the negative consequent is exhausted when it is interpreted as a bi-conditional. Otherwise, it yields the models:

    [o]   ¬Δ
           Δ
    . . .

which are not equivalent to the disjunction, circle or triangle, because the implicit model might contain neither a circle nor a triangle.

Counterfactual Conditionals

The interpretation of counterfactual conditionals depends on invoking counterfactual situations. When someone asserts:

If there had been a circle . . .

then listeners know that the speaker is assuming that there is not a circle, but that they are to envisage a once possible, but now counterfactual, context in which there is a circle:

Actual: ¬o
Counterfactual: [o]
                  . . .

The consequent:

. . . there would have been a triangle.

implies that there is not a triangle, but asserts that in the counterfactual situation where there is a circle, there is a triangle:

Actual: ¬o   ¬Δ
Counterfactual: [o]   Δ
                  . . .

The implicit model allows that there was once a real possibility in which there wasn't a circle but there was a triangle. Speakers can overrule the normal interpretation of a counterfactual (Wilson, 1975, p.122). The following assertion:

If there had been a circle then there would have been a triangle, and in fact there was a circle and so there was a triangle.

updates the model of actuality with the initial model of the counterfactual set:

Actual: o   Δ

The Relations Between Antecedent and Consequent

There is nothing too puzzling about the interpretation of neutral conditionals, because by definition there is no salient relation between antecedent and consequent. Yet no-one is likely to assert a conditional merely on the grounds that its consequent is true in the context specified by its antecedent. Despite the fact that it is true, one would hardly claim, for instance:

If Mrs Thatcher loses the election then one day it will rain.

On the contrary, one asserts a conditional where there are grounds for relating the antecedent to the consequent: the real possibility referred to by the antecedent has some bearing on the real possibility referred to by the consequent (cf. Barwise, 1989, Ch. 5).

The relations that can hold between antecedent and consequent may depend on a common referent or on general knowledge—a distinction that applies generally to relations in discourse (Johnson-Laird, 1983, Ch. 14). An example of a referential relation is:

If there is a circle then it is not large.

This relation rules out as impossible a certain contingency. There cannot be a case where the consequent of the conditional is false (the circle is large), and the antecedent is false (there isn't a circle). Hence, modus tollens is blocked. General knowledge enables certain rhetorical effects to be achieved by using conditionals with manifestly false constituents, e.g.:

If Thatcher wins the next election then pigs will fly.

Knowledge can also provide a framework that establishes a relation between antecedent and consequent (Goodman, 1947). The most important frameworks in which one state of affairs constrains another are those that establish inferential, causal, or deontic relations, e.g:

If the number hadn't been divisible by 2 then it wouldn't have
    been even.
    (An inferential relation.)
If the vase hadn't been dropped then it wouldn't have broken.
    (A causal relation.)
If we hadn't promised then we needn't have gone.
    (A deontic relation).

In these cases, general knowledge informs the choice of what to represent in the models of the conditionals. We can illustrate this point by considering the difference between different sorts of causal assertion (Miller and Johnson-Laird, 1976, Sec. 6.3.5). On the one hand, the assertion:

If the vase hadn't been dropped then it wouldn't have broken.

makes a strong claim that one event caused another:

Actual: d   b
Counterfactual: ¬d   ¬b

The possibility of one event without the other is not even countenanced. On the other hand, an assertion of exactly the same syntactic form:

If the vase hadn't been fragile then it wouldn't have broken.

does not make a causal assertion, but rather stipulates that one state of affairs allowed another to occur:

Actual: f   b
Counterfactual: ¬f   ¬b
                         f   ¬b

where the second counterfactual model allows that even though the vase is fragile, it need not have broken, e.g., if it hadn't been dropped. The difference in the interpretation of these two conditionals depends, of course, on general knowledge. A third sort of conditional, such as:

If the vase hadn't been touched then it might not have broken.

makes only a weak causal claim:

Actual: t   b
Counterfactual: ¬t   ¬b
                        ¬t   b

Causation is often treated by theorist and lay person alike as a primitive unanalyzable notion, but the concept can be taken to pieces in terms of real possibilities and counterfactual situations (Miller and Johnson-Laird, 1976, Sec. 6.3.5). Table 4.1 summarizes the models for the main causal relations. Because models are related to truth tables, these analyzes could be expressed in a new form of truth table that distinguishes between real and counterfactual contingencies. There is no need for any further decomposition of causation once models reflect the epistemological status of possibilities. "A caused B" in the strong sense means nothing other than that A happened and (then) B happened, and that had A not happened, then B would not have happened. In other words, it is a real impossibility for A to happen without B happening.

A similar analysis can be made of deontic matters. For example, the conditional:

Table 4.1
The major causal relations. The actual and counterfactual
models fall within the framework of physical principles

1. Strong causation:

	a caused c		a prevented c	
	a	c	a	¬c
Actual	a	c	a	¬c
Counterfactual	¬a	¬c	¬a	c

2. Weak causation:

	a caused c		a prevented c	
Actual:	a	c	a	¬c
Counterfactual:	¬a	¬c	¬a	c
	¬a	c	¬a	¬c

3. Allowing relation:

	a allowed c		a allowed not c	
Actual:	a	c	a	¬c
Counterfactual:	¬a	¬c	¬a	c
	a	¬c	a	c

If we had promised then we would have had to go.

makes a strong claim about obligation:

Actual: ¬p   ¬g
Counterfactual: p   g

The models in this case represent, not physical possibilities, but what is deontically possible, i.e., what is permissible. Physically it is, alas, all too possible to break promises, but as the models show, the only permissible course of action is to fulfil a promise. The relevant framework of knowledge—physical, deontic, or inferential—affects not only the interpretation of conditionals, but also the interpretation of modal auxiliary verbs such as "can" and "must" (Johnson-Laird, 1978). It leads to the fleshing out of different models of conditionals to reflect the underlying relation between antecedent and consequent.

The model theory of the meaning of conditionals can be summarized in three principles:

1. An indicative conditional is interpreted by constructing an explicit model of its antecedent, which is exhaustively represented, and to which is added a model of the consequent. An alternative implicit model allows for cases in which the antecedent does not hold.

2. A counterfactual conditional is interpreted in the same way except that the models of its antecedent and consequent are of

counterfactual situations, and there is an explicit model of the actual situation.

3. Conditionals may elicit richer models in which more states are rendered explicit. This fleshing out of models occurs in several circumstances, e.g. when a referential relation, or one based on general knowledge, holds between antecedent and consequent.

According to this theory, a conditional is true if the proposition asserted by its consequent is true in the context described by its antecedent; it is false if the proposition asserted by the consequent is false in the context described by the antecedent. Knowledge, however, can establish that the antecedent condition is irrelevant to the truth or falsity of the consequent, e.g. "If you had needed some money then there was £10 in the desk". Where the antecedent of an indicative conditional is false, the interpretation will yield no truth value unless the models have been fleshed out to include explicit information about this possibility. The same principle applies *mutatis mutandis* to counterfactuals. They can have a complete truth table, but one contingency in it will be an actual state, one or more may be counterfactual situations, and at least one contingency will be a real impossibility.

DEDUCTION WITH CONDITIONALS

The Paradoxes of Implication

Our aim in formulating a semantics of conditionals was to elucidate deductions with them. Apart from the studies that we described in the previous chapter, the main phenomena of conditional reasoning are effects of content. There is, however, one formal problem that any theory of conditionals must confront. Material implication supports two valid deductions that appear to be paradoxical when the relation is expressed using a conditional. A false antecedent warrants a conditional with any consequent whatsoever:

1. You are not a millionaire.
   ∴ If you are a millionaire then it will rain tomorrow.

Likewise, a true consequent warrants a conditional with any antecedent whatsoever:

2. The weather is fine.
   ∴ If World War III started yesterday then the weather is fine.

If you doubt the validity of these deductions, then a glance at the truth table should settle your mind:

p	q	if p then q
T	T	T
T	F	F
F	T	T
F	F	T

As you see, the conditional is true whenever its antecedent is false (the last two rows of the table), and whenever its consequent is true (the first and third rows). Because either condition suffices to establish the truth of the conditional, the corresponding deductions must be valid. Theorists therefore face a choice: to abandon the truth-table analysis of conditionals (even if it is supplemented by inferences based on general knowledge), or to accept the validity of these apparently paradoxical deductions and to explain why they seem improper. We shall embrace the second alternative.

A conditional with a negated antecedent, as we have seen, has the same truth conditions as a disjunction. Hence, if someone asserts:

If Shakespeare didn't write the sonnets, then Bacon did.

and Shakespeare did write the sonnets, then the assertion is true. And, likewise, if Bacon wrote the sonnets, the assertion is true. Both of the following deductions are therefore valid:

1. Shakespeare wrote the sonnets.
   ∴ If Shakespeare didn't write the sonnets then Bacon did.
2. Bacon wrote the sonnets.
   ∴ If Shakespeare didn't write the sonnets then Bacon did.

They do not seem to be valid for the same reason that the corresponding deductions with disjunctions do not seem to be valid:

1′. Shakespeare wrote the sonnets.
   ∴ Shakespeare wrote the sonnets or Bacon did.
2′. Bacon wrote the sonnets.
   ∴ Shakespeare wrote the sonnets or Bacon did.

All four deductions throw semantic information away. They thus violate one of the fundamental constraints on human deductive competence (see

Chapter 2). And that is why they do not seem to be valid, even though they are.

The Selection Task: Matching Bias

The best known phenomena of conditional reasoning occur in Wason's selection task (see e.g. Wason, 1966; Wason and Johnson-Laird, 1972; Wason, 1983). In the original version of the task, four cards are put in front of a subject. Each card has on its uppermost face a single symbol, say: A, B, 2, and 3; and the subjects know that every card has a letter on one side and a number on the other side. The experimenter then presents a neutral conditional:

If a card has an A on one side then it has a 2 on the other side.

The subjects' task is to select those cards that they need to turn over in order to determine whether the rule is true or false.

The majority of subjects select the A card, or the A and the 2 cards. Surprisingly, they fail to select the card corresponding to the case where the consequent is false: the 3 card. Yet, if the A had a 3 on its other side, the rule would be false; and so, by parity of reasoning, if the 3 had an A on its other side, the rule would also be false. In short, the correct selection consists in the card that renders the antecedent true and the card that renders the consequent false, because the combination of true antecedent and false consequent shows that the conditional itself is false.

The selection task calls for more than a deduction: subjects have to explore different possibilities, to deduce their consequences for the truth or falsity of the rule, and on this basis to determine which cards to select. The task has generated a large literature, which is not easy to integrate, and one major investigator, Evans (1989), has even wondered whether the paradigm tells us anything about deduction as opposed to heuristic biases. Part of Evans's concern arises from a phenomenon that he and his colleagues discovered, the so-called "matching" bias. When conditionals contain negated antecedents or consequents, subjects appear to ignore the presence of the negation in constructing an instance that falsifies the conditional. They merely match their selections to the cards mentioned in the conditional. They do not ignore negations, however, in constructing instances to render a rule true, or in coping with other connectives, such as disjunction.

If people succumb to matching bias in constructing false instances of conditionals, then they are also likely to succumb in carrying out the selection task. Evans and Lynch (1973) confirmed this prediction. Given a rule, such as:

If there is not an S on one side of a card then there is a 9 on the other side.

then about two thirds of the subjects select the S card, which renders the antecedent proposition false. These subjects thus appear to ignore the negation. A comparable effect occurs with the rule:

If there is an S on one side of a card then there is not a 9 on the other side.

Most subjects select the card that renders the antecedent true, and over half of them select the card that renders the consequent false. In this case, the subjects are correct, though presumably because they are merely matching their selections to the items mentioned in the rule.

Evans (1989, p.33) argues that the matching bias is "a complex, linguistically determined relevance judgement rather than a simply (sic) availability or response priming effect." He explains it by making two hypotheses. First, a conditional statement:

If (not) p then (not) q

is always about p and q regardless of the presence of negation. This assumption is similar to our earlier argument that a negation leads to a representation of the affirmative case too. Second, the effect is overridden in a verification task by another, more powerful, linguistic factor: "The use of *if* invites one to entertain the supposition that the antecedent condition is true ... the listener is strongly invited to consider the hypothesis (mental model, possible world) in which the antecedent and consequent conditions are actually fulfilled." (Evans, 1989, p.32).

The matching bias, as Evans allows, can be reconciled with the model theory. We argued earlier that conditionals with negative constituents elicit representations of the corresponding positive items. Hence, a conditional with a negative antecedent:

If there is not an A then there is a 2

may elicit the models:

2

[A]

Similarly, a conditional with a negated consequent:

If there is an A then there is not a 2

may elicit the models:

[A]
   2
. . .

As we will see, these interpretations then yield the observed phenomena. The subjects are reasoning, but their representation of the conditional has been influenced by the presence of negation.

The Selection Task: Realistic Content

With certain realistic rules or regulations, such as:

If a person is drinking beer then the person must be over 18.

subjects are more likely to reason correctly in the selection task. They choose the card corresponding to the case where the consequent is false: not over 18 (Griggs and Cox, 1982). Theories based on formal rules, as Manktelow and Over (1987) argue, cannot easily account either for the failure to select the false consequent with a neutral conditional or for its selection with these realistic conditionals. There is no difference in the logical form of realistic and neutral conditionals that could account for the results. Moreover, those arch-formalists, the Piagetians, claim that children have a capacity for falsification as soon as they attain the level of formal operations. Piaget describes this ability in the following terms: to check the truth of a conditional, if p then q, a child will look to see whether or not there is a counter-example, p and not-q (Beth and Piaget, 1966, p.181). Yet adults conspicuously fail to do so with neutral conditionals in the selection task.

Several reasons have been put forward to explain why a realistic conditional may elicit the correct selection. They are all variants on the theory that people use content-specific rules of inference. The simplest hypothesis is that subjects recall specific counterexamples from their memory of actual or similar cases, and use this knowledge to guide their selection (Griggs and Cox, 1982). A more plausible hypothesis allows for analogies (e.g., D'Andrade, cited in Rumelhart and Norman, 1981; Manktelow and Evans, 1979; Griggs, 1983; cf. also Riesbeck and Schank, 1989). Although both hypotheses lack clear boundary conditions, neither of them seems to embrace the finding that a general deontic framework can also improve performance. This finding was predicted by a third variant on content-specific rules: "pragmatic reasoning schemas" (Cheng and Holyoak, 1985; Cheng, Holyoak, Nisbett, and Olivier, 1986). These are rules of inference supposedly induced from experience, and they concern causation, permission, and obligation. The permission schema, for example, consists in four rules (or productions in a production system):

1. If the action is to be taken then the precondition must be satisfied.
2. If the action is not to be taken then the precondition need not be satisfied.
3. If the precondition is satisfied then the action may be taken.
4. If the precondition is not satisfied then the action must not be taken.

When a conditional, such as:

If a person is drinking beer then the person must be over 18.

cues the schema, then rule 4 directly elicits the idea that if a person is not over 18 then they must not drink beer. And this rule leads to the selection of the card corresponding to the false consequent: not over 18.

A variant of this idea has been advanced by Cosmides (1989), who argues that human evolution has led to a specific inferential module concerned with violations of social contracts. She shows that a background story eliciting such ideas can lead subjects to make a surprising selection: they choose instances corresponding to not-p and q for a conditional rule of the form, if p then q. In the context of the story, the rule:

If a man has a tattoo on his face then he eats cassava root.

tends to elicit selections of the following cards: no tattoo, and eats cassava root. We believe that there is a simple alternative explanation for this result. The subjects treat the rule as meaning:

A man may eat cassava root only if he has a tattoo.

Such an assertion, as we argued in the previous chapter, calls for models of the following sort:

[eating cassava]   tattoo
¬ eating cassava   [¬ tattoo]
       . . .

which, as the next section shows, leads to the subjects' choice of instances. There is no need to postulate a specific inferential module concerning the violation of social contracts (see also Griggs, 1984; Cheng and Holyoak, 1989).

Knowledge undoubtedly influences deduction, but is it represented by content-specific rules? There is no evidence for this form of representation; it could be represented by general assertions, which are used to construct models of the sort shown in Table 4.1. One further difficulty with pragmatic schemas is their use of unanalyzed modal auxiliaries, such as "may" and "must", which could be analyzed in terms of possible and permissible states of affairs.

The Model Theory of the Selection Task

The model theory assumes that reasoners use their knowledge, however it is represented, in constructing models of premises. The selection task is carried out in the following way:

1. The subjects consider only those cards that are explicitly represented in their models of the rule.
2. They then select those cards for which the hidden value could have a bearing on the truth or falsity of the rule.

This account is a simple modification of an earlier theory (Johnson-Laird and Wason, 1970) in which models of the rule now serve in place of truth tables.

A critical factor according to this theory is whether the models include explicit representations of negative instances. A neutral conditional, such as:

If there is an A then there is a 2

yields the models:

[A]   2
   . . .

The subjects will consider both cards, but will select only the "A" card, because it alone has a hidden value that could bear on the truth or falsity of the conditional. If they interpret the rule as a bi-conditional:

    [A]   [2]
...

then they will select both cards. Rules with a negated antecedent or a negated consequent, as we argued earlier, tend to elicit models of the positive items, e.g:

        2
    [A]

and so subjects will tend to make the same selections as those for affirmative conditionals. Hence, performance with neutral conditionals reflects a bias towards selecting those cards that match the cards in the explicit model (cf. Evans, 1987; 1989; Klayman and Ha, 1987). There may be an independent bias towards verifying the rule (Wason and Johnson-Laird, 1972). And, according to the model theory, the card corresponding to the false consequent will be selected only if the models of the conditional are fleshed out to represent it explicitly, e.g.:

    [A]   2
          ¬2

where since [A] is exhausted in the first model ¬2 must occur with ¬ A. An insightful performance may further depend on an explicit representation of what is not possible, i.e. the real impossibility given the rule:

    [A]   [¬2]

In short, the model theory predicts that people will select the card falsifying the consequent whenever the models are fleshed out with explicit representations of that card. This prediction makes sense of the five experimental manipulations that have been found to yield the correct selections, and neither memory for counterexamples nor pragmatic reasoning schemas can account for all of them:

1. Change the form of the rule. This manipulation includes the use of rules, such as "All circles are black", that elicit models of a single entity rather than of two separate entities (Wason and Green, 1984). It also

includes the use of conditionals with negated consequents, or the use of disjunctions (Wason and Johnson-Laird, 1969). We predict that changing the rule to an "only if" formulation should also enhance performance.

2.   Change the content of the rule. This tactic includes the use of contents that trigger memories for violations (Johnson-Laird, Legrenzi, and Legrenzi, 1972), or memories for analogous events (Griggs and Cox, 1982; Klaczynski, Gelfand, and Reese, 1989).

3.   Change the context of the rule. This tactic includes the use of a relevant deontic framework for the interpretation of the rule (Cheng and Holyoak, 1985; Cheng et al, 1986; Cosmides, 1989). General knowledge need not be represented by pragmatic reasoning schemas; it can nevertheless lead to the explicit representation of negative instances (see Table 4.1).

4.   Change the content of the cards, by labelling them explicitly with negations (Cheng and Holyoak, 1985, Expt 2; Jackson and Griggs, 1990).

5.   Change the task so that subjects are more likely to envisage all the alternatives explicitly. This manipulation includes reducing the choice to one between the consequent and the negated consequent (Johnson-Laird and Wason, 1970; Wason and Green, 1984; Oakhill and Johnson-Laird, 1985a), instructions to test violations of the rule (Valentine, 1985; Chrostowski and Griggs, 1985), and the verbalization of the reasoning behind one's selections (Berry, 1983; but cf. Klaczynski et al, 1989).

The Suppression of Valid Deductions

The selection task challenges formal theories because the only effects of content that they can explain are those on the interpretation of premises. A more recently discovered effect of content challenges the foundation of all formal theories: the assumption that the rule of modus ponens is part of mental logic. To describe the effect, we need first to consider certain fallacies.

Ordinary reasoners given the premises:

If she meets her friend then she will go to a play.
She did not meet her friend.

tend to draw the conclusion:

Therefore, she did not go to a play.

The inference is known (after its categorical premise) as denying the antecedent, and it is fallacious unless the first premise is interpreted as a bi-conditional. The following premises:

If she meets her friend then she will go to a play.
She went to a play.

lead to an analogous fallacy known (after its categorical premise) as affirming the consequent:

Therefore, she met her friend.

These fallacies might have led rule theorists to suppose that people are equipped with two invalid rules of inference for material implication:

1. If p then q
   not-p
   ∴ not-q

and:

2. If p then q
   q
   ∴ p

Rule theorists, however, have not in general adopted this idea, because they have been able to suppress the fallacies. They can do so by presenting an extra premise that establishes an alternative antecedent bringing about the same consequent (Rumain, Connell, and Braine, 1983; Markovits, 1984, 1985). Thus, where the original conditional is:

If she meets her friend then she will go to a play.

the additional presentation of:

If she meets her brother then she will go to a play.

blocks the bi-conditional interpretation of the original conditional. The subjects realize that she could have gone to a play even if she did not meet her friend. When the two conditionals are accompanied with the appropriate categorical premise, subjects tend no longer to deny the antecedent or to affirm the consequent.

If the fallacies can be blocked by providing extra information, then, as rule theorists such as Rumain, Connell, and Braine (1983) have argued, there cannot be mental inference rules corresponding to them. But, suppose that additional information could suppress valid deductions. What, then? By their own argument, rule theorists ought to claim that there cannot be inference rules for them, either. The question arises because Byrne (1986, 1989a) has devised a simple manipulation that suppresses modus ponens and modus tollens.

Given the conditional:

If she meets her friend then she will go to a play.

and the appropriate categorical premise, nearly everyone makes the modus ponens deduction, and a substantial proportion of people make the modus tollens deduction. Byrne suppressed these valid deductions by presenting an extra premise with the original conditional:

If she meets her friend then she will go to a play.
If she has enough money then she will go to a play.

The new premise reminds subjects of an additional condition that is necessary to bring about the consequent. Thus, both antecedents seem jointly necessary for the consequent to occur. When subjects are presented with these two conditionals and the categorical premise, they tend not to make the modus ponens deduction. The group of subjects who received only the original conditional tended to make modus ponens (96%), but the group who received the additional premise showed a striking suppression of the deduction (38%). There was a similar suppression of modus tollens. As one would expect, however, the new premise did not suppress the fallacies.

A distinguished rule theorist describes his concept of a formal rule of inference as follows:

> By a formal logical rule, I take it, we mean a rule that applies to a string in virtue of its form. That is, the rule can apply whenever a string is described as having a certain form.... The question of whether there is a psychological version of this rule in the minds of normal people (not trained in logic) turns on whether they have a secure intuition, applying equally to any content, that [the rule applies]. I take it that they have. And for me, that's an end of it.

> (John Macnamara, personal communication, 1989)

Byrne has shown that people do not have a secure intuition that modus ponens applies equally to any content. Hence, by Macnamara's criterion, one may doubt the existence of a rule for modus ponens in mental logic.

The suppression of modus ponens casts no doubt whatsoever on its validity as a rule of inference, but it does support our thesis that people make deductions not by following such rules but by building models. For the conditionals that suppress the fallacies, their knowledge leads them to models in which each alternative antecedent brings about the same consequent. For the conditionals that suppress the valid deductions, the subjects' knowledge leads them to construct one model in which both antecedents occur and an implicit alternative model. These premises therefore suppress the valid deductions because only one of the necessary conditions is asserted categorically.

The Spontaneous Use of Conditional Descriptions

One final question about the various theories: what do they imply about the spontaneous use of conditionals in descriptions? For rule theories, people should use an assertion of the form, if p then q, whenever q can be inferred from p (Braine, 1979; Braine and O'Brien, 1989). We have found that when subjects are asked to summarize a truth table succinctly, they hardly ever use a conditional to describe material implication or equivalence. According to the model theory, a conditional has the initial models:

$$[p] \quad q$$
$$\dots$$

and so a truth table presents too much information to assimilate, and also too many contingencies that have no explicit representation in the models. What should elicit a conditional, however, is a set of contingencies that corresponds to these two models. But, how is one to convey the content of the implicit alternative model?

Over a series of experiments, we developed a procedure in which the subjects have to paraphrase sentences (Byrne and Johnson-Laird, 1990a; Byrne and Johnson-Laird, 1990b). In the critical experiment, we presented subjects with sets of three simple sentences, such as:

Laura has an essay to write.   (e)
The library stays open.   (l)
Laura studies late in the library.   (s)

and their task was to combine them into a single sentence using any words whatsoever. Three factual sentences, such as these, are likely to yield a model of an actual sequence of events:

e   l   s

and this model should be described using factual conjunctions, such as "and", and "when". To elicit a conditional, we needed to suggest an implicit alternative, and so we used a modal verb that signified a real possibility. In place of the simple factual assertion:

Laura studies late in the library.

we used the modal assertion:

Laura can study late in the library.

which implies that studying late is a possibility rather than a fact. We tested a group of 9 adult subjects with the factual sentences and a separate group of 18 subjects with the modal sentences. The group with factual materials used conditional descriptions on only 2% of trials, but the modal group used them on 36% of trials.

CONCLUSIONS

Conditionals are problematical, but the theory of mental models makes sense of them. It accounts for how people understand them, how they reason with them, and how they use them in describing the world. Their initial interpretations, especially with a neutral conditional, produce one explicit model of the antecedent and consequent, and one implicit model that allows for alternative possibilities. These models lead to a defective truth table, an inability to make a modus tollens deduction, and a lack of insight into the selection task. When the models are fleshed out with explicit information, particularly from a knowledge of the relations between events, then judgements conform to a complete truth table, modus tollens is deduced, and an insightful choice in the selection task become feasible.

CHAPTER 5

Reasoning about Relations

Comparisons are invidious, but they are the stuff of many deductions in daily life:

Harold was better than Ted.
Maggie was worse than Ted.
Therefore, Harold was better than Maggie.

They hinge on relations that are *internal* to propositions, and so the propositional calculus cannot capture their validity, because it is not sensitive to the internal structure of premises (see Chapter 1). A proper logical analysis calls for the resources of the predicate calculus. Nevertheless, such relational deductions are easy to make, and seldom elicit errors. They are trivial, although it has proved far from trivial to understand how people make them.

Our plan in this chapter is to begin with these simple relational deductions, so-called "three-term series" problems. We will discover that despite many experimental studies these problems are too impoverished to discriminate among competing accounts of how people solve them. And so we will turn to more complex relational deductions that depend on at least two dimensions, e.g.:

The volume control is on the right of the tone control.
The tuner is above the tone control.
The clock is above the volume control.
Therefore, the tuner is on the left of the clock.

We will report empirical studies of these deductions that have enabled us to reach a conclusion about the reasoning mechanism.

THREE-TERM SERIES PROBLEMS

When logicians analyze relations, they focus on their logical properties. For example, the relation "in front of" is transitive, that is, it supports valid deductions of the form:

A is in front of B.
B is in front of C.
Therefore, A is in front of C.

Intransitive relations, such as "directly on top of", also support valid deductions:

A is directly on top of B.
B is directly on top of C.
Therefore, A is *not* directly on top of C.

Non-transitive relations, such as "next to", do not warrant either sort of deduction. If:

A is next to B.
B is next to C.

then A may be next to C if they are arranged in a circle, or it may not be if they are arranged in a line. Hence, there is no valid conclusion.

Other logical properties include symmetry and reflexivity, and their cognates. Symmetric relations, such as "in the same place as", give rise to the following sort of deduction:

A is in the same place as B.
Therefore, B is in the same place as A.

Reflexive relations, such as "identical to", yield the following sort of logical truth for any individual:

A is identical to A.

Relations yield still other sorts of deduction, and many of them have no recognized logical label, e.g.:

The police managed to prevent the man from assassinating the prime minister.
Therefore, the police prevented the man from assassinating the prime minister.
Therefore, the man did not assassinate the prime minister.
Therefore, the man did not kill the prime minister.

We have outlined three broad approaches to the psychology of reasoning: formal rules, content-specific rules, and mental models. Theories of relational reasoning also fall into these main categories. Rule theories require representations of the logical properties of relations, which can be expressed, as we saw in Chapter 1, by meaning postulates. Meaning postulates for the relation, "in front of", for example, would include the following in which each variable is universally quantified:

If x is in front of y and y is in front of z then x is in front of z.
(transitivity)
If x is in front of y then y is not in front of x.
(asymmetry)
If x is in front of y then y is behind x.
(converse relation)

Alternatively, there could be just one general postulate for each logical property, e.g.:

If xRy, and yRz, then xRz
(transitivity)

and all relevant relations could be tagged to indicate which postulates apply to them (Bar-Hillel, 1967).
A deduction, such as:

1. The circle is in front of the triangle.
2. The cross is behind the triangle.
   Therefore, the circle is in front of the cross.

can be made by first instantiating the meaning postulate that allows a relation to be transformed into its converse:

3. If the cross is behind the triangle, then the triangle is in front of the cross.
   (instantiation of conversion postulate)

and by instantiating the postulate for transitivity:

4. If the circle is in front of the triangle and the triangle is in front of the cross, then the circle is in front of the cross. (instantiation of transitivity postulate)

The conclusion can then be proved using the standard rules for connectives:

5. The triangle is in front of the cross. (modus ponens from 2 and 3)
6. The circle is in front of the triangle and the triangle is in front of the cross. (conjunction of 1 and 5)
7. The circle is in front of the cross. (modus ponens from 4 and 6)

Where rule theories diverge is in their representation of logical properties, such as transitivity. They could be captured in postulates, which are assertions to be taken as true, or in content-specific rules of inference, which enable one assertion to be derived from others. The latter often take the form of productions in computer programs (see Chapter 2), e.g.:

(Condition (And (in front of x y)(in front of y z))
(Action (in front of x z))).

Such programs have indeed been proposed for spatial inference (e.g., Ohlsson, 1981, 1984; Hagert, 1983, 1984; Olson and Bialystok, 1983).

Historically, the first theory of how people could carry out a three-term deduction was proposed by Hunter (1957). His starting point was William James's idea (1890, p. 646) about a series of the form:

$a > b > c \ldots > z$

James argued that "any number of intermediaries may be expunged without obliging us to alter anything in what remains written". Hunter's theory adopts the same principle, but posits two operations to bring the premises into the required linear order: the conversion of a premise from the form, b < a, to the form, a > b, and the re-ordering of premises from, say:

b > c
a > b

into the order:

a > b
b > c

The rule for conversion depends on content because not all premises can be validly converted; and the expunging of intermediaries is similarly content-specific. Hence, Hunter's operations are akin to content-specific rules.

Clark (1969) proposed an explicitly content-specific theory. It stresses the factors that lead to greater difficulties in relational deductions, as reflected in longer response times. In certain antonymic pairs of expressions, such as:

better - worse
taller - shorter
bigger - smaller

the first term can be used in a neutral way to refer to the relative positions of two items on the dimension in question, whereas the second term conveys information about which end of the dimension the pair is to be found. To assert, for example:

Maggie is worse than Ted.

suggests that neither of them is much good. Psycholinguistic evidence has shown that these so-called "marked" terms are slightly harder to understand than their related "unmarked" terms. And Clark demonstrated the same phenomenon in three-term series problems. He also hypothesized that the specifics of a relation are harder to comprehend than the general information it conveys about the dimension. For example, one readily grasps from the previous assertion that Maggie and Ted are bad, but it is a little harder to determine their relative demerits. From these principles, he was able to predict the difficulty of different three-term series problems. His theory, however, concerns factors affecting performance, and was not intended to account for the complete sequence of processes that lead to the right answer.

Model theories of relational deductions were also among the earliest to be proposed (e.g. DeSoto, London, Handel, 1965; Huttenlocher, 1968).

We have implemented a computer program that is based on the model theory (an extension of one described in Johnson-Laird, 1983, Ch. 11), and that can carry out three-term and other, more complicated, relational deductions. It uses neither meaning postulates nor rules of inference. The transitivity of the relation, "in front of", for example, is nowhere explicitly represented, but is an emergent property from the meaning of the relation and its use in constructing models. The meaning is itself represented by a piece of code that is used by the compositional procedures that combine meanings according to syntax (see Chapter 9). The meaning of the premise is used to build models, to verify assertions in models, and to search for alternative models that falsify putative conclusions. It states, in effect, the direction in which a spatial model should be scanned in order to establish that one entity is in front of another from the observer's point of view, i.e. the positions on the line of sight should be scanned while holding the horizontal axis constant. Expressions such as "in front of" have, in addition to this *deictic* meaning that depends on the speaker's point of view, a meaning that depends on the *intrinsic* parts of certain entities, e g , people and cars have fronts and backs (soo e.g. Mlller and Johnson-Laird, 1976, Sec 6.1). It calls for a similar procedure based on the entities themselves rather than a line of sight.

In the deduction based on the premises:

The circle is in front of the triangle.
The cross is behind the triangle.

The first premise leads to the construction of a minimal spatial array that satisfies the truth conditions of the premise (assuming the appropriate viewpoint):

Δ
O

The information in each subsequent premise can be added to the model, inserting tokens in the appropriate place in the array to satisfy the meaning of the premises. Thus, the second premise yields:

+
Δ
O

The conclusion:

The circle is in front of the cross.

contains only referents that are in the model, and so a procedure is called to verify the assertion in the model. It evaluates the assertion as true in the current model, and so another procedure is called to try to falsify it by finding an alternative model of the premises. This procedure fails in the current case, and so the conclusion is valid.

The premises:

The circle is in front of the triangle.
The cross is behind the circle.

yield the initial model:

+
Δ
O

that supports the conclusion:

The triangle is in front of the cross.

But, in this case, the falsification procedure succeeds in constructing an alternative model of the premises in which the conclusion is false:

Δ
+
O

The two models do not support any relation in common between the triangle and the cross, and so no valid deduction can be made about them.

Experimental results corroborated Clark's linguistic theory. But they are also consistent with the construction of a spatial array whose top represents the highest or positive end of a scale. Subjects prefer to work from the top down, and to construct an array from an "end-anchored" premise, i.e. one in which the first noun phrase refers to an item at one end of the array. Although imagery *per se* does not seem to play a large role in transitive deductions (Richardson, 1987), the evidence implies that subjects do construct a linear array of items (e.g., Barclay, 1973). Similarly, when the relevant entities are far apart in the array, subjects are faster to make decisions about the relation between them (Potts, 1978; Newstead, Pollard, and Griggs, 1986). They also make more inferences from sequences of conditionals that are transitive than from those that are not transitive—a phenomenon that again suggests that they try to construct integrated representations (Byrne, 1989b). Nevertheless, the rule and model theories make much the same predictions for three-term series problems.

In response to the impasse, some theorists have proposed that reasoners use both rules and models, either at different points during the process (e.g. Johnson-Laird, 1972; Sternberg and Weil, 1980; Sternberg, 1985), or as alternative strategies (Egan and Grimes-Farrow, 1982; Ohlsson, 1984). A more radical way around the impasse is to examine problems for which the theories do make different predictions. A promising form of relational reasoning, which is fundamental to understanding the world—for planning routes, locating entities, and envisaging layouts—depends on two-dimensional spatial relations.

TWO-DIMENSIONAL SPATIAL DEDUCTIONS

When people understand spatial descriptions, they imagine symmetrical arrays in which adjacent objects have roughly equal distances between them (Ehrlich and Johnson-Laird, 1982). They can represent these descriptions in two ways: one is close to the linguistic structure of the sentences, and the other is close to the structure of the situation that is described (Mani and Johnson-Laird, 1982). How then do they make deductions about spatial relations?

Consider the following problem:

I. A is on the right of B
    C is on the left of B
    D is in front of C
    E is in front of B
    What is the relation between D and E?

Hagert (1983, 1984) has proposed a rule theory that includes the rules shown in Table 5.1. In combination with rules for propositional connectives, they allow an answer to the question to be derived:

D is on the left of E.

and Table 5.2 presents the derivation.

Here is a second problem:

II. B is on the right of A
    C is on the left of B
    D is in front of C
    E is in front of B
    What is the relation between D and E?

Table 5.1
Some inference rules for one-dimensional and two-dimensional deductions (from Hagert, 1983)

a. Left (x, y) & Front (z, x) → Left (front (z, x), y)
    where the right-hand side signifies "z is in front of x, which is on the left of y".

b. Left (x, y) & Front (z, y) → Left (x, front (z, y))
    where the right-hand side signifies "x is on the left of z, which is in front of y".

c. Left (x, y) & Left (y, z) → Left (x, left (y, z))
    where the right-hand side signifies "x is on the left of y, which is on the left of z".

d. Left (x, y) ↔ Right (y, x)

e. Left (front (x, y), z) → Left (x, z) & Left (y, z) & Front (x, y)

f. Left (x, front (y, z)) → Left (x, y) & Left (x, z) & Front (y, z)

g. Left (x, left (y, z)) → Left (x, y) & Left (x, z) & Left (y, z)

h. Left (x, y) → ¬ Right (x, y)

i. Right (x, y) → ¬ Left (x, y)

Table 5.2
The derivation of a spatial deduction using Hagert's (1983) rules

The premises:
1. A is on the right of B
2. C is on the left of B
3. D is in front of C
4. E is in front of B
   Hence, D is on the left of E.

The derivation:

5.	C is on the left of B and D is in front of C	(conjunction of 2 & 3)
6.	D is in front of C, which is on the left of B	(rule a applied to 5)
7.	D is on the left of B, and C is on the left of B, and D is in front of C	(rule e applied to 6)
8.	D is on the left of B	(conjunction elimination applied to 7)
9.	D is on the left of B & E is in front of B	(conjunction of 4 & 8)
10.	D is on the left of E which is in front of B	(rule b applied to 9)
11.	D is on the left of E, and D is on the left of B, and E is in front of B	(rule f applied to 10)
12.	D is on the left of E	(conjunction elimination, 11)

It can be solved using exactly the same derivation. The first premise is irrelevant in both problems, and the remaining three premises are identical. Hence, if people are using rules, there should be little difference in difficulty between problem I and problem II.

In contrast, the model theory predicts a difference. The premises of problem I support the model:

C   B   A
D   E

D is on the left of E in this model, and it is a valid conclusion because the procedure that revises models cannot construct an alternative model to refute it. The premises yield a one-model problem with a valid conclusion.

Problem II supports at least two distinct models:

C   A   B   A   C   B
D   E   D   E

but both of them support the same conclusion:

D is on the left of E.

and no alternative model falsifies it. The premises yield a multiple-model problem with a valid conclusion. For one-dimensional problems, the validity of a deduction is confounded with the number of models that it requires: one model problems support a valid deduction, multiple-model problems do not. Two-dimensional problems, however, allow us to disentangle the two variables. And the model theory predicts that the second problem should be harder than the first, because it should be harder to make deductions based on more than one model.

A third sort of problem is exemplified by the premises:

III. B is on the right of A
    C is on the left of B
    D is in front of C
    E is in front of A
    What is the relation between D and E?

In this case, there is no valid answer; and both the rule and the model theories predict that this sort of problem should be hardest of all. According to the rule theory, it is difficult because all potential derivations have to be tried before one can respond that the problem has no valid answer. According to the model theory, the problem is difficult because it requires at least two models to be constructed in order to appreciate that there is no valid conclusion relating D and E:

```
C   A   B        A   C   B
D   E            E   D
```

It is a multiple-model problem with no valid conclusion about D and E, and so it should be harder than the one-model problem. It should also be harder than the multiple-model problem with a valid conclusion, where the valid conclusion emerges even if only one model is constructed—the conclusion is true in every model of the premises.

We tested the predictions of the two theories in an experiment in which 15 subjects made one-dimensional and two-dimensional deductions about the layouts of everyday objects, such as cups and plates (Byrne and Johnson-Laird, 1989b). The percentages of correct conclusions were as follows:

One-dimensional problems:
    Valid conclusion
    (one model)   69%
    No valid conclusion
    (multiple model)   19%
Two-dimensional problems:
    Valid conclusion
    (one model: e.g. problem I)   61%
    Valid conclusion
    (multiple model: e.g. problem II)   50%
    No valid conclusion
    (multiple model: e.g. problem III) 18%

We expected that the one-dimensional problems would be easier than the two-dimensional ones, but there was no reliable difference between them. As both theories predicted, the valid problems were easier than the invalid ones. The crucial finding, however, occurred with the two-dimensional problems. The one-model problems with a valid conclusion were reliably easier than the multiple-model problems with a valid conclusion. This difference supports the model theory, and runs counter to the rule theory.

A stronger test between the two theories would pit them directly against one another, in cases where the rule theory predicts a difference in one direction, and the model theory predicts a difference in the opposite direction. Our next experiment made such a comparison, using a fourth sort of problem:

IV. A is on the right of B
     C is on the left of B
     D is in front of C
     E is in front of A
     What is the relation between D and E?

This problem does not contain any premise that directly asserts the relation between the pair of items, A and C, to which E and D are respectively related. It is therefore necessary to deduce the relation between A and C from the first two premises:

1. A is on the right of B
2. C is on the left of B

These premises yield, according to the formal rules (see Table 5.1), the following sequence of inferences:

3. B is on the right of C
   (modus ponens from 2 and instantiation of rule d)
4. A is on the right of B and B is on the right of C
   (conjunction of 1 and 3)
5. A is on the right of C
   (modus ponens from 4 and instantiation of transitivity)

This conclusion and the remaining two premises now permit an analogous derivation to the one for problem II, where B and C were the relevant pair of items and directly related in the second premise.

Problem IV requires a longer derivation than problem II, and so it should be harder according to the rule theory. Problem IV, however, supports just one model:

C   B   A
D   E

whereas problem II requires more than one model. Hence, the two theories make exactly opposite predictions.

We tested the predictions in a second experiment in which 18 subjects carried out three sorts of two-dimensional problem: one model problems with a valid conclusion (such as IV), multiple model problems with a valid conclusion (such as II), and multiple model problems with no valid conclusion (such as III). The problems concerned everyday objects, and the layouts were in one of four orientations:

		1			2			3			4	
A	B	C		E	D		D	C		A	E
D		E		A	B	C		B		B	
							E	A		C	D

The percentages of correct conclusions were as follows:

Valid conclusion (one model: IV)	70%
Valid conclusion (multiple model: II)	46%
No valid conclusion (multiple model: III)	15%

These results support the model theory, but not the rule theory. Despite the fact that the derivation for IV is much longer than the derivation for II, problem IV was reliably easier. Problems with no valid conclusion were, as both theories predict, hardest of all.

Both experiments show that it is easier to make a valid deduction when a description corresponds to just a single layout as opposed to two or more layouts. The phenomenon is explained if people reason by imagining the state of affairs described in the premises, drawing a conclusion from such a mental model, and searching for alternative models that might refute the conclusion.

Could our instruction to imagine the layouts have led the subjects to adopt a strategy otherwise alien to them? We used the instruction, which was casually mentioned during the subjects' introduction to the task, in order to avoid any problems in the interpretation of "on the right of", "on the left of", and the other spatial terms. Only the deictic sense yields the deductions of the sort used in the experiment, and a simple way to ensure that the subjects made this interpretation rather than the one based on intrinsic parts was to tell them that the layouts were being described from a particular point of view. It is unlikely that this instruction could be powerful enough to cause subjects to adopt a wholly unnatural reasoning strategy. Indeed, several authors have lamented the difficulty of inducing reasoning strategies by explicit instructions (e.g. Dickstein, 1978), while others have denied a significant role for imagery in relational reasoning (Newstead, Manktelow, and Evans, 1982; Richardson, 1987). The critical feature of the model theory is the structure of the representations used in reasoning —they should be the same as the structure of the world, not the structure of sentences—rather than that they should be experienced as images.

ALTERNATIVE RULE THEORIES FOR SPATIAL DEDUCTIONS

Our experiments are damaging for rule theories of the sort shown in Table 5.1. Could a theory with different rules account for our results? One alternative is worth describing because it illuminates the peculiar difficulties that confront rule theories. It postulates such principles as:

If x is on the left of y, and w is in front of x,
and z is in front of y, then w is on the left of z.

The first premise in problems I and II is irrelevant, but the application of this rule to the remaining premises yields the conclusion directly:

D is on the left of E.

Because a large number of such rules would be necessary to deal with the full set of spatial relations, we can invoke general postulates of the same structure:

If x is related to y on one dimension,
and w is related to x on an orthogonal dimension
and z has the same orthogonal relation to y,
then w is related to z in the same way as x is related to y.

This general postulate has the advantage that it captures the content of many specific postulates, because it can be applied to any rotation or reflection of the configuration:

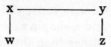

Yet, a theory based on this rule still makes the wrong predictions. It matches the premises of the difficult problem directly, where C is directly related to B:

II. B is on the right of A
     C is on the left of B
     D is in front of C
     E is in front of B

and so the second premise corresponds to the clause in the postulate:

If x is related to y on one dimension...

There is no such correspondence in the case of the easy problem, IV, where it is necessary, as we showed, to deduce the relevant relation (between A and C). Hence, the postulate predicts the opposite of the observed difference. One might be tempted to invoke a rule that does match problem IV directly, e.g.:

If x is related to y on one dimension,
and y is related to z on the same dimension,
and v is related to x on an orthogonal dimension,
and w is related to z on the orthogonal dimension,
then v is related to w in the same way as x is related to z

which can be used for any orientation of the configuration:

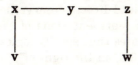

Unfortunately, the rule does not match the premises of the other easy problem, I, and so now this problem should be difficult. In short, the three sorts of valid problem that we have studied put any rule theory on the horns of a dilemma. If the theory explains the ease of problem I it cannot explain the ease of problem IV, and vice versa. And, if the inferential system has all of the rules that we have considered, then no problem should be harder than any other.

CONCLUSIONS

The model theory overcomes the difficulties for rule theories because it separates the representation of the premises from subsequent deductive processing. There are many possible models corresponding to the possible layouts of objects, but any deduction can be made by the same process—the search for alternative models that refute the relation established in a model. For rule theories, however, the process of deduction depends on the particular rules and postulates that are used in deriving the conclusion, and so different deductions depend on different rules. The need for a derivation's length, in addition, to predict the difficulty of a deduction places an impossible load on the theory. The model theory readily accommodates such deductions as:

The door is taller than it is broad.
The table is wider than the door is tall.
Therefore the table is wider than the door is broad.

Reasoners can construct a model of the situation from their knowledge of the meaning of the relational terms, and they can compare the relative sizes of the objects in any model that satisfies the premises. To derive the conclusion using formal rules, however, calls for a complicated procedure. It is necessary to use postulates that interrelate such predicates as "broad", "wider", and "taller", and that enable the relative sizes of different dimensions to be compared.

Critics sometimes argue that the use of spatial models smuggles in inference rules by the back door. But, the procedures in our computer program that operate to construct and to inspect arrays are certainly not formal inference rules, which, by definition, lead directly from verbal premises to verbal conclusions. Likewise, the representations of the meanings of relations are not meaning postulates that specify logical properties. The essence of the semantic entry for "on the right of", for example, merely ensures that one object is on the right of another in a model (see Chapter 9 for the details of how such meanings can be represented). The meaning does not in itself specify that the relation is transitive, but this logical property emerges as soon as the meaning is put to use in building models.

The same point can be made by considering the definition of "greater than" in the theory of recursive functions. One number, x, is greater than another, y, if and only if x is the successor of y or the successor of some other number, z, that is greater than y. This recursive definition depends only on the concept of the successor of a number—a mathematical function that, given a natural number, such as 5, delivers its successor: 6. When you learn to count, you master this function. It is in no sense transitive, i.e. if x is the successor of y, and y is the successor of z, then x is *not* the successor of z. Nevertheless, the transitivity of "greater than" is an emergent property of the recursive definition. The general message of recursive function theory is that the richness of computable mathematical functions and relations is likewise emergent from different assemblies of a handful of simple building blocks (Rogers, 1967).

Other critics have suggested that the use of arrays trades unfairly on a visual metaphor. Our computer program is unable to exploit the metaphor and yet it is certainly capable of modelling the deductive process. The construction of a model depends on understanding the meaning of a relational term. The logical properties of the relation then emerge from its use in constructing models. Indeed, there is an important asymmetry between the meaning of a relation and its logical properties. Logical properties can emerge, as they do in our program, from meaning. But, meaning cannot emerge from logical properties. Many distinct relations have identical logical properties, e.g. both "on the right of" and "on the left of" are transitive, asymmetric, and irreflexive. No matter how many other logical properties a rule theory adduces, it will never be able to distinguish between the meanings of these two relations.

Our aim in this chapter was to reach a conclusion about how people make relational deductions. We have argued that they do so by imagining the state of affairs described by the premises. Rule theorists may indeed concede that spatial deductions are based on mental models rather than formal rules. We will show in subsequent chapters that relational reasoning is fundamental to many abstract deductions, and that the model account extends to them too.

CHAPTER 6

One Quantifier at a Time: The Psychology of Syllogisms

Until the nineteenth century, logic was almost entirely Scholastic syllogisms; and until the latter half of this century, the psychology of reasoning followed suit. A syllogism has two premises that each contain a single quantifier, e.g.:

> Some athletes are bodybuilders.
> All bodybuilders are characters.
> Therefore, some athletes are characters.

Although an attempt has been made to characterize the mental processes of syllogistic reasoning in terms of formal rules (see Braine and O'Brien, 1984), most theories are based on models. Our chief concern in this chapter is therefore to decide among competing ideas about the sorts of models that underlie syllogistic reasoning. Our strategy will be first to describe the logic of syllogisms, next to consider some experimental findings that enable us to choose among the theories, and finally to present some new evidence that corroborates our choice.

The premises and conclusion of an orthodox syllogism are in one of four distinct "moods":

All A are B	affirmative universal
Some A are B	affirmative existential
No A are B	negative universal
Some A are not B	negative existential

In the example above, the terms in the premises are in the following "figure":

A - B   (athletes - bodybuilders)
B - C   (bodybuilders - characters)

There are four possible figures for the premises, where B is the "middle" term, which occurs in both premises, and A and C are the "end" terms, which occur in conclusions:

A - B   B - A   A - B   B - A
B - C   C - B   C - B   B - C

The first two of these figures are asymmetrical because the middle term is located in different places in the two premises; and the second two figures are symmetrical because the middle term is located in the same place in both premises. Given that each premise can be in one of four moods, there is therefore a total of 64 distinct forms of premises. Scholastic logicians recognized that the order of the premises had no logical effect, and so they adopted the convention that the subject of the conclusion was whichever end term occurred in the second premise. (Our example violates this convention, and follows Aristotle's method of laying out syllogisms—he was a better psychologist than the Scholastic logicians.) Until the 1970s, psychologists followed Scholastic logic and, as a result, they ignored half of the possible forms of syllogism. In fact, there is a total of 512 possible syllogisms because each pair of premises can be combined with eight possible conclusions (four conclusions in the order A - C, and four conclusions in the order C - A). Few of these possibilities are valid: even when either order of terms may occur in the conclusion, only 27 pairs of premises yield valid conclusions (see Johnson-Laird and Steedman, 1978; Adams, 1984). Some of these 27 are so easy that a nine year old child can spontaneously draw a correct conclusion, whereas others are so hard that barely any adults perform better than chance with them.

Early studies of syllogistic deduction were vitiated by methodological flaws. Subjects could use guessing and other non-inferential processes, because they had only to evaluate given conclusions; and no study came close to examining all 512 forms of syllogism. In the 1970s, however, some experimenters asked subjects to generate their own conclusions, and this procedure enabled all 64 forms of premises to be investigated (Johnson-Laird and Huttenlocher, reported in Johnson-Laird, 1975; Johnson-Laird and Steedman, 1978). A summary of the results of four such experiments is given in Table 6.1. The Table presents the

Table 6.1

The percentages of correct conclusions for the 27 valid syllogisms (from four experiments). The numbers in parentheses are the mean rank-orders of the difficulty of the problems. These results are for both the conclusion stated and its converse where appropriate. The table also shows the models for the syllogisms. For simplicity, we have omitted the wholly implicit individuals normally signified by three dots.

| | **AB–BC Figure** | | | |
| | **1st premise** | | | |
2nd premise	*All A–B*	*Some A–B*	*No A–B*	*Some A–not B*

All B–C	[a] b] c
	[a] b] c
	All A–C 89 (3.5)
		a [[b] c]
		a [[b] c]
		Some A–C 88 (2.6)
			[a] [a] c [a] c
			[a] [a] c [a] c
			      [[b] c] [[b] c] [[b] c]
			      [[b] c] [[b] c] [[b] c]
			Some C–not A 11 (24.5)	

Some B–C			[a] [a] c [b] c
			[a] [a] c [b] c
			      [b] c [b] c [b] c
			      [b] c [b] c [b] c
			Some C–not A 20 (20.7)	

No B–C	[a] b]
	[a] b]
	      [c]
	      [c]
	No A–C 74 (6.2)
		a [b] a [b] a [b]
		a [b] a [b] a [b]
		         [c] a [c] a [c]
		         [c] a [c] a [c]
		Some A–not C 38 (15.2)		

Some B–not C				

BA-CB Figure

	1st premise			
2nd premise	All B-A	Some B-A	No B-A	Some B-not A
All C-B	[c] b] a [c] b] a All C-A 63 (8.1)		[c] b] [c] b] [a] [a] No C-A 70 (7.0)	
Some C-B	c [b] a] c [b] a] Some C-A 86 (3.2)			
No C-B	[c] [c] a [c] a [c] [c] a [c] a [tb] a] [tb] a] [tb] a] [tb] a] [tb] a] [tb] a] Some A-not C 8 (25.2)	[c] [c] a [c] [c] a [b] a [b] a [b] a [b] a Some A-not C 15 (22.2)	c [b] c [b] [a] c [b] c [b] [a] [a] c [a] [a] c [a] Some C-not A 38 (13.5)	
Some C-not B				

AB-CB Figure

	1st premise			
2nd premise	*All A-B*	*Some A-B*	*No A-B*	*Some A-not B*
All C-B			[a] [a] [b [c]] [b [c]] No A-C 79 (4.1)	a a a a a [b [c]] a [b [c]] [b [c]] a [b [c]] Some A-not C 34 (15.4)
Some C-B			[a] [a] c [a] [a] c [b] c [b] c [b] c [b] c [b] c [b] c Some C-not A 28 (15.9)	
No C-B	[a b] [a b] [c] [c] No A-C 75 (5.7)	a [b] a [b] a [b] a [b] a [b] a [b] [c] [c] a [c] [c] [c] a [c] Some A-not C 19 (20.5)		
Some C-not B	[a b] [a] b] c [a b] c [a] b] c c c c c Some C-not A 41 (13.0)			

BA-BC Figure
1st premise

	All B-A	Some B-A	No B-A	Some B-not A
2nd premise				

```
                          BA-BC Figure
                           1st premise

             All B-A          Some B-A        No B-A              Some B-not A

2nd premise
All B-C    [a [b] c] [a [b] c] [a [b] c]   a [b] c    [a]  [a]  [[b] c]  [a]  c     [a]             [a] [[b] c]
           [a [b] c] [a [b] c] [a [b] c]   a [b] c    [a]  [a]  [[b] c]  [a]  c     [a] [[b] c]     [a] [[b] c]
                        a                              [[b] c]    c [b] c  [[b] c]   [[b] c]   [b] c
           Some A-C  19 (21.7)    Some A-C  68 (8.1)   [[b] c]      [b] c  [[b] c]   [[b] c]   [b] c
                                                       Some C-not A  16 (23.1)       Some C-not A  31 (17.1)

Some B-C   [a [b]] c                                   [a]      c
           [a [b]] c                                   [a]      c
           Some A-C  69 (8.2)                                 c
                                                       [b] c   [b]    c
                                                       [b] c   [b]    c
                                                       Some C-not A  23 (18.6)

No B-C     [a [b]]   [a [b]]       a [b]    a [b]
           [a [b]]   [a [b]]       a [b]    a [b]
              [c] a  [c] a [c]        [c] a   [c] a [c]
              [c]    [c]    [c]       [c]     [c]    [c]
           Some A-not C  15 (23.8)  Some A-not C  26 (18.9)

Some B-not C  [a [b]]
              [a [b]]
              [a [b]] [c]  [a [b]] [c]
                 [c]       [a [b]] [c]
              Some A-not C  51 (11.5)
```

percentages of correct conclusions for the 27 valid problems, and the mean rank of each problem's difficulty over the four experiments. (It also shows the models for each problem, which we will explain later.) Despite the differences in subjects (American, English and Italian) and languages, the experiments yield a high degree of concordance in the rank orders of difficulty (Kendall's co-efficient of concordance, $W = 0.975$, $p < 0.001$). For the 37 problems with no valid conclusions interrelating the end terms, the results are more variable, but they too yield a reliable concordance ($W = 0.84$, $p < 0.001$). The easiest problem in Table 6.1 had 89% correct conclusions; the hardest problem had only 8%. How then are we to account for the vast differences in difficulty from one syllogism to another?

THE CAUSES OF DIFFICULTY IN SYLLOGISTIC REASONING

The Atmosphere Hypothesis

One long-standing proposal is that reasoners are influenced by the "atmosphere" created by the mood of the premises. Whenever at least one premise is negative, they choose a negative conclusion; whenever at least one premise contains the existential quantifier, "some", they choose an existential conclusion; otherwise they chose an affirmative and universal conclusion (see e.g. Woodworth and Sells, 1935; Begg and Denny, 1969; Wetherick and Gilhooly, 1990). Because the effect is apparently stronger for valid than for invalid conclusions, there must be—as Woodworth and Sells allowed—an additional inferential mechanism. Hence, several recent theories have assumed that atmosphere governs merely the initial formulation of putative conclusions (see Madruga, 1984; Inder, 1987; Polk and Newell, 1988). But, as we will show, the atmosphere effect, if it exists, plays little part in deduction, and the evidence that appears to support it has an alternative explanation.

The Conversion Hypothesis

Another long-standing account attributes errors to the fallacious conversion of premises (Chapman and Chapman, 1959). Immediate inferences of the form:

Some A are B
Therefore, Some B are A

and:

> No A are B
> Therefore, No B are A

are valid. But, inferences of the form:

> All A are B
> Therefore, All B are A

and:

> Some A are not B
> Therefore, Some B are not A

are invalid. There are two ways in which conversion could occur. One is a process of direct verbal conversion from "All A are B" to "All B are A". The other is a consequence of a mental representation of "All A are B" that fails to allow that there may be B's that are not A's, i.e., it represents the two sets as co-extensive. One theory of performance posits that every premise is verbally converted, whether validly or invalidly (Revlis, 1975; Revlin and Leirer, 1978), but the evidence rules out this idea. If every premise were converted then the figure of a problem should not affect the accuracy of performance, yet in fact it does (Johnson-Laird and Bara, 1984). Conversion errors appear to arise from an incomplete representation of premises. Indeed, although people often judge that all four moods of premise imply their converses (Wilkins, 1928; Newstead, 1990), the errors can be blocked by instructions (Dickstein, 1975), or by the use of unambiguous premises (Ceraso and Provitera, 1971).

The Figural Effect

A third set of proposals about syllogistic reasoning concern so-called "figural" effects. Although their proper interpretation is controversial, the figure of a problem can undoubtedly affect the form of the conclusions that subjects draw, their accuracy, and the speed of response (see e.g. Johnson-Laird and Bara, 1984). Premises in the figure:

> A - B
> B - C

tend to elicit conclusions of the form:

A - C

whereas premises in the figure:

B - A
C - B

tend to elicit conclusions of the form:

C - A

In other words, the order of the premises has no effect, because when only one premise has an end term as subject, that term tends to occur as the subject of the conclusion—regardless of the order in which the premises are presented. Accuracy is affected as a by-product of this bias. Where premises, such as:

None of the A is a B
All of the B are C

support only a valid conclusion of the form:

Some of the C are not A

which runs counter to the bias, the task is exceptionally difficult. We have only ever encountered one subject who performed at a better than chance level with such problems. With premises in the two symmetrical figures:

A - B
C - B

and:

B - A
B - C

there is no overall response bias, although there are some effects within figures (see Johnson-Laird and Bara, 1984).

At least three hypotheses have been advanced to account for the figural effects. When the effects were first discovered, they were explained in terms of a directional bias built into the mental representations themselves (Johnson-Laird, 1975; Johnson-Laird and

Steedman, 1978). This hypothesis was abandoned, however, when it was discovered that figure affects the difficulty of forming an initial model. Johnson-Laird and Bara (1984) accordingly proposed that reasoners had to carry out mental operations on syllogistic premises in order to bring the two middle terms into contiguity. This notion can be traced back to Hunter's (1957) theory of three-term series problems (see Chapter 5). Premises in the figure:

A - B
B - C

already occur in an order in which the two occurrences of B follow one another, and so there is no need for any operation to bring them into contiguity. They will be easy to integrate, and so they elicit the highest proportion of valid conclusions and the smallest proportion of "no valid conclusion" responses. Premises in the figure:

B - A
C - B

yield contiguous occurrences of the middle term provided that their initial interpretation is based on the second premise and the interpretation of the first premise is then renewed in order to add its information to the model. Hence, the premises will yield conclusions of the form, C - A, on the assumption that the first information into working memory is the first information out of it (see Broadbent, 1958, p. 236). They will also elicit slightly fewer correct conclusions and slightly more "no valid conclusion responses" because of the increase in difficulty in making an integrated interpretation. These difficulties will be exacerbated with the figure:

A - B
C - B

because it is now necessary to switch round the entire representation of the second premise in order to bring the two middle terms into contiguity. The greatest effect, however, will occur with the figure:

B - A
B - C

which calls for subjects either to renew their interpretation of the first premise in order to switch it round or else to switch round their

Table 6.2

The effects of figure on correct conclusions, erroneous "no valid conclusion" responses, and latencies. These results are from Johnson-Laird and Bara, 1984, Experiment 3, and the latencies are only for one-model problems because there were insufficient correct conclusions drawn to the other sorts of syllogism.

| | Figures | | | |
	A - B B - C	B - A C - B	A - B C - B	B - A B - C
Percentages of valid conclusions	51	48	35	22
Percentages of erroneous "No valid conclusion" responses	4	11	34	34
Latencies (sec) of correct conclusions (one-model problems)	11.6	12.9	18.7	22.1

interpretation of the second premise and then re-new their interpretation of the first premise. This figure will elicit the smallest proportion of valid conclusions and the largest proportion of "no valid conclusion" responses, whether or not correct.

A third hypothesis about the figural effect has recently been advanced by Wetherick and Gilhooly (1990). They argue that it arises from a rhetorical principle. The asymmetrical figures have only one end term that functions as the subject of a premise, and so reasoners use that term as the subject of their conclusion. This idea is plausible, but it fails to explain the observed trend over the four figures in difficulty, latency, and "no valid conclusion" responses. Table 6.2 shows these trends in one experiment, and other experiments yield similar results. They are what one would expect if reasoners are carrying out mental operations to bring the middle terms into contiguity. Whatever the true account of the effects of figure, it cannot explain syllogistic reasoning in full—if only because it would shed no light on how reasoners represent the meaning of the premises or derive conclusions from them.

FORMAL RULES FOR SYLLOGISTIC REASONING

No-one has proposed a full theory of syllogistic inference based on formal rules, perhaps because the lengths of formal derivations for valid syllogisms fail to account for the differences in their difficulty. Table 6.3 presents two typical derivations: one for an easy problem and one for a difficult problem. Both derivations consist in exactly the same sequence of rules. Yet the easy problem has a mean rank of 2.6 in difficulty with 88% correct conclusions, whereas the difficult problem has a mean rank of 18.9 in difficulty with only 26% correct conclusions (see Table 6.1). Hence, we can be confident that subjects are not using these derivations. Since the rules for connectives are identical to those postulated by psychologists, the discrepancy may arise from the rules for quantifiers.

Because some immediate inferences with quantified premises, such as:

All psychologists are either clinicians or experimenters.
Therefore, all psychologists who are not clinicians are
    experimenters.

are easy, Braine and Rumain (1983, p. 296) have argued that reasoners have an inference rule that moves from premise to conclusion in a single step:

a's are either F or G
Therefore, *a's* that are not F are G

This rule condenses into a single step the three stages of quantified deduction—elimination of quantifiers, reasoning by connectives, and restoration of the quantifiers. Rules of this sort, however, have yet to be proposed in a form that is powerful enough to cope with the full set of syllogisms.

EULER CIRCLES AND VENN DIAGRAMS AS REPRESENTATIONS

Most theories of syllogistic reasoning have been based on models of one sort or another. Some postulate that reasoners construct Euler circles, or equivalent strings of symbols (see Erickson, 1974; Guyote and Sternberg, 1981). In this case, each set is represented by a separate circle in the Euclidean plane, and the relations between sets are graphically depicted by relations between circles (see Figure 2.2 in Chapter 2). Hence, a premise of the form, "All A are B", calls for two Euler diagrams: in one, the circle denoting A is properly included in the circle denoting B in order to represent the proper inclusion of the set A within the set B, and in the other the two circles are co-extensive in order to represent the co-extension of the two sets. Unfortunately, the number of Euler

Table 6.3
Formal derivations in the predicate calculus of (a) an easy syllogism, and (b) a difficult syllogism.

Problem (a): 88% correct conclusions

1.	$(\exists y)(Ay \ \& \ By)$	Some of the athletes are bakers.
2.	$(\supset z)(Bz \rightarrow Cz)$	All of the bakers are canoeists.

Stage 1:   Instantiation of the premises:

3.	$Aj \ \& \ Bj$	(existential instantiation of 1)
4.	$Bj \rightarrow Cj$	(universal instantiation of 2)

Stage 2:   Propositional reasoning

5.	Aj	(conjunction elimination from 3)
6.	Bj	(conjunction elimination from 3)
7.	Cj	(modus ponens from 4 and 6)
8.	$Aj \ \& \ Cj$	(conjunction of 5 and 7)

Stage 3:   Generalization of the conclusion

9.	$(\exists x)(Ax \ \& \ Cx)$	(existential generalization of 8)

∴ Some of the athletes are canoeists

Problem (b): 26% correct conclusions

1.	$(\exists x)(Bx \ \& \ Ax)$	Some of the bakers are athletes.
2.	$(\supset y)(By \rightarrow \neg Cy)$	None of the bakers are canoeists.

Stage 1:   Instantiation of the premises:

3.	$Bj \ \& \ Aj$	(existential instantiation of 1)
4.	$Bj \rightarrow \neg Cj$	(universal instantiation of 2)

Stage 2:   Propositional reasoning

5.	Aj	(conjunction elimination from 3)
6.	Bj	(conjunction elimination from 3)
7.	$\neg Cj$	(modus ponens from 4 and 6)
8.	$Aj \ \& \ \neg Cj$	(conjunction of 5 and 7)

Stage 3:   Generalization of the conclusion

9.	$(\exists x)(Ax \ \& \ \neg Cx)$	(existential generalization of 8)

∴ Some of the athletes are not canoeists

---

representations does not correlate with the difficulty of deductions: some easy syllogisms call for many representations, whereas some difficult syllogisms call for few. For example, premises of the form:

Some of the A are B
All the B are C

need 16 different Eulerian combinations, whereas premises of the form:

All of the B are A
None of the C is a B

need only 6 different Eulerian combinations (see Johnson-Laird and Bara, 1984). Yet the first problem is the simplest of all (88% correct conclusions) and the second problem is the hardest of all (8% correct conclusions). Although at least one critic has promised to devise an alternative theory based on Euler circles that avoids this problem (see Ford, 1985), it has not been forthcoming. The theories that do exist posit a limit on the number of combinations that human reasoners can construct (Erickson, 1974; Guyote and Sternberg, 1981). This assumption curtails the competence of human reasoners. If people can examine, say, only four possible combinations, then they do not have, even in principle, the competence to make valid deductions.

A superior method for syllogistic inference uses Venn diagrams (see Figure 2.3 in Chapter 2). Three overlapping circles, each representing a set, are drawn within a rectangle representing the universe of discourse. Universal premises are represented by shading out the appropriate regions, and existential premises are represented by placing crosses in the appropriate regions. Newell (1981) has explored a psychological analogue of this method based on strings of symbols, but it does not account for the differences in difficulty among syllogisms.

MENTAL MODELS FOR SYLLOGISTIC REASONING

We need a theory that explains both rational competence—the possibility of reaching the right conclusion for the right reason—and the pattern of performance, including errors and difficulties. These goals inspired the original model theory, and it gradually evolved into a general explanation of reasoning and comprehension (see Johnson-Laird, 1983). We will consider a more recent version of the model theory, but its general principles should be familiar by now. Reasoners construct a set of models of the premises that makes explicit the minimum amount of information; they formulate a parsimonious conclusion based on this set; and to test for validity, they search for counterexamples, perhaps fleshing out the initial models in order to do so. If there is no such counterexample, the conclusion is valid.

In previous versions of the theory, an assertion such as:

All of the athletes are bakers.

was represented by a single model of the form:

```
a = b
a = b
  o b
```

where each line represents a separate individual (the number of individuals is arbitrary), "a" represents an athlete, "b" represents a baker, and "o" represents an optional individual who may, or may not, be present in the situation referred to by the premise. We now believe that reasoners are more likely to adopt the convention used for connectives, in which an annotation indicates that a set has been exhaustively represented. Hence, they initially represent the premise above using the following sort of model:

```
[a]    b
[a]    b
  . . .
```

where the square brackets indicate, as before, that a set has been exhaustively represented in the model, i.e. members of the set cannot occur elsewhere in the model, and the three dots allow for other sorts of individual yet to be made explicit. The number of individuals remains arbitrary, but, for simplicity, is likely to be small. A fully explicit model for the premise could take the form:

```
 [a]    [b]
 [a]    [b]
[¬a]    [b]
[¬a]   [¬b]
```

where again, each line represents a different individual, and "¬" represents negation. Although the initial model seems to support the converse assertion: "All the bakers are athletes", this explicit model refutes it, because it contains a baker who is not an athlete.

The initial model of an existential assertion "Some of the athletes are bakers" takes the form:

    a   b
    a   b
    . . .

where neither of the sets is exhaustively represented.

The initial model of a negative universal, such as, "None of the athletes is a baker" takes the form:

    [a]
    [a]
          [b]
          [b]
          . . .

in which both sets are exhaustively represented

Finally, the model for a negative existential, such as, "Some of the athletes are not bakers" takes the following form:

    a
    a
    a   [b]
          [b]
          . . .

This model supports the converse assertion—a common fallacy—but it is falsified by constructing the alternative model:

    a
    a
    a   [b]
    a   [b]
          . . .

Readers familiar with Scholastic logic will note that exhaustive representation corresponds exactly to the traditional notion of a "distributed" term.

The information from a second premise is added to the model of the first premise. In all cases, we shall assume that there is no doubt about the existence of members of the relevant sets—an assumption that is generally warranted in daily life and that we made explicit in our experiments. The procedure that adds information is straightforward in the case of the following problem:

All the athletes are bakers.
All the bakers are canoeists.

The model of the first premise is:

    [a]   b
    [a]   b
     . . .

The information from the second premise can be readily added, but there are trivial indeterminacies: there may or may not be bakers who are not athletes, and there may or may not be canoeists who are not bakers. We assume that reasoners build the following sort of initial model:

    [[a]   b]   c
    [[a]   b]   c
     . . .

where the notation:

    [[a]   b]   c

signifies that a is exhausted with respect to b, and b is exhausted with respect to c. It follows that one way of fleshing out the model explicitly is consistent with the set of athletes being properly included in the set of canoeists, and another way of fleshing out the model explicitly is consistent with the two sets being co-extensive. It is not necessary, however, to flesh out the model in order to draw the parsimonious conclusion:

All the athletes are canoeists.

and there is no way of fleshing out the model to refute this conclusion: it is valid and depends on the construction of just one model. It is indeed one of the easiest of syllogisms.

The procedure is more complicated in the case of the following problem:

All of the bakers are athletes.
None of the bakers is a canoeist.

It yields the model:

```
[a    [b]]
[a    [b]]
            [c]
            [c]
      . . .
```

which supports the conclusion:

None of the canoeists is an athlete.

This is the most common error with this problem. The following model refutes this conclusion:

```
[a    [b]]
[a    [b]]
a            [c]
             [c]
      . . .
```

and the two models together support the conclusion:

Some of the canoeists are not athletes.

This conclusion, in turn, is refuted by the model:

```
[a    [b]]
[a    [b]]
a            [c]
a            [c]
      . . .
```

Some subjects may at this point be tempted to conclude that there is no valid conclusion. In fact, all three models support a conclusion that cannot be refuted:

Some of the athletes are not canoeists.

Ths multiple-model problem is, not surprisingly, one of the hardest syllogisms.

In general, the model theory accounts for the difference in difficulty among the valid syllogisms: problems that require just one model are easier than those that require more than one model. The theory also accounts for the most common errors that occur with the difficult syllogisms—they are the conclusions that are supported by just one model of the possible models of the premises. Table 6.1 above summarizes the models that can be constructed for the 27 valid syllogisms. There are 10 one-model problems (with 76% correct conclusions over the four experiments) and 17 multiple-model problems (with only 25% correct conclusions). It is a striking fact that the rank order of difficulty of the problems is almost perfectly correlated with the predictions of the theory.

The correct evaluation of problems with no valid conclusion requires, in principle, more than one model to be constructed. Consider, for example, the premises:

None of the athletes is a baker.
None of the bakers is a canoeist.

They support the initial model:

[a]
[a]
    [b]
    [b]
        [c]
        [c]
     . . .

which yields the conclusion, "None of the athletes is a canoeist". This conclusion is refuted by an alternative model, but its construction calls for a more explicit representation:

[a]   ¬b   [c]
[a]   ¬b   [c]
¬a   [b]   ¬c
¬a   [b]   ¬c
 . . .

There is no simple conclusion interrelating the end terms that is true in both models, and so a correct response is, "no valid conclusion".

The model theory explains why some invalid syllogisms are easier than others. Those problems that are in the symmetrical figures will be more likely to elicit a "no valid conclusion" response if only because it is harder to form an initial model in these figures. A further factor concerns the role of items that are not initially represented as exhausted. For example, the premises:

All of the canoeists are bakers.
Some of the bakers are athletes.

elicit the initial model:

    [[c]   b]   a
    [[c]   b]   a
            . . .

which yields the conclusion:

Some of the canoeists are athletes.

This conclusion can be falsified provided that one bears in mind an alternative disposition of the middle term:

    [[c]   b]
    [[c]   b]
            b   a
            b   a
            . . .

Problems that hinge on unexhausted terms are more difficult than those, such as the previous problem, that do not.

THREE STUDIES OF SYLLOGISMS

The model theory identifies two potential sources of difficulty and error in syllogistic reasoning:

1. If more than one model has to be constructed (e.g. by making implicit information explicit) to reach the right response, then the problem will be more difficult than a one-model problem. This factor explains the difference in difficulty among the valid syllogisms, and it accounts for the characteristic errors made on the multiple-model problems.

2. The integration of the information from the two premises is affected by their figure.

The theory accounts for the results of the experiments on straightforward syllogistic reasoning. We have also tested it in three additional ways in which its predictions appear to differ from those of any rule theory, although, as we have remarked, no comprehensive rule theory for syllogistic reasoning has yet been proposed.

The Effects of Belief

The first set of studies was carried out by Oakhill and her colleagues, and examined the effects of beliefs about the world on deduction. According to rule theories, any effect of belief or prejudice on deduction can operate only by biasing the initial interpretation of the premises or else by acting as a post-deductive "censor" that throws out conclusions offensive to the reasoner's views about the world. There cannot be any effect on the process of deduction itself because formal rules are by definition blind to content. The model theory also predicts these effects, but in addition it suggests that the deductive process itself can be affected by beliefs. In particular, reasoners will search for refuting models more assiduously if their initial conclusion is unbelievable than if it is believable.

There is a long tradition of studies of belief and syllogistic reasoning (e.g. Janis and Frick, 1943; Henle and Michael, 1956; Kaufmann and Goldstein, 1967). Unfortunately, many of these studies are flawed. For example, where the subjects were asked to evaluate given conclusions, their beliefs could act as a "censor" without having any effect on reasoning. Oakhill and her colleagues, however, investigated the conclusions that the subjects drew for themselves (Oakhill and Johnson-Laird, 1985b; Oakhill, Johnson-Laird, and Garnham, 1989). Their principal finding concerned problems based on such premises as:

All of the Frenchmen are wine drinkers.
Some of the wine drinkers are gourmets.

According to the model theory, subjects are likely to construct an initial model of the form:

    [[f]   w]   g
    [[f]   w]   g
        . . .

which supports the conclusion:

Some of the Frenchmen are gourmets.

A panel of judges independently rated such putative conclusions as being highly believable (i.e. 6.6 on a seven-point scale). Hence, the theory predicts that reasoners should tend not to search for counterexamples. In another condition, however, the premises had the same form but an important difference in content:

All of the Frenchmen are wine drinkers.
Some of the wine drinkers are Italians.

They yield a model of the form:

```
[[f]    w]    i
[[f]    w]    i
       . . .
```

which supports the conclusion:

Some of the Frenchmen are Italians.

The panel judged such putative conclusions as unbelievable (1.6 on the seven-point scale). Hence, in this case, the subjects should search more assiduously for a refuting model, e.g.:

```
[[f]    w]
[[f]    w]
       w      i
       w      i
       . . .
```

In short, the model theory predicts that the believability of the *initial* putative conclusion should affect the likelihood of the correct "no valid conclusion" response. Initial conclusions do not occur in rule theories and so these theories cannot make this prediction. It was corroborated by the results of the experiments. Evans, Barston, and Pollard (1983) report similar findings for the evaluation of given conclusions; and Markovits and Nantel (1989) have discovered that the effects of belief are stronger for conclusions that subjects generate themselves than for those they evaluate.

Memory for Conclusions

The second test of the theory also concerned initial putative conclusions. In the case of invalid syllogisms, as we have seen, the model theory predicts that reasoners construct a model, consider the putative conclusion that it supports, often only to reject it as a result of constructing an alternative model. In contrast, rule theories predict that the "no valid conclusion" response is elicited by a failure to derive any conclusion interrelating the end terms. We tested these opposing claims in an experiment that examined the subjects' ability to recall their responses to sixteen problems (see Byrne and Johnson-Laird, 1989c; in press). Eight problems supported a valid conclusion, and eight did not. The sixteen subjects drew their own conclusions to these problems, which were presented in a random order. Subsequently, we gave them an unexpected "recognition" test in which they had to pick out the conclusion that they had drawn from a set of four conclusions. The choice, however, *never included a "no valid conclusion" response to an invalid problem*. Instead, it contained the initial putative conclusion predicted by the model theory, which subjects should have fleetingly considered if only to reject. The crucial data are the recognition choices for those trials (27%) where subjects had correctly responded "no valid conclusion" in the reasoning task. In these cases, the subjects realized that their "no valid conclusion" response was not amongst the choice set on 20% of occasions, and they could not identify their conclusion on 6% of occasions. In every single case of the remaining 74% of responses, the subjects chose the initial conclusion predicted by the model theory.

The phenomenon is difficult for rule theories to explain. Because there are no proofs for invalid syllogisms, it is difficult to see how the subjects could have reached *any* conclusion if they had responded "no valid conclusion". One might argue that the subjects were not really remembering conclusions from earlier in the experiment, but rather that they were reasoning from the premises once again. Although this possibility cannot be eliminated, it still corroborates the model theory and counts against rule theories.

"Only" as a Quantifier

The third study exploited an important feature of the model theory. It distinguishes between the representation of premises, and the inferential procedure that operates on the representation. The representation of premises depends on their meaning; the inferential procedure of searching for a counterexample is entirely general and can be applied to any sort of model. It follows that the theory can be easily extended to accommodate a new quantifier. It is necessary only to describe the contribution of the new quantifier to models of assertions containing it. Once this semantics has been specified, the reasoning procedure can operate on the models, and there is no need for new procedures for the quantifier. The parsimony of the model theory contrasts with rule theories, which must describe both the meaning of the new quantifier and its rules of inference.

We exploited this factor to extend the model theory to cope with "only", which is a connective (see Chapter 3) and a quantifier:

Only the bakers are athletes.

This assertion has the same truth conditions, as Keenan (1971) has argued, as:

All the athletes are bakers.

But, we suspected that there was a revealing difference between their mental representations. The assertion containing "only" makes explicit right from the start not merely that some bakers are athletes but also that anyone who is *not* a baker is also *not* an athlete. Hence, the initial model contains explicit negative information. Could there be a baker who is not an athlete? In fact, the correct interpretation of "only" calls for such a possibility, but reasoners initially are likely to construct the following model:

```
[b    [a]]
[b    [a]]
[[¬b]  ¬a]
 . . .
```

where, once again, the three dots represent a region of uncertainty that could be fleshed out ultimately to contain:

```
b    ¬a
```

A fully explicit model for "all the athletes are bakers" is as follows:

```
 a    b
 a    b
¬a    b
¬a   ¬b
```

Hence, the two models are equivalent in content, but the equivalence is not immediately apparent because the initial model for "all" makes explicit just the affirmative information, whereas the model of "only" makes explicit both affirmative and negative information.

The difference between the models leads to a testable prediction. Because the model for "only" is more complex than the one for "all", it should be harder to make deductions from "only" than from "all". We tested this prediction in an experiment that compared problems, such as:

Only the a's are b's
Only the b's are c's

with equivalent problems, such as:

All the b's are a's
All the c's are b's

where the content of the premises concerned sensible everyday relations (Johnson-Laird and Byrne, 1989). The problems based on "only" (26% correct) were reliably harder than the problems based on "all" (46% correct). A second experiment also confirmed that problems based on "only" were affected by the number of models that had to be constructed: one-model problems were significantly easier (55% correct) than multiple-model problems with a valid conclusion (15% correct). Once again, the erroneous conclusions to the multiple-model problems were primarily those supported by just one model of the premises (56% of errors).

An incidental observation was very damaging to the atmosphere hypothesis: where both premises were based on "only" just 16% of conclusions contained it, whereas 45% of conclusions contained "all". Likewise, where one premise was based on "only", just 2% of conclusions contained it. This result runs counter to the atmosphere hypothesis, which is still often assumed by theories of syllogistic reasoning (e.g. Madruga, 1984; Polk and Newell, 1988). In our view, the apparent evidence supporting the hypothesis derives, in fact, from the natural consequences of building models based on the meaning of the premises, and then using a procedure to construct parsimonious conclusions. This claim is supported by the well-known fact that the majority of valid conclusions to the 27 premise pairs correspond to the predictions of the atmosphere effect. Hence, even a computer program that used the first-order predicate calculus might seem to be abiding by the atmosphere effect. The bias towards "all" rather than "only" corroborates our assumption that "only" elicits explicit negative information. Negation is a well-known cause of difficulty (Wason, 1959; Clark and Clark, 1977), and so subjects avoid using the negative quantifier when they can use an affirmative one.

Our theory of models has used conceptual tags to represent various sorts of abstract information, such as "¬" to represent negation. Some theorists have argued that representations should eschew such tags and represent only directly perceptible physical information (Inder, 1987; cf. also Levesque, 1986). There are indeed ways to avoid them—by maintaining a linguistic representation of the premises, for example—but there is reason to believe that people do represent abstract concepts (Johnson-Laird, 1983, Ch. 15; Polk and Newell, 1988). The final experiment that we will report in this chapter provides evidence that reasoners represent negation directly in their models.

The model theory predicts that deductions based on what is explicit in a model should be easier than those that depend on fleshing out implicit information. Hence, the following premises:

All authors are bankers.
Mark is an author.

should readily yield the conclusion:

Mark is a banker.

whereas the premises:

All authors are bankers.
Mark is not a banker.

should less readily yield the conclusion:

Mark is not an author.

In this case, the model has to be fleshed out with negative information about the set of individuals who are not bankers before the conclusion can be derived. The corresponding problems based on "only" yield a different prediction, granted our assumption that their models will contain explicit negative information right from the start. Hence, there should be no difference between the premises:

Only bankers are authors.
Mark is an author.

and:

Only bankers are authors.
Mark is not a banker.

26 subjects made all four sorts of deduction, and the results corroborated the theory:

"All"	Affirmative	96% correct
	Negative	73% correct
"Only"	Affirmative	90% correct
	Negative	86% correct

If subjects reason on the basis of models, then the interaction is explicable only if they represent negation explicitly for the premises based on "only".

CONCLUSIONS

In this chapter, we have considered deductions from premises containing single quantifiers, and we have shown how a theory based on models is able to account for deductive competence and for systematic patterns of performance. It predicts which problems will be difficult and it predicts which errors ordinary individuals will make with them. Rule theories in contrast have had relatively little to say about these deductions, but nevertheless we were able to present experimental evidence that any rule theory is likely to have difficulty in explaining. For example, the believability of a putative conclusion influences whether or not subjects stick with it or else search for counterexamples to it. Reasoners appear to construct such initial conclusions even when their ultimate response is "no valid conclusion", and this phenomenon certainly cannot be accounted for in terms of formal rules. Finally, we have shown how the theory can be readily extended to a new quantifier, "only". One problem that we have not resolved, however, concerns the form of models. Some theorists have proposed that they correspond to Euler circles, or to Venn diagrams, or to strings of symbols equivalent to these representations. Although we have expressed some doubts about such theories—they place combinatorially explosive demands on working memory, for example—we know that they continue to exert an appeal to some cognitive scientists. Hence, in the next chapter, we will extend the model theory to deal with premises that contain more than one quantifier. One of the main reasons for considering such deductions is that Euler circles and Venn diagrams are not powerful enough notations to represent them.

CHAPTER 7

Many Quantifiers: Reasoning
with Multiple Quantification

There are some cubists, musicians, and authors.
All cubists are painters.
Lisa is one of the cubists and Paul is one of the musicians.
Every painter is staying in the same hotel as every author.
None of the authors is staying in the same hotel as any of the
    musicians.
What follows?

You should be able to deduce:

Therefore, Lisa is not in the same hotel as Paul.

This conclusion depends on a series of deductions. Some are based on
premises containing one quantifier, and some on premises containing
two quantifiers, e.g.:

Every painter is staying in the same hotel as every author.

Proofs of multiply-quantified deductions call for the most powerful of
logics—the predicate calculus, which includes the propositional calculus
but also additional machinery to analyze the internal structure of
sentences. In this chapter we will examine how people make such
deductions, and one of our aims is to determine the form of
representation that they use. Neither Euler circles nor Venn diagrams

are powerful enough. They cannot, for instance, represent such assertions as "Every painter is staying in some hotel or other" and "There is some hotel in which every painter is staying". The deduction above surely calls for a system that deals with the whole gamut of inferences without a shift from one sort of representation to another. Hence, Euler circles or Venn diagrams are unlikely to be used even for singly-quantified premises.

Given the logical power required for multiply-quantified inferences, it is hardly surprising that they have not previously been investigated by psychologists. The studies that we will report, which were carried out in collaboration with Patrizia Tabossi (see Johnson-Laird, Byrne, and Tabossi, 1989), will allow us to draw an informative contrast between rule theories and model theories.

A RULE THEORY FOR MULTIPLE QUANTIFIERS

Here is a simple but robust result. When we presented adults with these premises:

> None of the painters is in the same place as any of the
>   musicians.
> All of the musicians are in the same place as all of the authors.

the majority of them drew the valid conclusion:

> None of the painters is in the same place as any of the authors.

But, when we presented them with these premises:

> None of the painters is in the same place as any of the
>   musicians.
> All of the musicians are in the same place as some of the
>   authors.

only a few drew the valid conclusion (or an equivalent of it):

> None of the painters is in the same place as some of the authors.

Why is there this difference in accuracy? Some putative accounts of quantified deduction can be immediately eliminated. For example, the difference cannot be attributed to the "atmosphere" of the premises, which we discussed in the previous chapter. Likewise, the conversion of premises is hardly relevant because "in the same place" is a symmetric relation. And, as will show presently, the difference is not caused by ambiguity in the scope of quantifiers (see Chapter 1 for an account of scope).

There is a large linguistic literature on the analysis of quantified sentences, and many linguists are committed to the view that sentences have a logical form that explicitly represents quantificational structure, binding relations, and other such matters (see Chapter 2). And at least one linguist, Janet Fodor (1982), has put forward a model account of the meaning of quantifiers. But, perhaps because of the dearth of experimental studies, no psychological rule theory of reasoning with multiple quantifiers has so far been proposed. If people use rules, however, then the rules are likely to be related to those of the predicate calculus—just as the linguistic theories of logical form posit structures that can be related to that calculus.

A rule theory can account for differences in difficulty in terms of two factors: the respective lengths of the derivations, and the relative availability or ease of applying the rules of inference that are required in the derivations. Both factors depend on the particular set of rules postulated by the theorist. Proofs in the predicate calculus, as it is usually formalized, depend on three stages, which we illustrated in Chapter 1: the replacement of quantified variables by hypothetical individuals, the use of rules for connectives to derive conclusions about these individuals, and the restoration of quantifiers in place of them. If the second stage is to be compatible with existing psychological theories of *propositional* reasoning, then it must depend on a set of "natural deduction" rules (see Table 2.2). The three stages might be collapsed into one for certain deductions (see Braine and Rumain, 1983), but this stratagem is neither feasible nor plausible for multiply-quantified deductions because, as we will now show, a series of deductions based on connectives has to be made after the elimination of the quantifiers.

A three-stage derivation for the easy problem above is presented in Table 7.1, in which "∀" denotes the universal quantifier, "any", and "∃" denotes the existential quantifier, "at least some". The derivation is possible only because the relation "in the same place as" is both transitive and symmetric, and these properties are stated in the form of meaning postulates.

The derivation has a large number of steps for such a simple deduction. Even this number depends on a simplification: we have used the rule for modus tollens, which according to the psychological theories of propositional reasoning normally calls for the lengthier process of a *reductio ad absurdum* (see Table 2.2). The difficult problem above has an almost identical derivation. It requires exactly the same number of

Table 7.1

A formal derivation in the predicate calculus. For simplicity, we have restricted quantifiers to particular sorts of individuals.

The premises can be symbolized as:

1.	$(\forall P)(\forall M)\neg(PSM)$	(None of the P is in the same place as any of the M)
2.	$(\forall M)(\forall A)(MSA)$	(All of the M are in the same place as all of the A)
3.	$(\forall x)(\forall y)(\forall z)(xSy \ \& \ ySz \rightarrow xSz)$	(transitivity of "in the same place as")
4.	$(\forall x)(\forall y)(xSy \rightarrow ySx)$	(symmetry of "in the same place as")

Stage 1: Instantiation of quantifiers

5.	$(\forall M)\neg(pSM)$	(universal instantiation of P in 1)
6.	$\neg(pSm)$	(universal instantiation of M in 5)
7.	$(\forall A)(mSA)$	(universal instantiation of M in 2)
8.	(mSa)	(universal instantiation of A in 7)
9-11.	$(pSa \ \& \ aSm) \rightarrow pSm$	(universal instantiations of X, Y, and Z in 3)
12, 13.	$(mSa) \rightarrow (aSm)$	(universal instantiations of X and Y in 4)

Stage 2: Propositional reasoning

14.	$\neg(pSa \ \& \ aSm)$	(modus tollens from 6 and 11)
15.	$\neg(pSa)$ or $\neg(aSm)$	(de Morgan's law from 14)
16.	(aSm)	(modus ponens from 8 and 13)
17.	$\neg(pSa)$	(disjunctive rule from 15 and 16)

Stage 3: Re-introduction of quantifiers

18.	$(\forall A)\neg(pSA)$	(universal generalization of a in 17)
19.	$(\forall P)(\forall A)\neg(PSA)$	(universal generalization of p in 18)

The conclusion corresponds to:

None of the P is in the same place as any of the A.

steps, and differs only in that the existential quantifier, "some", in the second premise has to be existentially instantiated, and so the quantifier restored at the end of the derivation is also existential. There is no principled way in which the derivations for the two sorts of problems can be made to differ in length. For example, if instead of transitivity and symmetry, we adopt a principle of "negative transitivity":

For any x, y, and z, if x is in the same place as y, and y is *not* in the same place as z, then x is *not* in the same place as z

then the effect is to shorten both of the derivations by the same amount.

If subjects are using formal rules of this sort, the only feasible explanation of the difference in difficulty between the two problems is that some aspect of reasoning with an existential quantifier causes problems. As we will see, this possibility is eliminated by the results of our experiments. Rule theories fail to elucidate our initial result, and so we now turn to the model theory.

THE MODEL THEORY FOR MULTIPLE QUANTIFIERS

According to the model theory, people reason from a premise, such as:

None of the painters is in the same place as any of the
  musicians.

by constructing a model of the state of affairs that it describes. They assume that there are a certain number of individuals of each sort, say, three of each, and they represent them as being in different places:

  I [p] [p] [p] I [m] [m] [m] I

where each "p" represents a painter, each "m" represents a musician, different places are represented by demarcating spatial locations with vertical barriers, and the fact that a set of individuals has been exhaustively represented is shown by square brackets. The model is constructed on the basis of the meaning of the sentence, and we will describe the process in more detail later.

The information from the second premise:

All of the musicians are in the same place as all of the authors.

can be added to the model:

  I [p] [p] [p] I [m] [m] [m] [a] [a] [a] I

This model supports the conclusion:

None of the painters is in the same place as any of the authors.

There is no alternative model that satisfies the premises yet refutes this conclusion, and so it is valid. The problem is accordingly a one-model problem with a valid conclusion.

The first premise of the difficult problem is the same as before:

None of the painters is in the same place as any of the
  musicians.

and yields again the same sort of model:

  I [p] [p] [p] I [m] [m] [m] I

The second premise is:

All of the musicians are in the same place as some of the
authors.

which yields the following model:

  I [p] [p] [p] I [m] [m] [m] a a I

where the authors are not exhaustively represented. This model
supports the same conclusion as before:

None of the musicians is in the same place as any of the authors.

And, in fact, over a quarter of our subjects erroneously drew such a
conclusion. With this problem, however, the search for an alternative
model that refutes the conclusion will be successful because the set of
authors is not exhausted, e.g.:

  I [p] [p] [p] a I [m] [m] [m] a a I

Some subjects conclude:

Some authors are in the same place as all the painters.

This is an extraordinary conclusion to draw from the premises if one is
reasoning by rule, but the model theory makes sense of it. Subjects
consider what is true in this second model, and forget about the first
model (if they ever constructed it). A few prudent subjects, in fact, draw
the conclusion but with a modal qualification:

Some authors *could* be in the same place as all the painters.

This conclusion is valid because it requires only a single model to satisfy
a conclusion qualified by "could". As one would expect, these modal
conclusions are drawn more often for multiple-model problems (20%
modal conclusions in our experiment) than for one-model problems (2%
modal conclusions). The present premises, in fact, support a stronger
conclusion, which holds over all of their models:

Some of the authors are not in the same place as any of the painters.

or equivalently:

None of the painters is in the same place as *some* of the authors.

This second problem is thus a valid multiple-model one, and the theory correctly predicts that it should be harder than the one-model problem.

EXPERIMENTAL TESTS OF THE TWO THEORIES

The model theory explains the difference in difficulty between the easy and the difficult pair of problems, but we also investigated other sorts of deduction. There are a large number of doubly-quantified pairs of premises, because each premise can express one of twelve underlying relations, namely:

1. $(\forall A)$ $(\forall B)$ (ARB)
2. $(\exists A)$ $(\forall B)$ (ARB)
3. $(\exists B)$ $(\forall A)$ (ARB)
4. $(\forall B)$ $(\exists A)$ (ARB)
5. $(\forall A)$ $(\exists B)$ (ARB)
6. $(\exists A)$ $(\exists B)$ (ARB)

and their respective negations. The arrangement of the terms in the two premises can also be in one of the four so-called "figures" (see Chapter 6). Because we could not test subjects on all of the possible problems, we chose sets of problems that could distinguish between the rule and model theories.

In our first experiment in collaboration with Tabossi, we gave 18 doubly-quantified problems to students at the University of Bologna. The problems included twelve with valid conclusions, which all required derivations of the same length according to the rule theory based on the principle of "negative transitivity". Six, however, were one-model problems, and the other six were multiple-model problems. The results corroborated the model theory. The subjects made more correct deductions from the one-model problems (68%) than from the valid multiple-model problems (13%). These results ruled out any simple response-priming or matching explanation of performance. The correct conclusion to the one-model problems always matched the logical form of one of the premises, e.g.:

All the X are in the same place as all the Y.
Some of the Y are in the same place as all the Z.
∴ All the X are in the same place as all the Z.

And, in several cases, the same condition applied for the valid multiple-model problems, e.g.:

None of the X is in the same place as some of the Y.
All of the Y are in the same place as some of the Z.
∴ None of the X is in the same place as some of the Z.

The match did not facilitate performance.

The results are not consistent with a rule theory using the principle of "negative transitivity". They are consistent, however, with a rule theory using separate postulates for transitivity and symmetry. It was this version of the rule theory that our second experiment was designed to test.

We gave a set of 12 valid problems to 18 adult subjects. We also gave them six problems with no valid conclusions interrelating the end terms. Each of the valid problems had one affirmative and one negative premise, and they all had formal derivations of the same length according to the rule theory (see Table 7.1). But, according to the model theory, half of them are one-model problems and half of them are multiple-model problems. The results again corroborated the model theory: there were more correct deductions from the one-model problems (67%) than from the multiple-model problems (16%). Moreover, in this experiment, we gave the subjects problems based on three different relations: "in the same place as", "equal in height to", and "related to" in the simple consanguineal sense, which subjects spontaneously treat as transitive and symmetric. If subjects are constructing images, as distinct from models (see Johnson-Laird, 1983, Ch. 7), then the imageability of the relation might well have affected their performance. In fact, it did not.

The experiment also eliminated the possibility that guessing explains the difference in performance between one-model and multiple-model problems. One-model problems might be easier than multiple-model problems because they have a greater number of correct, though weaker, conclusions. The subjects would then have a correspondingly greater chance of guessing the right conclusion for the one-model problems. In this experiment, however, the subjects' correct conclusions to the one-model problems were all of the form:

None of the X is in the same place as any of the Y.

and did not reflect the range of possible answers predicted by the guessing hypothesis.

We have now eliminated both a rule theory based on negative transitivity and a rule theory based on transitivity and symmetry. Yet, a defender of rules might argue that we have not made a fair test. We have shown merely that rules fail to predict observed differences—albeit differences predicted by the model theory. A more stringent test should examine cases where the rule theory predicts a difference in difficulty that is not predicted by the model theory. Our third, and final, experiment provided this test.

We gave 11 adult subjects a set of multiply-quantified problems. We chose some problems that required only 14 line derivations because their proofs depended solely on transitivity, and not on symmetry. For example, premises of the following sort:

All of the P are related to all of the M.
All of the M are related to all of the A.

yield the valid conclusion:

∴ All of the P are related to all of the A.

when "related to" is used in the simple consanguineal sense. As Table 7.2 shows, the derivation of this conclusion requires only the postulate of transitivity.

We compared these problems to ones that required 19-line derivations, which depended on both transitivity and symmetry (see Table 7.1). The rule theory predicts that the more steps there are in a derivation, the harder a problem should be, and so it predicts a difference between these two sorts of problem. The 14-line problems are all one-model problems and so the theories are agreed that these problems should be easy. But, some of the 19-line problems are one-model, and some of them are multiple-model. Hence, in these cases, the two theories diverge.

Table 7.3 summarizes all the problems that we used in the experiment, and states the percentages of correct responses. As it shows, performance conformed to the model theory, and not to the rule theory. The 14-line problems (73% correct) were easier than the 19-line problems (55% correct). But this apparent corroboration of the rule theory is undermined by the effects of the number of models—as a glance at Table 7.3 confirms. The 19-line valid problems are easy (71%) when they require only one model, but difficult (23% correct) when they require multiple models.

Table 7.2

A formal derivation in the predicate calculus based only on the property of transitivity

The premises can be symbolized as:

1.	($\forall$P)($\forall$M) (PRM)	(All of the P are related to all of the M)
2.	($\forall$M)($\forall$A)(MRA)	(All of the M are related to all of the A)
3.	($\forall$x)($\forall$y)($\forall$z)(xRy & yRz → xRz)	(transitivity)

Stage 1:   Instantiation of quantifiers

4.	($\forall$M) (pRM)	(universal instantiation of P in 1)
5.	(pRm)	(universal instantiation of M in 4)
6.	($\forall$A)(mRA)	(universal instantiation of M in 2)
7.	(mRa)	(universal instantiation of A in 6)
8–10.	(pRm & mRa) → pRa	(universal instantiations of X, Y & Z in 3)

Stage 2:   Propositional reasoning

11.	(pRm & mRa)	(conjunction of 5 and 7)
12.	(pRa)	(modus ponens from 10 and 11)

Stage 3:   Re-introduction of quantifiers

13.	($\forall$A) (pRA)	(universal generalization of a in 1?)
14.	($\forall$P)($\forall$A) (PRA)	(universal generalization of p in 13)

The conclusion corresponds to:

All of the P are related to all of the A.

The results also ruled out differences between existential and universal quantifiers, and differences in scope ambiguity, as alternative explanations of the phenomena. Although people usually interpret the scope of quantifiers as following their surface order in a sentence (Johnson-Laird, 1970), we controlled for its potential effect in this experiment. A telling contrast occurred between one pair of problems. The subjects drew 64% correct conclusions from the one-model premises:

None of the painters is related to any of the musicians.
Some of the musicians are related to all of the authors.

but they drew only 23% correct conclusions from the multiple-model premises:

None of the painters is related to any of the musicians.
All of the musicians are related to some of the authors.

The quantifiers in both problems are the same, and the only linguistic difference between them is in the order of the quantifiers in the second premise. Hence, there is no intrinsic difference in difficulty between

Table 7.3
The problems used in Experiment 3 (each problem was presented
once in figure 1 and once in figure 2).

Type of problem	All-All All-All	All-Some All-All	All-Some All-Some	All-Some Some-All
Number of models	one	one	one	multiple
Lines in derivations	14	14	14	none (no valid conclusion)
Percentage of correct conclusions	82	78	60	14

Type of problem	None-any All-All	None-any Some-All	None-any All-Some	None-some Some-All
Number of models	one	one	multiple	multiple
Lines in derivations	19	19	19	none (no valid conclusion)
Percentage of correct conclusions	78	64	23	32

existential and universal quantifiers. Likewise, in both problems the second premise is theoretically ambiguous in scope. For example, "All of the musicians are related to some of the authors" could mean that the musicians are related to one and the same set of authors (For some y, for any x, such that y is an author and if x is a musician, then x is related to y), or else it could mean merely that each musician is related to some authors (For any x, for some y, if x is a musician then y is an author and x is related to y). And there is nothing intrinsically difficult about this second premise of the multiple-model problem, because it also occurs in the following one-model problem:

All of the painters are related to some of the musicians.
All of the musicians are related to some of the authors.

to which the subjects drew 60% correct conclusions.

THE DIFFERENCES BETWEEN RULES AND MODELS

Our results refute any rule theory resembling the predicate calculus, but could there not be some alternative formulation that might save the hypothesis of mental rules of inference? Obviously, we cannot rule out this possibility, but we can show that it is extremely unlikely. A rule theory starts with a representation of the logical form of premises, which depends in the case of our materials solely on their linguistic structure. Hence, what is needed is a linguistic difference between the various problems that leads to much longer or more difficult derivations for the multiple-model problems. We have searched for such a factor, but our search has failed. Our experiments have eliminated the following potential factors:

1. An atmosphere or response-priming effect, in which there is a match between the form of the correct conclusion and the form of the premises (ruled out by the first experiment).
2. Affirmative versus negative premises (ruled out by the second experiment, in which all the problems with valid conclusions had one affirmative premise and one negative premise).
3. The greater number of valid conclusions for the one-model problems than for the multiple-model problems (ruled out by the second experiment, where the subjects drew only the strongest valid conclusion to the one-model problems).
4. A difference in difficulty between existential and universal quantifiers (ruled out by the third experiment).
5. Ambiguities in the scope of quantifiers (ruled out by the third experiment).
6. A difference in difficulty between certain premises as a whole (ruled out by the third experiment).

It is therefore highly improbable that any aspect of the logical form of premises creates the observed pattern of performance.

A crucial distinction between the two sorts of theory is that formal derivations depend on variables whereas the manipulation of models does not. Models do not normally contain variables, because the work of instantiation is a part of comprehension. Universal quantifiers are instantiated by mental tokens that exhaust the relevant set, whereas existential quantifiers are instantiated by sets of mental tokens that do not exhaust the relevant set. The model theory has separate procedures that operate, in effect, to instantiate and to generalize, but because these procedures operate on models, rather than on logical forms, the theory is able to predict the relative difficulty of deductions.

A further advantage of the model theory is that, unlike a rule theory, it accounts for comprehension and the formulation of conclusions, and so reasoning itself depends solely on searching for counterexamples. Most of the theoretical work is done once one has an analysis of the *meanings* of expressions, i.e. an account of how they are mapped into models. It is therefore relatively easy to extend the theory to embrace a new quantifier, connective, or relational term: the same general procedures for constructing and interpreting models apply, and it is necessary only to specify the truth conditions (with respect to models) of the new expression. Its logical properties emerge from the process of using it to build and to interpret models, and do not have to be laid down explicitly in rules of inference or meaning postulates.

Any theory of the interpretation of multiply-quantified assertions must allow for the occurrence of an indefinite number of quantifiers, even within the same noun phrase, e.g.:

Some of the relatives of every employee of all the friends of the president ....

and so the interpretation of quantifiers almost certainly depends on a mechanism that operates compositionally, that is, it builds up the interpretation of an expression from the meanings of its constituents according to the syntactic relations between them. We have implemented a computer program (see Chapter 9) that works on such a "rule-by-rule" basis in which for each syntactic rule, there is a structural semantic principle for assembling the procedure that will construct the required set of models. An analogous assumption is standard in the semantics of the predicate calculus, and in those analyses of natural language inspired by model-theoretic semantics (see e.g. Partee, 1975; Barwise and Etchemendy, 1989b). A critical difference, however, is that the program *constructs* models of multiply-quantified assertions, whereas the existence of a set of models is taken for granted in model-theoretic semantics, which provides only an account of how to assign truth or falsity to an assertion with respect to models. Hence, in theory, the procedure representing the meaning of an assertion has to be used to do different jobs, from building a model to verifying the assertion in relation to an existing model.

The search for alternative models of the premises to refute a putative conclusion could, in theory, be carried out in a purely random way provided that the same models are not sampled more than once. A random alteration can be made to a model and, if the result is still consistent with the premises, the conclusion can be evaluated with respect to it. A model is finite and there are only a finite number of alterations that can be made to it. Hence, sooner or later, they will have been exhausted. Although ordinary individuals seem not to possess any simple deterministic search procedure, they probably do not search entirely at random, either. Two principal factors are likely to play a role: the occurrence of a choice in the initial construction of a model, and the occurrence of sets that are not exhaustively represented. Both are clues to the possibility of constructing alternative models that might refute the conclusion drawn from the initial model. At present, however, we have too little information to characterize the details of the search. It may differ from one individual to another, though the consistent pattern of errors that we have observed suggests that many common factors are at work.

CONCLUSIONS

Once a compositional semantics has been specified for quantifiers and relations, then it can be used to construct models on the basis of the meaning of assertions, to formulate conclusions that hold in models, and to evaluate alternative models that may be counterexamples to putative conclusions. The same meanings can be used to control all these processes. Although we have reported only three experiments on deduction from premises containing more than one quantifier, their results are clear cut. They show that people reason by building models rather than by using formal rules of the sort currently embodied in psychological theories of deduction. Such theories predict differences in difficulty that are not observed, and they fail to predict differences that are observed. In contrast, the model theory explains the phenomena.

CHAPTER 8

Meta-deduction

The main domains of deduction are propositional, relational, and quantificational reasoning; and we have now shown that the model theory accounts for human competence and patterns of performance in all three of them. But, as we mentioned in Chapter 2, reasoners can *know* that they have made a valid deduction, and these meta-deductive intuitions prepare the way for the development of self-conscious methods of checking validity. Without this higher-level, or meta-deductive, ability human beings could not have invented logic, they could not make deductions about other people's deductions, and they could not devise psychological theories of reasoning. In this chapter, we are going to examine what little is known about meta-deduction, and advance a model theory of the ability—one that we will compare with a theory based on formal rules. We will distinguish between *meta-logical* reasoning, which depends on an explicit reference to truth and falsity, and *meta-cognitive* reasoning, which depends on reference to what others may be deducing.

Meta-logical deduction is exemplified by the following sort of argument:

Every time I argue from premises of the form:
    If p then q
    p
to the conclusion q, I notice that when the premises are true, the conclusion is true. And I am unable to construct a counterexample in which the premises are true and the conclusion is false. This formal pattern of inference must be valid.

147

In discussing certain conditionals in Chapter 4, we ourselves engaged in the following meta-logical argument:

> If you doubt the validity of these deductions, then a glance at the truth table should settle your mind ... the conditional is true whenever its antecedent is false ... and true whenever its consequent is true .... Because either condition suffices to establish the truth of the conditional, the corresponding deductions must be valid.

There is indeed historical evidence that semantic intuitions precede logical formalization (see Kneale and Kneale, 1962). In short, without the ability to reason about which patterns of inference preserve truth, human beings would lack both logical and psychological accounts of deduction.

Meta-cognitive reasoning is deduction about other people's deductions. As social psychologists and sociologists have long understood, it plays a key part in human interactions (see e.g. Goffman, 1959; Nisbett and Ross, 1980). In public places, for instance, much of our deliberate behaviour is designed to ensure that other people will infer that our activities are legitimate. A man loitering on a street corner will ostentatiously keep looking at his watch, and frowning in irritation, to make clear to the world at large that he is waiting for someone. He does not need to keep checking the time, but his action legitimizes his presence there. He has calculated what others are likely to think and adjusted his behaviour so that they will think what he wants them to think.

A RULE THEORY
OF META-LOGICAL DEDUCTION

Both meta-logical and meta-cognitive deductions, we believe, are abilities that depend on ordinary deductive powers. They call upon these powers much as a computer program calls upon a subroutine to carry out some humdrum operation. Both meta-abilities are also a source of logical puzzles, and, as we will show, it is through these puzzles that they can be investigated in the psychological laboratory. Meta-logical puzzles depend on reference to truth and falsity, either directly or indirectly. They have many forms, and here are three examples (with solutions at the end of the chapter):

1. There are three people: one who always tells the truth, one who always lies, and one who sometimes lies and sometimes tells the truth.
   A says: I am the person who sometimes lies.
   B says: That is true.
   C says: I am not the person who sometimes lies.
   Who is who?

2. One of the following people is Napoleon:
   A says: no more than one of us is telling the truth.
   B says: I am Napoleon.
   C says: I am Napoleon.
   Who is Napoleon?

3. Only given both of the following premises:
   It is raining tonk the match is cancelled.
   The match is not cancelled.
   can a valid deduction be made to the conclusion:
   It is not raining.
   What interpretations does "tonk" have?

The use of puzzles to investigate meta-logical deduction has been pioneered by Rips (1989), who studied a series of "knight-and-knave" puzzles (Smullyan, 1978). Imagine, for example, that there are only knights, who always tell the truth, and knaves, who always lie. Given:

Lancelot says "I am a knave and so is Gawain".
Gawain says "Lancelot is a knave".

then what are Lancelot and Gawain? The puzzle can be solved in the following way. Lancelot cannot be telling the truth because he asserts that he is a knave, that is, a person who always tells lies. Hence, he *is* a knave. Because the first clause of his assertion is then true, the second clause must be false in order for his assertion *as a whole* to be false. It is therefore false that Gawain is a knave: he is a knight. And indeed he is, because he correctly asserts that Lancelot is a knave. As the puzzle illustrates, if a liar asserts, A and B, it does not follow that both propositions are false. The assertion is a conjunction and so it will be false if just one of its constituents, say B, is false.

Rips attempts to cut meta-logical deduction down to the size of ordinary deduction: he accounts for it merely by adding some extra rules to his formal theory (see Chapter 2). He adds content-specific rules that define knights and knaves:

a. If S says P and S is a knight, then P.
b. If S says P and S is a knave, then not P.
c. If S is not a knight then S is a knave.
d. If S is not a knave then S is a knight.

He postulates a single deterministic procedure for solving problems:

1. Assume that the first person mentioned in the problem is a knight, and then draw as many deductions as one can from this assumption.
2. If these deductions lead to a contradiction, abandon the assumption and assume instead that the first-mentioned person is a knave (and make as many deductions as one can from this assumption).
3. Assume that the second person is a knight, and so on.
4. Continue until all the consistent sets of assumptions have been established, and report what is constant to all these sets. If any individuals have no constant identity within them, then their status as a knight or knave is not determined.

The basic inferential strategy is a *reductio ad absurdum*: any assumption is abandoned if it yields a contradiction. Table 8.1 summarizes how Rips's program solves a meta-logical problem.

According to the theory, the difficulty of a problem depends on the number of steps in the derivation, and Rips reports two experiments that appear to support this prediction. Nevertheless, we shall argue that his theory fails to do justice to meta-logical deduction.

Our first concern is that Rips's theory does not reflect the importance of truth and falsity. The proper definition of a knight is as follows:

If S says P and S is a knight, then P is true.

But Rips uses the definition:

If S says P and S is a knight, then P.

This so-called "disquotational" approach eliminates any reference to "truth" and "falsity", and handles meta-deduction in a purely syntactic way. It will work for the particular puzzles that Rips considers, but as a general solution it has well-known problems (see Austin, 1970; Barwise and Etchemendy, 1987). For example, an assertion, such as:

It is true that it is raining.

Table 8.1

A summary of Rips's (1989) program solving a puzzle
(see the text for a statement of rules a - d)

The premises:
1. A says, "B is a knave".
2. B says, "A is a knight if and only if C is a knight".

The derivation:

3.	A is a knight	(hypothesis)
4.	B is a knave	(rule a applied to 3 and 1)
5.	not (A is a knight if and only if C is a knight)	(rule b applied to 4 and 2)
6.	C is knave	(Rips says that the program uses a rule to make this deduction from 5 and 3, though he does not list the rule in his program)
7.	B is a knight	(hypothesis)
8.	not (B is a knight)	(7 contradicts 4)
9.	B is a knave	(rule d applied to 8)
10	C is a knight	(hypothesis)
11	not (C is a knight)	(10 contradicts 6)
12	C is a knave	(rule d applied to 11)

The program has thus obtained one consistent set of assignments:
    A is a knight, B is a knave, and C is a knave.

*It now explores the consequences of assuming that A is a knave. In fact, they turn out to be
as follows:*
    A is a knave, B is a knight, and C is a knave.

The solution is therefore that C is a knave, and that the identities of A and B are not determined.

refers to a statement and ascribes a truth value to it, whereas the
assertion:

It is raining.

refers to a state of affairs. If the two statements are treated on a par, as
they would be on Rips's account, then this important referential
distinction is lost. There is also no way in which a disquotational
approach could capture the fundamental definition:

A valid deduction is one in which the conclusion must be true given
that the premises are true.

People can understand this statement, and they certainly grasp the
meaning of "true" and "false".

Rips's approach is consistent with his claim that cognitive psychology has to do without semantic notions of truth and reference (Rips, 1986). There is an historical irony about this claim. The heyday of the purely formal approach to logic was brought to an end by the development of meta-logic. Thus, Tarski showed how to define truth in a model-theoretic semantics for the predicate calculus, and Gödel proved certain theorems about the relations between the calculus and its semantics, e.g. the predicate calculus is "complete" in that it provides a formal derivation for any theorem that is valid in the semantics (see Chapter 1). The very book from which the knight-and-knave puzzles were taken (Smullyan, 1978) goes on to consider Gödel's proof that no consistent formal system can capture all arithmetic truths. Without the notion of truth, there is no notion of validity or meta-logic, and there can be no theory of how logical and psychological theories themselves are developed.

Our second concern is Rips's assumption that reasoners have a single deterministic procedure for solving meta-logical puzzles. In fact, they are almost certainly much less systematic in their approach until they have had considerable experience with the problems. We asked several subjects to think aloud as they grappled with the following problem:

A says, "I am a knave and B is a knave".
B says, "A is a knave".
What are A and B?

The diversity of their approaches was immediately obvious. One subject said:

My first thought is that the initial sentence seems like a contradiction. But two people saying that A is a knave makes it more probable that A is a knave. Possibly B is a knave if A says he is. But A could be lying about whether he is a knave or B is a knave, or maybe he's not lying at all. Therefore, there's no way of knowing whether either of them is telling the truth.

A slightly more insightful individual said:

If A is a knave, he wouldn't say that he's a knave ... seems to be contradictory. One is stuck then. It's impossible for anyone to say they're a knave. You don't know whether A is lying or not. B says A is a knave; so he could be lying or telling the truth. I can't think of anything else ...

And a third subject, who solved the problem, said:

A says B is a knave. If B is telling the truth—anything A says is a lie. So if A says "I am a knave". Oh, no, he says "and": the whole thing could be a lie. He could be telling the truth about the first part, so let's say A says "I am a knave", and B says "A is a knave". I am going to say that's right. So the second part of A's assertion, B is a knave, is a lie. So B is a knight. Let's assume it's not true: A is a knight. If he was a knight and could only tell the truth, then both things he says must be true. And I don't think that could work out. If everything he says is true, then both parts must be true, so he can't be a knight, because the first part contradicts it. If B is a knight, then that leads us back to the initial conclusion. So, A is a knave and B is a knight.

Obviously, meta-logical problems are not easy for people who have not encountered them before (the subjects in Rips's first experiment drew only 20% correct conclusions). Unlike, say, a simple syllogism, where the answer emerges rapidly and almost automatically, people can and do reflect about these problems. They spontaneously make meta-logical remarks, e.g. the remark above about the key role of "and". Notwithstanding the well-known reservations about the interpretation of protocols, we draw just one conclusion from the examples above: there is not just one deterministic procedure that people use to make a meta-logical deduction. Different individuals may use different methods, and, we suspect, the same individuals may use different methods on different occasions of testing. In short, an adequate theory must allow for a diversity of strategies.

THE MODEL THEORY
OF META-LOGICAL DEDUCTION

Our theory of meta-logical deduction depends on two principal components: a procedure for making ordinary deductions, and a higher-level component that uses various strategies that put this deductive machinery to work (Johnson-Laird and Byrne, 1990). The first component uses mental models to carry out straightforward propositional deductions (see Chapter 3), such as:

A or B, or both
Not A
Therefore, B

The second component is an ability to reflect on deductive problems (and on processes of thought), and uses the ordinary deductive machinery as a sub-component. People typically have no existing procedures for dealing with meta-logical relations, and so their first efforts are tentative and exploratory: they may, like a logician, pursue the consequences of certain assumptions about the truth or falsity of premises, they may notice certain interesting patterns in a puzzle, or, like the subject in our third protocol above, they may grasp the consequences of circular assertions. With experience of the puzzles, they may develop more systematic strategies—perhaps as a result of forming "chunks" out of sequences of moves that they have frequently used (Newell, 1990). Hence, meta-logical skill is a higher-order inferential ability that depends on existing deductive procedures.

We will now describe four potential meta-logical strategies that all use models for ordinary propositional deductions. We will show how they lead to certain predicted patterns of difficulty and that these predictions are corroborated by the known data. We have modelled all four strategies by adding components to our existing program that makes propositional deductions by building models.

The program deals with the most general assertions, such as "Proposition A asserts that proposition A itself is false", which we abbreviate as "A asserts that not A". It parses such premises as:

A asserts that not B and C.
B asserts that not A.

and builds up a set of models representing their meaning by using a compositional semantics (with one semantic rule for each syntactic rule in the grammar). The parse yields a set of models for each premise in which the assertor, e.g. A, is represented along with a set of models corresponding to what is asserted by this individual, e.g.:

$\neg$B   C

Because the meta-logical procedures use the ordinary deductive procedures as a sub-component, it is necessary to translate "true" and "false" into the "disquotational" language of that sub-component. This approach suffices for these problems because of the following semantic principle:

An assertion of the form, not p, is *true* if and only if, p is *false*.

Thus, in the domain of these problems, one can move freely from the falsity of p, to the assertion: not p, and *vice versa*. We have already described our misgivings about a disquotational analysis of meta-logical assertions in general.

The first meta-logical strategy that we implemented was Rips's strategy, but we used models instead of formal rules of inference: reasoners follow up to the bitter end the *full chain* of consequences of making the contrasting pair of assumptions about an individual assertor. In our view, this strategy often makes intolerable demands on working memory. Nevertheless, we implemented it in our program, and Tables 8.2 and 8.3 present two examples of its use, and the first of these tables also shows the form of the output from our program. The first example requires the reasoner to follow up the consequences of a set of disjunctive models (see Table 8.2). In our view, this requirement renders the strategy most improbable, especially granted that this problem was amongst the easiest for the subjects in Rips's first experiment (29% correct). The strategy is less complicated for the second example (Table 8.3). Yet, the problem was one of the most difficult that Rips investigated, and only 12% of his subjects solved it.

The contrast between these two examples led us to doubt whether ordinary reasoners use the strategy in Rips's theory. The need to follow up disjunctive consequences puts too great a load on working memory (see also the "double disjunctions" of Chapter 3). We therefore implemented a revised strategy based on simple chains of deduction.

A *simple chain* is constructed in the following way. Reasoners follow up the consequences of assuming the truth of the first premise, but they abandon the strategy whenever it becomes necessary to follow up disjunctive models. If they have not been forced to abandon the strategy, they then consider the consequences of assuming the falsity of the first premise, and again abandon the strategy whenever it is necessary to follow up disjunctive models. A further difference from Rips's full chain is that the procedure does not go on to consider the consequences of other premises. The second strategy that we implemented depends on circular assertions, such as:

A asserts that not A and B.

The circularity catches most people's attention. As the three protocols quoted earlier show, reasoners are likely to grasp that the assertion appears to be self-refuting. Many people at this point can go no further. Some, however, grasp that if A's assertion is false, then the first clause is true, and so the second clause must be false. This *circular* strategy accordingly depends on a simple procedure. It first assumes that the assertor is telling the truth, and follows up only the immediate

Table 8.2
A summary of the full chain strategy solving a problem that elicited 29% correct responses

Problem 1:
    A asserts that not B and C
    B asserts that not A
    C asserts B

1.   Hypothesize that A is telling the truth.
    Conjoin A with the set of models representing A's assertion:
        A ¬B C

2.   Follow up ¬B, i.e. combine ¬B with the negation of B's assertion:
        ¬B A
    This is consistent with the previous model.

3.   Follow up C:
        C B
    which contradicts the model in 1. The actual output of the program, which
    summarises the process thus far, is as follows:
    MAKING A CHAIN FROM THE PREMISE A ASSERTS THAT COMMA
    NOT B AND C
    CHAIN hyp A → A -B C, neg-hyp B → -B A, hyp C → C B,
        ⇒ A CONTRADICTION

4.   Hypothesize that A is telling a lie:
    Conjoin ¬ A with the negation of A's assertion:
        ¬A B   C
        ¬A ¬B ¬C
        ¬A B ¬C

5.   Follow up each of the consequences within each of these models.
    Hypothesizing B and then C from the first model yields a consistent consequence:
    ¬A B C; hypothesizing not B yields a contradiction: A; and hypothesizing B and
    then not C yields another contradiction. Hence, the outcome is:
        ¬A B C

6.   It follows that not A and B and C.

consequence of this assumption, i.e. it does not consider the consequences of this consequence (unlike the full chain). Next, it assumes that the assertor is making a false assertion, and follows up only the immediate consequence of this assumption. The circular strategy solves a problem if one of these two assumptions leads to a contradiction and the other leads to an assignment of a truth value to all the individuals in the problem.

Table 8.3
A summary of the full chain strategy solving a problem that
elicited 12% correct responses

Problem 2:
    A asserts that not B
    B asserts that A and C
    C asserts that not A

1.   Hypothesize that A is telling the truth.
    Conjoin A with the set of models representing A's assertion:
        A   ¬B

2.   Follow up ¬B, i.e. combine ¬B with the negation of B's assertion:
        ¬B   ¬A   C
        ¬B   A   ¬C
        ¬B   ¬A   ¬C
    The only model consistent with the model in 1 is:
        ¬B   A   ¬C

3.   Follow up ¬C:
        ¬C   A
    which is consistent with the previous result.

4.   Hypothesize that A is telling a lie: conjoin ¬A with the negation of A's assertion:
        ¬A   B

5.   Follow up B:
        A   C
    which contradicts the model in 4.

6.   It follows (from 2 and 3) that A, not B, and not C.

Here is an example. Given the problem:

A asserts that not A and not B.
B asserts that B.

the program assumes that A is true, which yields a contradiction at once, because A asserts that not A. It then assumes that A is false, which yields the model, ¬A B. The solution is accordingly: not A and B. For problems that do not contain any circular assertions, the strategy is impotent.

So far, all the strategies that we have described rely on making hypothetical assumptions and then following up their consequences to various degrees. There is an alternative tactic that can be used once one has discovered that a particular hypothesis leads to a contradiction. Consider the premises:

A asserts that A and B.
B asserts that not A.

There is a circular assertion, but the circular strategy fails, because it is necessary to trace two links (from A to B, and from B back to A, in order to discover that A must be false). Likewise, the simple chain fails because it is necessary to follow up the disjunctive consequences of negating A & B, i.e. ¬A B, ¬A ¬B. But, once ¬A has been discovered as a consequence of hypothesizing A, there is a simple matching tactic that is a direct consequence of comparing models: ¬A is the case, and the content of B's assertion is ¬A, and therefore B's assertion must be true.

We have implemented this *hypothesize-and-match* strategy using again the model deductive procedure to carry out the essential work. The strategy assumes that the first assertion, A, is true. If the consequence is a contradiction, it then attempts to match ¬A to the content of the other assertions. If some other assertion, B, has a matching content, then B is true. This consequence can in turn be matched with the content of other assertions, and so on. It is possible to implement a mis-match strategy in which the falsity of B is derived from its inconsistency with some known truth, but we believe that this strategy is likely to be beyond the competence of most people.

The final strategy that we implemented also makes use of matching. It is likely to be developed from encounters with the following sort of premises:

A asserts that not C.
B asserts that not C.
C asserts that A and not B.

Reasoners may notice that since A and B make the same assertion, they are either both telling the truth or both lying. C, however, does not assign the same status to both of them. Hence, C is false. Both A's assertion and B's assertion match this conclusion, and so both are telling the truth. There are two tactics underlying this *same-assertion-and-match* strategy: first, the detection of two assertors that make the same assertion, which in turn is inconsistent with a third assertion; and, second, the use of a match between the resulting conclusion (¬C) and the content of specific assertions (A and B both assert not C). The strategy also detects where two individuals make opposing assertions about the same individual, and assigns falsity to any assertion that treats the two individuals as of the same status.

In summary, we have implemented Rips's full chain and four simpler strategies:

1. Simple chain: assume that the assertor in the first premise tells the truth, and follow up the consequences, but abandon the procedure if it becomes necessary to follow up disjunctive consequences. Assume that the assertor in the first premise is lying and do likewise.
2. Circular: if a premise is circular, follow up the immediate consequences of assuming that it is true, and then follow up the immediate consequences of assuming that it is false.
3. Hypothesize-and-match: if the assumption that the first assertor A is telling the truth leads to a contradiction, then attempt to match ¬A with the content of other assertions, and so on.
4. Same-assertion-and-match: if two assertions make the same claim, and a third assertor, C, assigns the two assertors to different types, or *vice versa*, then attempt to match ¬C with the content of other assertions, and so on.

Doubtless, reasoners develop still further strategies depending upon the particular problems that they encounter, but we have not yet attempted to model them.

THREE PREDICTIONS OF THE MODEL THEORY

The four simple strategies are all based on the assumption that ordinary individuals have a limited capacity for models of premises. Hence, they cannot cope with the consequences of a disjunctive set of models; they have only a limited ability to follow up the consequences of assumptions; and they find positive matches easier than negative mismatches. The model theory accordingly makes three main predictions about performance with meta-logical problems, granted some minimal competence with them.

The first prediction is that problems that can be solved by using one of the four simple strategies will be easier than those that require more powerful strategies such as the full chain proposed by Rips. In order to test this prediction, we re-analyzed the results of Rips's first experiment, which he kindly made available to us. There were 28% correct conclusions to the problems that can be solved by a simple strategy, but only 14% percent correct conclusions to the problems that cannot be solved in this way (Mann-Whitney $U = 7$, $p < 0.001$, one tail, by materials).

The second prediction is that the difficulty of a problem will depend on the number of clauses that it is necessary to use in order to solve the problem. This number obviously relates to the number of clauses in the statement of the problem, but the two notions are distinct as we can illustrate by considering two contrasting cases.

The first problem has the premises:

A asserts that not A and B.
B asserts that B.

The circular strategy applied to the first premise yields the conclusion that A is false and hence B is false. The program in effect merely traverses a circular loop from A back to A, and then the link from A to B. The consequences of B's assertion can be followed up, but they play no part in discovering the solution. The second problem has the premises:

A asserts that A and not B.
B asserts that A.

In this case the circular strategy fails to solve the problem, because it is necessary to consider both premises. The hypothesize-and-match strategy proceeds as follows: assume that A is true, and it follows that not B. From not B, it follows that not A, which contradicts the assumption. Given not A, B is not true because B asserts that A. Hence, the solution is: not A and not B. The program in effect traverses the link from A to B, and then the link from B back to A, in order to discover the contradiction; finally, it matches the negation of A with the link from B to A in order to draw a conclusion about B. This problem should therefore be harder than the first one.

This second prediction, as we have illustrated, can be couched in terms of the number of links that have to be traversed in order to solve a problem. Hence, the prediction is almost independent of the processing theory that we have proposed, and is likely to be made by any sensible analysis of meta-logical problems. Indeed, we suspect that the number of links to be traversed is one of the main contributors to the number of steps that Rips's program requires in order to solve a problem. The two problems above are in fact taken from his second experiment, and show how in this case our simpler account makes the same predictions as his theory. There is a corollary to our prediction. For many problems, the number of clauses (links) that have to be explored depends on the particular premise with which the process of reasoning begins. Hence, an experimental manipulation of this variable should affect performance.

The third prediction is a consequence of the model theory. Other things being equal, the hypothesis that an assertion is true should be easier to process than the hypothesis that an assertion is false. The operation of negating a set of models takes work. It calls, as we have seen, for the construction of the complement of a set of models. This prediction is corroborated by a result from Rips's second experiment, which by his own account presented some difficulty for his theory. The finding was that certain ways of couching a problem, such as:

A: I am a knave or B is a knight.
B: I am a knight.

are easier than others, such as:

A: I am a knave or B is a knave.
B: I am a knight.

A simple chain for the first problem hypothesizes that A is a knight, from which it follows that B is too, and B's assertion is consistent with this conclusion. The hypothesis that A is a knave immediately yields a contradiction since A's assertion would then be true. Therefore, A and B are both knights. The second problem, however, calls for a slightly more complex process. The hypothesis that A is a knight leads to the conclusion that B is a knave, and so it is now necessary to negate B's assertion to discover that it is consistent with this conclusion. Hence, the procedure carries out a negative operation that is not required for the first problem. This dichotomy runs through the complete set of Rips's problems and accounts for the difference in difficulty between them.

META-COGNITIVE DEDUCTION

Deductions about other people's deductions also depend on a higher-level component that can use the ordinary deductive machinery in various strategies. They, too, can be investigated experimentally by way of puzzles. Here, for example, is a species of meta-cognitive puzzle that we have devised:

There are two sorts of people: logicians, who always make valid deductions; and politicians, who never make valid deductions.
A says that either B is telling the truth or else B is a politician (but not both).
B says that A is not telling the truth (i.e. lying).
C deduces that B is a politician.
Is C a logician?

The puzzle can be solved in the following way. Suppose that A is telling the truth, then there are two alternatives: B is telling the truth, or else B is a politician. But, B asserts that A is lying, and so the first alternative leads to a contradiction. Hence, if A is telling the truth, it follows validly that B is a politician. Now, suppose that A is lying. It is then not the case that either B is telling the truth or is a politician, i.e. it follows that if and only if B is telling the truth then B is a politician. But, if B is lying then A is not lying—a consequence that contradicts the assumption. Hence, B is telling the truth, and so it follows that B is a politician. In conclusion, whether A tells the truth or lies, it follows that B is a politician. Because C deduces this valid conclusion, C must be a logician.

Problems that depend for their solution on deducing what one person can deduce about another person's deductions have been investigated in some unpublished studies carried out by George Erdos of the University of Newcastle. He gave his subjects meta-cognitive puzzles of the following well-known variety (see Fujimura, 1913/1978; Anno and Nozaki, 1984; Dewdney, 1989):

Three wise men who were perfect logicians were arrested by the Emperor on suspicion of subversion. He put them to the following test. The three men were lined up in a queue facing in the same direction, and a hat was placed on the head of each of them. The men could not see their own hats, but the man at the back of the queue (A) could see the two hats in front of him, the man in the middle (B) could see the one hat in front of him, and the man at the front (C) could see no hat. The Emperor said: "If one of you can tell me the colour of your own hat, I will set all three of you free. There are three white hats and two black ones from which your hats have been drawn. I will now ask each of you if he can tell me the colour of his hat. You may answer only 'yes', 'no', or 'I don't know'". A who could see the two hats in front of him said, "I don't know". B heard A's answer and said, "I don't know". C heard the two previous answers. What was C's answer?

The problem can be solved by considering the deductions made by the logicians. B deduces that if A had seen two black hats in front of him:

	A	B	C
		black	black

A could have said "yes" because A would have known that his own hat must be white. But since A said "I don't know", B concludes that A did not see two black hats, i.e. A must have seen one of the following disjunctive possibilities:

A	B	C
	white	white
	black	white
	white	black

C, in turn, deduces that if B had seen a black hat, then B would have said "yes" because, by the previous deduction, B would have known that his own hat must be white. Hence, B must have seen a white hat (and not known of course whether his own hat was black or white). Hence, C concludes that his own hat is white, and he answers "yes" to the Emperor.

This type of sequential argument generalizes to any number, n, of individuals provided that the Emperor makes his selection from n white hats and n - 1 black hats. Thus, where there are four men wearing hats, D, who sees no hats can argue as follows: "If I am wearing a black hat, then the other three will see it and know that at most there are only two remaining black hats for them. This case is therefore identical to the three-hat problem. If none of the three has said 'yes', then that implies that I have a white hat."

These meta-cognitive problems are not easy to solve. The size of their problem spaces is not large, but some problems with a small problem space can be very difficult (see e.g. Kotovsky and Simon, 1989). In our view, the source of difficulty is two-fold. First, meta-cognitive problems place a considerable load on working memory whenever a reasoner has to construct a model of one person's model of another person's model of the situation. This pre-requisite may call for a disjunctive set of models to be constructed and retained, e.g. C's deduction hinges on B's representation of the three possibilities that A could have seen. Erdos also reports that subjects often correctly deduce that A cannot see two black hats, but when they come to consider B's situation they forget that B can make this deduction too. Second, the particular strategy to be adopted is not one that ordinary individuals are likely to be equipped with prior to the experiment. Like a meta-logical deduction, they have to reflect upon the problem and to discover for themselves the information latent in each of the logicians' answers. This task can be made easier, as Erdos has shown, by first giving the subjects a simple two-hat problem. Finally, it is worth noting that his subjects did not find it helpful to be presented with a table of all the possible combinations of hats. In our view, this "hint" is analogous to presenting a truth table: it swamps subjects with information.

CONCLUSIONS

Psychology is a "recursive" discipline because a plausible theory of high-level cognition should reveal how the theory itself could have been created as a result of the theorist's high-level cognition. A theory of meta-deduction should therefore provide some insight into its own development. Our theory postulates a capacity to think about thinking—to reflect on patterns of deduction and the preservation of truth, to reflect on what one has deduced for oneself, and to reflect on the implications of what others can deduce. This general meta-cognitive capacity enables people to construct models of thought, and to construct models of those models, and so on, recursively (see Johnson-Laird, 1983, Chapter 16). In this way, simple reasoning strategies can be invented by logically untutored individuals. The same ability can be used by logicians to create formal calculi for deduction, and then to reflect upon the relations between these calculi and their semantics. And, most importantly, the ability can be used by cognitive scientists to construct theories about itself.

The Solutions to the Three Puzzles
at the Start of the Chapter

1. A says: I am the person who sometimes lies.
    B says: That is true.
    C says: I am not the person who sometimes lies.

A cannot be the truth-teller, and so A either sometimes lies or always lies. If the former, then B is the truth-teller, and so C must be the liar—but C cannot be the liar because C would then be telling the truth. Therefore, A always lies. In which case, B must be the person who sometimes lies, and so C is the truth-teller.

2. A says: no more than one of us is telling the truth.
    B says: I am Napoleon.
    C says: I am Napoleon.

Suppose A's assertion is true, then A must be Napoleon because B and C must be lying. Suppose A's assertion is false, then more than one person is telling the truth, but that is impossible because B and C can't both be telling the truth. Hence, this possibility is eliminated: A *is* telling the truth, and so A is Napoleon.

3. It is raining tonk the match is cancelled.
    The match is not cancelled.
    Therefore, it is not raining.

Given a truth-table of the contingencies, the second premise rules out the first and third contingencies, and the conclusion calls for the first and second contingencies to be ruled out, and, since the third is ruled out, it calls for the fourth contingency to be true:

Raining	Match cancelled	Second premise	Conclusion
T	T	F	F
T	F		F
F	T	F	
F	F		T

Hence, the premise with "tonk" must rule out the second contingency and allow that the fourth is true. If it ruled out both the first and second contingencies, the inference could be made from the tonk premise alone. Hence, its entry must be either: T F F T (material equivalence), or T F T T (material implication).

CHAPTER 9

Deduction, Non-monotonic Reasoning, and Parsimonious Conclusions: How to Write a Reasoning Program

In this chapter, we describe how to build a deductive program that reasons on the basis of models. Our aim is to help others to develop such programs, and to present solutions to two long-standing problems in Artificial Intelligence (AI). The first problem is to find a way to combine valid deduction with non-monotonic reasoning, and the second problem is to devise a procedure for drawing parsimonious conclusions.

We begin with non-monotonic reasoning, which occurs whenever additional information leads to the withdrawal of an earlier conclusion (see Chapter 2). We outline a program that combines a novel method of non-monotonic reasoning with valid deduction. This combination is not a luxury for model-based reasoning. It is essential for coping with the fact that the construction of a model from a premise may call for certain arbitrary assumptions to be made. Finally, we consider the formulation of parsimonious conclusions. Infinitely many valid conclusions follow from any set of premises, and so the designer of a program that draws its own conclusions is forced to ask: which particular conclusion should the program draw? In practice, programmers in both AI and psychology usually avoid this question by the simple expedient of devising programs that evaluate only given conclusions (see e.g., Newell, Shaw, and Simon, 1963; Reiter, 1973; Bledsoe, 1977; Robinson, 1979; Moore, 1982; Rips, 1983; Wos, 1988). Human reasoners, according to our theory of competence, spontaneously aim for a conclusion that re-expresses the semantic information in the premises more parsimoniously (see Chapter 2). But the problem of parsimony is too important to be left to psychologists. It crops up in an entirely different context—the design of electronic circuits, such as those for computers, made up from so-called "Boolean units" that carry out elementary logical operations. The search for the simplest circuit equivalent to a given circuit is exactly the same task as the search for a maximally parsimonious re-description of a set of premises in the propositional calculus.

NON-MONOTONIC REASONING: FORMAL THEORIES

The maintenance of a consistent data-base in a large-scale computer program is analogous to the maintenance of a coherent set of beliefs. When formal rules for the predicate calculus are used to check consistency, two main difficulties arise. The first difficulty is that the predicate calculus is only *semi-decidable*, that is, if a deduction is valid then in principle a derivation for it can always be found, but if it is invalid, then it may lead the program into an endless loop and so the fact that it is invalid may never be forthcoming. One pays this price for adopting a calculus that is powerful enough to apply to infinite sets, but there is no need to pay it for everyday matters. Reasoning can be based directly on finite sets of models for which there is a full decision procedure. The second difficulty for formal rules is non-monotonic reasoning. From the premises:

Dogs have four legs.
Fido is a dog.

it follows validly:

Fido has four legs.

But, suppose that you learn that Fido was born with only three legs. Naturally, you will withdraw the conclusion. Yet, in logic, it remains valid because no subsequent information can subtract from the set of conclusions that follow validly from premises. Logic is monotonic (see Chapter 2). Hence, *prima facie* everyday inference cannot be based on the predicate calculus.

An alternative course of action suggested by the case of Fido is to argue that the premise, "Dogs have four legs", is false. It should be replaced by one that makes all relevant information explicit:

If a dog is born intact, has not been in any accidents, and has not had a leg amputated, and so on ..., then it has four legs.

But it is difficult to implement this idea because there can never be any guarantee that all the relevant conditions have been captured. In daily life, people often have to reason from incomplete information. Perhaps, the premise could be framed along the following lines:

If x is a dog and x is not abnormal then x has four legs.

This principle of "circumscription" underlies McCarthy's (1980, 1986) attempt to extend the predicate calculus so that it is non-monotonic, but the approach turns out to require a higher-order predicate calculus, which is not even semi-decidable (see Chapter 1).

A coherent data-base can be organized by representing explicitly the dependence between different assertions in a "truth-maintenance" system (Doyle, 1979). The system stores information to the effect that one assertion depends on another as its justification or reason. Hence, when all the reasons for an assertion are expunged as a result of subsequent information, the assertion itself is withdrawn. People could modify their beliefs in the same way, but it is a costly procedure, and perhaps they merely maintain a moderately coherent set of beliefs. A theory of this process has been proposed by Harman (1986), who distinguishes between deduction and a reasoned change in view. He suggests that people have basic dispositions to recognize that some propositions immediately imply others, and to recognize that some propositions are immediately inconsistent with others. A theory of the coherence amongst facts and hypotheses has been developed by Thagard (1988), who has devised a program that can decide between competing theories on the basis of their coherence with the data. What establishes that one proposition coheres with another, however, is a primitive unanalyzed notion in the theory.

Formal rules might solve the problem of maintaining consistency if they were made *non-monotonic* (see e.g. Doyle, 1982). A non-monotonic "logic" allows for the withdrawal of a conclusion in the light of subsequent information. It typically relies on default values (Minsky, 1975). The concept of dog, for example, includes a variable which denotes number-of-legs, and, if there is no information to the contrary, then by default this variable is set equal to four. The mechanism is analogous to Wittgenstein's (1953) notion of a criterion. He argued that many concepts have no essential conditions. Instead they depend on criteria. The criteria for doghood include having four legs, hair, a head and a tail, the ability to bark, and so on. Criteria are not necessary conditions for doghood—a particular dog might be three-legged, bald, mute, and tail-less. Criteria are not inductions based on observation—how could one count the number of legs on dogs until one had some way of identifying dogs? Criteria are fixed by the conventions governing the use of a concept.

Several sorts of non-monotonic logic have been based on extensions of formal logic. Reiter (1980) introduced default rules of inference of the form:

If A, and it is consistent to infer B, then infer B.

Hence, given the proposition, Fido is a dog, one can infer that Fido has four legs provided that this proposition cannot be disproved. McDermott and Doyle (1980) stated defaults, not as rules of inference, but as postulates of the form:

If A and B-is-not-disprovable then B.

where the operator "Is-not-disprovable" is akin to the operator "possibly" in a modal logic. Moore (1985) introduced an "autoepistemic" logic that models the reasoning of ideally rational agents about their own beliefs:

If A and not (agent-believes not B) then B.

where the operator "agent-believes" reflects the beliefs of the relevant individual (see also Niemalä, 1988).

In our view, it is a mistake to try to accommodate default reasoning within a system based on formal rules—if only because such systems tend not to be even semi-decidable in the sense we described above (Reiter, 1980). A more natural approach emerges from the way that the model theory deals with the indeterminacy of discourse (Johnson-Laird, 1983). No matter how carefully someone describes a situation, their remarks will be consistent with many alternative states of affairs. If they say, for instance:

The boy stood on the burning deck.

then there are infinitely many configurations of boy and deck that would satisfy the assertion. Model-theoretic semantics accommodates them all, but this infinitude is far too big to fit inside anyone's head (Partee, 1979). We have assumed instead that people normally need to construct just a single model of such an assertion. One model has the advantage that it fits inside the head without pre-occupying working memory to the exclusion of all else. It has the disadvantage that it may not correspond to the situation that is described. So, how can people work with just one model? A parallel question in the philosophy of mathematics is: how can an individual proving a geometric theorem work with just one diagram (see Beth, 1971, Ch. IV)? The answer to both questions is that it is always possible to *change* the model. Before we can demonstrate how models are changed, however, we need to show how they are constructed in the first place. The process is complicated, and so we devote the next section to it, and afterwards return to non-monotonic reasoning.

THE CONSTRUCTION OF MODELS OF PREMISES

Parsing and Compositional Semantics

The first task in constructing a model from a verbal premise is to parse the premise. This operation calls for a grammar that enables the meaning of the premise to be built up compositionally, i.e. from the meanings of its constituents and the syntactic relations amongst them. A compositional semantics can be set up by pairing each grammatical rule with a semantic procedure so that whenever the parser uses a rule in analyzing a sentence it also carries out the semantic procedure. The words in the lexicon likewise have syntactic categories and semantic procedures.

Suppose that the program, like the one mentioned in Chapter 5, is to build a model from the following spatial description:

The circle is on the right of the triangle.
The cross is in front of the line.
The line is on the left of the triangle.

The grammar needs a rule which, omitting details, specifies that a sentence can consist of a noun phrase followed by a predicate:

Sentence → NP Predicate

The grammar also needs the rule:

Predicate → V-copular Relation NP

which specifies that a predicate can consist of a copular verb followed by a relation followed by a noun phrase, e.g. "is in front of the triangle".

These sorts of rules make up a context-free grammar, i.e. only one symbol occurs on the left-hand side of each rule, and so regardless of this symbol's context it can have the constituents on the right-hand side of the rule. Although such a grammar may lack the power to cope with any sentence in a natural language, it can certainly cope with a considerable fragment of English (Gazdar, Klein, Pullum, and Sag, 1985). It can also be parsed using a variety of algorithms, and, as Chomsky (1959) showed, the only memory needed for the results of interim computations is a stack to which access is made according to the principle: first-in, last out, i.e. solely to the topmost symbol on the stack. One simple type of parser carries out only two basic operations: it can *shift* a word from the sentence onto the stack, and it can *reduce* one or more symbols on the stack to a single symbol using a rule in the grammar or an entry in the lexicon. The rule above, for example, can be used to reduce the following symbols on the stack:

NP
Relation
V-copular

to one symbol:

Predicate.

Many sentences are locally ambiguous in that more than one rule is applicable at certain points in parsing them. One solution to this problem is to try one rule at a time, recording the history of the parse on a separate stack, and backtracking whenever the parse runs into a dead end, i.e. the parser goes back to the most recent unexplored alternative rule and tries it. These and other more efficient techniques are common-place in computer science (see Johnson-Laird, 1983, Ch. 13, for descriptions of them).

The general principle that we adopt is to build up a semantic representation on the parse stack. When it is evaluated in the context of existing models, it carries out the appropriate model-building operation. Hence, each item on the stack has two parts, its grammatical category and its semantic representation, e.g.:

NP   (Δ)
Relation   (1 0 0)
V-copular   (dummy)

The item on top of the stack derives from the noun phrase, "the triangle", and denotes a triangle, because the program treats definite descriptions as referring expressions. The next item derives from the relation, "on the right of", and its meaning consists in a set of parameters (1 0 0) that concern the co-ordinates of three-dimensional space: the value of the left-right dimension should be incremented (i.e. 1 is added to it), and the values of the other two dimensions, front-back and up-down, are held constant (i.e. 0 is added to them). The third item derives from the copular verb, "is", which has no meaning as far as the program is concerned, and so its semantic procedure, dummy, does no work. The semantic representations are constructed by the semantic procedures that are paired with grammatical rules and lexical entries. For example, the semantic procedure paired with the grammatical rule for forming predicates can be carried out on the contents of the stack above. The effect of the grammatical rule is to replace the three grammatical categories on the stack with one grammatical category, and the effect of the semantic procedure is to replace the three semantic representations with one:

Predicate ((1 0 0)(Δ))

which captures the meaning of "on the right of the triangle". The final result of parsing a premise, such as:

The circle is on the right of the triangle.

is the following pair on top of the stack:

Sentence ((1 0 0) (Δ) (O))

where the semantic representation captures the meaning, or "intension", of the premise.

Procedures For Constructing Models

We have so far treated the meaning of a premise as depending only on grammar and the meanings of words. Its *significance*—the particular proposition that it expresses—depends on a number of additional factors, and particularly on its context of use. Context in everyday discourse is a matter of general knowledge and knowledge of the circumstances of the utterance—the situation to which it refers, what has been said earlier, the participants in the discourse, and so on. For our purposes, however, context is the information that is already represented in the model of the discourse. It is this information that determines how to use the representation of meaning in constructing a model. If a sentence does not refer to any items in any existing models, e.g. it is the first premise of an argument, then the program uses the meaning of the sentence to build a new model. Given the premise:

The circle is on the right of the triangle.

the program uses the representation of its meaning:

((1 0 0) (Δ) (o))

to construct the smallest possible three-dimensional model:

Δ   o

This model represents the reference (or "extension") of the premise—the particular situation in which it is true, here as if viewed from above. If the premise refers to an item in an existing model, the program adds the new item to the model, using the representation of meaning to ensure that it is put into an appropriate position. If the premise refers to two items in separate models, then the program uses the representation of meaning to combine the two models appropriately.

Here is an example that illustrates the combination of two separate models. The first premise is:

The circle is on the right of the triangle.

and the procedure for starting models constructs the following minimal array:

Δ   o

The second premise is:

The cross is in front of the line.

and, because it does not refer to anything in the existing model, the program builds a separate model anew:

|
+

The third premise is:

The line is on the left of the circle.

and the representation of its meaning is used to combine the two existing models into one:

```
|  Δ  o
+  .  .
```

This example illustrates a critical feature of model-based reasoning programs. The three premises are indeterminate in the following sense: they do not establish a spatial relation between the line and the triangle. The only constraint is that both are on the left of the circle. The program merely selects whichever relation is more convenient. In effect, it makes an arbitrary assumption about the particular relation between the two items. Such assumptions keep the number of models to a minimum. If the program attempted to construct all possible models, it would soon exhaust its memory because the possibilities increase exponentially. An analogous case concerns "default" assumptions. The meaning of the word "triangle", for example, can specify an isosceles triangle by default, and this interpretation will be taken for granted initially. It can be revised later if necessary.

Models For Propositional Connectives

The same principles apply to the construction of models from sentences containing propositional connectives (see Chapter 3). Each connective is specified in the lexicon along with its grammatical category and meaning. In an AI program that we have implemented, the meaning of "and", for instance, is a procedure called "cart" that takes two sets of models and constructs their Cartesian product, eliminating redundant or inconsistent combinations. A pair of models, such as:

```
 a   ¬b
¬a    b
```

corresponds to a proposition of the form:

a or else b, but not both

where a and b might be, say, descriptions of spatial relations. Given this set and another, say, for "if b then c":

```
   a   ¬b        b    c
  ¬a    b       ¬b    c
               ¬b   ¬c
```

cart combines each model in the first set with each model in the second set, dropping those combinations that would contain both a proposition and its negation. It also ensures that there is only one instance of each proposition in each model:

```
   a   ¬b    c
   a   ¬b   ¬c
  ¬a    b    c
```

The meaning of "not" is a procedure called "negate", which returns the complement of a set of models. For example, the negation of the model:

```
   a   ¬b
```

is the set of models:

```
   a    b
  ¬a    b
  ¬a   ¬b
```

The meanings of the other propositional connectives are defined in terms of cart and negate. For instance, the definition of the semantics of a conditional is:

```
(defun sem-ifi (models1 models2)
  (append (cart models1 models2 )
          (cart (negate models1) models2)
          (cart (negate models1) (negate models2))))
```

The two sets of models to which sem-ifi is applied can themselves be of any degree of complexity.

Whenever the parser uses a rule of the grammar, it evaluates the semantic procedure paired with the rule. Hence, for example, when it parses the italicized constituent:

ifi *a*

it builds a model of the clause:

a

When it parses the next clause:

then *b*

it builds another model:

b

When it finally uses the rule that identifies all these constituents as themselves making up a sentence:

Sentence → *ifi* Sentence *then* Sentence

it evaluates an associated semantic procedure, which in turn applies the procedure corresponding to the meaning of the connective (sem-ifi) to the interpretations of the two clauses (the two sets of models) and returns the result:

$$
\begin{array}{ll}
a & b \\
\neg a & b \\
\neg a & \neg b
\end{array}
$$

Because the grammatical rules and their associated semantic procedures are recursive, the premises can be of an arbitrary degree of complexity.

The Construction of Quantified Models

The treatment of models for premises containing quantifiers is again along the same general lines. For illustrative convenience, consider a sentence about three separate finite sets of integers, x, y, and z, such as:

All x's are equal to the sum of some y and some z.

The sentence can be parsed compositionally to yield a representation of its meaning:

(All x)(Some y)(Some z)(x = y + z)

This representation is akin to many linguistic analyses of quantified sentences in that it makes explicit the scopes of the quantifiers (see Chapter 2). Its use, however, is quite different. The meaning of a quantifier is, in essence, the raw material for a recursive loop that is used in building or manipulating a model. Thus, the universal quantifier "all" elicits a recursion that deals with a set exhaustively, whereas the existential quantifier "some" elicits a recursion that does not. We will now consider how an initial model of the premise is constructed. Those who do not relish such details may skip to the section on verification.

The essential work is done by a recursive procedure that works its way through the representation:

(All x)(Some y)(Some z)(x = y + z)

to construct an end result such as:

x = ([8] [6]), y = (1 6 4 2), z = (7 7 3 2 4 4)

In which all x's are equal to some y plus some z, e.g. 8 = 1 + 7. The square brackets, as usual, indicate that the x's are exhaustively represented. The sizes of the sets are arbitrary, but for simplicity we assume small sizes.

The recursive procedure starts with the following sets that show merely the numbers of initial items to be constructed:

(/[x][x]) (/ y y) (/ z z)

The procedure needs to keep track of where it is in each set, and so "/" is a marker that indicates the current position, i.e. at the first item in each of the sets. The procedure then goes to the first quantifier in the list, (All x), and uses the *basic equation* stated in the premise to set up:

$ = y + z

where $ is the unknown corresponding to x, and y and z are the next items to be examined in the sets, i.e. the items after the markers. Sometimes, as we will see, existing values place constraints on the solution of the equation. Here, there are no such constraints, and so an arbitrary value is chosen for $, say, 8. The procedure recurses to the next quantifier (Some y) and sets up the equation:

8 = $ + z

which again does not constrain the value of $, and so an arbitrary value is chosen, say, 1. The procedure recurses to the final quantifier in the list (Some z) and sets up the equation:

$$8 = 1 + \$$$

which yields the value, 7. The current sets are accordingly:

(/ [8] [x]) (/ 1 y) (/ 7 z)

Because there are no further quantifiers in the list, the procedure updates the marker for z:

(/ [8] [x]) (/ 1 y) (7 / z)

which yields a new equation:

$$8 = 1 + \$$$

The current set of z's is then completed:

(/ [8] [x]) (/ 1 y) (7 7 /)

and the recursion for (some z) bottoms out. Control returns to the previous quantifier, but since the quantifier for z is an existential the possibility of generating new items has to be represented:

(/ [8] [x]) (1 / y) (7 7 / z z)

The next equation is:

$$8 = \$ + z$$

which returns, say, 6.

The recursive calls continue in this way until the values of z have been obtained for the new value of y:

(/ [8] [x]) (1 6 /) (7 7 2 2 /)

At this point, the recursion for (some y) bottoms out and control passes back to (all x):

([8] / [x]) (1 6 / y y) (7 7 2 2 / z z)

A new value for x is chosen, say, 6. The procedure does not automatically generate new items but checks first whether or not the sets already contain appropriate values. Hence, after it has added the value 4 to y, it does not need to add any new values to z in order to satisfy the equation:

6 = 4 + $

It generates another new value of y, say 2, and finishes off the process by generating the required values for z. Hence, the final values of the sets are:

[8 6] (1 6 4 2) (7 7 2 2 4 4)

The procedure is analogous to the standard interpretation of quantifiers in the predicate calculus (see Chapter 1) except that it *constructs* a model of the assertion. The universal quantifier, "all", leads to an exhaustive representation of a set, and once the set is complete no further items can be added to it; the existential quantifier, "some", does not lead to an exhaustive representation and so new items can be added at any point in the procedure. The order of the quantifiers in the semantic representation corresponds to their respective scopes: the first quantifier has the largest scope, the second has the next largest scope, and so on (see Chapter 1).

Verification

There remains one final, and important, possibility that can occur in the interpretation of a premise: all its referring expressions may already be represented in the set of models. For a spatial proposition, they may all be in one and the same model. For a premise containing propositional connectives or quantified expressions, the relevant entities may all be in the existing set of models. In these cases, the program uses the representation of meaning in order to *verify* the premise in the models. The premise may establish a new property or relation that has to be added to the model. Otherwise, it may have a truth value in the model, and in this case the program then tests whether the premise follows validly, or as a non-monotonic inference, from the previous premises.

THE COMBINATION OF VALID AND NON-MONOTONIC REASONING

The program reasons by searching for alternative models of the premises, and the key principle in these searches is that it is at liberty to undo both arbitrary and default assumptions. It treats each premise as a potential conclusion: if it is true in the current models, then a search is made for an alternative model that renders it false. This search tests validity, because if no model of the previous premises falsifies the current premise, then it follows validly from them. But, it may have been true merely by chance or by default—in which case, there is a model that falsifies it, and so the premise makes definite what was hitherto only a possibility. If the premise is false in the current models, then a search is made for an alternative model of the previous premises that renders it true. This search makes non-monotonic reasoning possible, because if there is such a model of the previous premises, then the premise was false merely by chance or by default, and so a new model accommodates it by changing the arbitrary or default assumption. However, it may have been false because the premises are genuinely inconsistent—in which case, there is no model that renders it true. The program operates according to the principle: *one situation, one model*. It can do so because the model can be changed, if necessary, to accept any new information that is consistent with the previous premises. The model serves as a representative sample from the set of possible models. Non-monotonic reasoning is essential for the program's operation; it is a process that is complementary to valid deduction.

That is the theory of reasoning at the "computational level". How is it implemented in an algorithm? In principle, as we mentioned in Chapter 7, the search for alternative models could be entirely random. We do not believe that human reasoners search in this way, and certainly it would be very wasteful in an AI program. A better strategy is based on negating putative conclusions. We will use spatial examples to explain how the procedure works, but the reader should bear in mind that the principle is general and, in its present form, far exceeds the capacity of human working memory.

Consider the following spatial description (problem II in Chapter 5):

The circle is on the right of the star.
The triangle is on the left of the circle.
The cross is in front of the triangle.
The line is in front of the circle.

which yields the following initial model:

Δ   *   o
+   . |

If the further assertion is made:

The cross is on the left of the line.

then both referents are already in the model, and the verifying procedure establishes that the premise is true in the model. This result triggers the test of validity. It attempts to construct an alternative model of the previous premises in which the *negation* of the current premise is true. Since the premise asserts that the cross is on the left of the line, its negation calls for the cross either to be in the same left-to-right orientation as the line or else to be on the right of the line. The test of validity works by constructing a model in which the negation is true, and assessing whether any of the previous premises are false in this new model. If not, then it has falsified the old model because all of the premises are true in the new model. If any previous premises are false in a new model, they are added to the list of assertions that need to be rendered true. The procedure changes the model to render the first such premise true without undoing the earlier change(s), assesses whether any other premises are false in this new model, and continuoo in this recursive way either until it finds a model that satisfies all the previous premisoo (and the negation of the current premise) or until it has exhausted all possible modifications. In the first case, the truth of the current premise was merely contingent on the way in which the initial model was constructed; in the second case, it is a valid deduction because there is no way of accommodating its negation in any model of the premises.

To revert to our example, the procedure's first task is to render true:

The cross is not on the left of the line.

and so it constructs the alternatives:

```
Δ  *  O
|  .  +
```

The model is inconsistent with the premise that the cross is in front of the triangle and the premise that the line is in front of the circle. Hence, the procedure satisfies the first of these premises:

```
.   * (Δ O)
|   .   +
```

where two items within the same parentheses are in the same left-to-right orientation, e.g. one might be above the other. The procedure then satisfies the second of these premises:

```
O  *  Δ
I  .  +
```

But this model is inconsistent with the premise that the circle is on the right of the star and the premise that the triangle is on the left of the circle. The first of these premises can be accommodated:

```
*  O  Δ
.  I  +
```

but the possibilities for accommodating the second premise have been exhausted. Hence, the procedure has failed to render the negated premise true. There is nowhere left to go, and so there is no counterexample to the current premise:

The cross is on the left of the line.

It follows validly from the previous premises.

The procedure for non-monotonic reasoning is similar. It starts with a premise that is false in the current model, and it changes the model to render the premise true. It then assesses whether there are any previous premises that are false in the modified model. If not, then the new model is the one that is required. But if some previous premise is false in the new model, then the procedure attempts to accommodate it recursively.

THE FORMULATION OF PARSIMONIOUS CONCLUSIONS

Human beings draw parsimonious conclusions for themselves; automated reasoning programs do not. The task is not trivial, and it is important because it is equivalent to the simplification of a Boolean circuit. The equivalence follows directly from the fact that the units in such circuits work like switches, e.g. an "and" unit only transmits a signal if both its inputs receive a signal, a "not" unit only transmits a signal if its input does not receive a signal, and so on. These elements are used to build computers, and various algorithms exist for simplifying their circuits (e.g., Karnaugh, 1953; Quine, 1955; McCluskey, 1956; Arevalo and Bredeson, 1978). The need to design Very Large Scale Integrated (VLSI) circuits has revived interest in the problem (see Dunne, 1988), but no general solution guaranteed to deliver a maximally parsimonious description of Boolean expressions has so far been proposed. Any solution is bound to be computationally expensive:

technically, the problem could be solved in polynomial time by an algorithm that makes correct choices in some non-deterministic way, i.e. the problem is NP-complete (Gimpel, 1965). Because an actual program cannot perform in this magical manner, it has to explore all the choices, and so the time it takes grows exponentially as a function of the number of elements in the circuit, or, equivalently, the number of connectives in the proposition.

The algorithm that we have developed, which is described in Johnson-Laird (1989), produces a maximally parsimonious conclusion that makes explicit all the information in the premises. It therefore delivers a circuit that is as simple as possible yet equivalent to the input circuit. By a *maximally parsimonious* description, we mean one that accurately describes a set of explicit propositional models, and that uses the smallest possible number of atomic propositions. For example, the assertion:

if, if c then a then b

is more parsimonious than the equivalent assertion:

if a then b and, b or c

They both describe the same set of models:

$$
\begin{array}{ccc}
a & b & c \\
a & b & \neg c \\
\neg a & b & c \\
\neg a & b & \neg c \\
\neg a & \neg b & c
\end{array}
$$

but the first assertion refers just once to each type of atom in the models. Other definitions of parsimony are possible. It can be defined in terms of the number of *connectives* that occur in a proposition, but this measure correlates with the present one. However the notion is defined, a maximally parsimonious description depends in part on the connectives that are available in the language (or the sort of units available for use in circuits). A plausible constraint is therefore to work within the confines of a standard formalization of the propositional calculus in which negation takes one argument, the connectives take two arguments, and they include conjunction ("and"), exclusive disjunction ("ore"), inclusive disjunction ("ori"), material implication ("ifi"), and material equivalence ("iff"). Any differences in parsimony then reflect matters of principle rather than superficial linguistics.

The algorithm, which has been implemented in a computer program called PropAi (for Propositional inference in Artificial Intelligence), has two main components: one parses input premises and constructs a set of explicit models of them, and the other parsimoniously describes any such set of models, or any set that is directly input to the program by the user. Such models, as the set above shows, are isomorphic to a single premise in "disjunctive normal form". The complexity of describing models, as opposed to building them, is shown by the fact that two thirds of the program is devoted to the task.

The program's output is a maximally parsimonious conclusion that is equivalent to the set of premises. Table 9.1 presents three typical examples of the program's performance based on examples chosen at random from text-books on logic. Each example shows the input to the program and its output, which in these cases includes both an evaluation of one of the premises and a maximally parsimonious conclusion that is semantically equivalent to all of them. The table also explains the use of commas in descriptions. Because the program evaluates each premise as a potential conclusion, it can also be used as a theorem-prover, and it readily solves all the propositional problems in Pelletier's (1986) sample.

The Use of Score-Tables

Given a set of models that each contain only two atoms, there is a simple procedure for describing the set. If the set contains four distinct models, it is equal to all possible models that can be constructed from the pair of atoms:

$$a \qquad b$$
$$a \qquad \neg b$$
$$\neg a \qquad b$$
$$\neg a \qquad \neg b$$

and its description is a tautology: a ori not a and, b ori not b. If the set has fewer models, the procedure tries the first connective in its lexicon, builds a set of models using it, and compares this model with the original set. It synthesizes a model from the next connective, and so on, until it discovers the correct one. It is also constrained to avoid the use of negation as far as possible.

The chief difficulty in finding parsimonious descriptions arises because each model can contain many atoms. In such cases, the set of models needs to be broken recursively into ever smaller pieces until each piece can be described using the procedure above. But, the method of

Table 9.1

Some typical examples of the outputs from the PropAi program. Commas
are used instead of parentheses: a comma calls for the connective following
it to be interpreted prior to the interpretation of the preceding connective,
e.g. w ori, ifi p then q is equivalent to: (w ori (ifi p then q)).

---

1.   *Input*

      w ori, ifi p then q
      ifi q then, c ori s
      ifi s then u
      not c and not u
      not w.

    Output

This premise follows from those that preceded it: not w.
The premises are equivalent to:
      not w and, not p and, not q and, not c and, not s and not u.

2.   *Input*

      ifi a then b and, ifi c then d
      ifi b then e and, ifi d then f
      not, e and f
      ifi a then c
      not a.

    Output

This premise follows from those that preceded it: not a.
The premises are equivalent to:
      not a and, , ifi b then e and, , ifi e then not f and, , not d ori f and, ifi c then d.

3.   *Input*

      ifi v then, s and, p and m
      ifi r then ifi g then ifi not l then not m
      ifi s then r
      ifi p then ifi c then g
      ifi l then not c
      c
      not v

    Output

This premise follows from those that preceded it: not v.
The premises are equivalent to:
      not v and, not l and, c and, , ifi p then g and, , ifi not r then not s and, ifi, m and g
      then not a.

---

decomposing models must be guaranteed to yield a maximally
parsimonious description. The way in which the program works is to use
what we refer to as "score-tables". A score-table re-organizes the
information in a set of models to make explicit which combinations of
atoms occur with a particular atom, or set of atoms, of interest. Certain

sorts of score-table provide an immediate way of dividing the set of models up into partitions that are easy to describe.

For example, the set of models:

a	b	¬c
a	¬b	c
¬a	b	c
¬a	¬b	¬c

yields, among others, the following score-table that makes explicit which combinations occur with a and ¬a:

Scores	Scored combinations	
(a)	b	¬c
(a)	¬b	c
(¬a)	b	c
(¬a)	¬b	¬c

Because all possible combinations of the scored atoms b and c occur, these combinations can be divided into two sets, Y and ¬Y, associated respectively with the two scores a and ¬a:

1.　　a　　Y
　　　¬a　　¬Y

where Y is equal to the scored combinations:

2.　　b　　¬c
　　　¬b　　c

and ¬Y is the complement of this set. The set of models has now been broken into the two partitions, 1 and 2, which can both be described by the simple procedure outlined earlier:

1.　　iff a then Y

and:

2.　　b ore c

The second description is then substituted for the "Y" in the first description to yield:

iff a then, b ore c

This description is maximally parsimonious because each atom in the original models is referred to only once.

Not all sets of models can be described by referring to each atom no more than once. A maximally parsimonious description of the following models:

```
 a      b     c
¬a      b    ¬c
¬a     ¬b    ¬c
```

must contain more than one instance of the same atomic proposition, e.g.:

iff a then c and, ifi a then b.

What can be proved, however, is that any set of models whatsoever always has a score-table of at least one of six types, and that these six types can be used to construct the most parsimonious descriptions that are possible (see Johnson-Laird, 1989).

The program scores models in order to describe them, and it begins to construct the set of all possible score-tables, starting with single atoms as scores, then pairs of atoms, and so on. The most parsimonious description of a set of models may have to be derived, not from a score based on only a single atom, but from one based on several. Such a score-table will yield a maximally parsimonious description only if it is one of the six types. A set of models may, for example, fail to yield one of the six types until it is scored for several atoms. Hence, the scoring procedure stops only if it discovers an optimal score-table, e.g. a binary score for all the possible scored combinations (as in the penultimate example). Otherwise, it continues until it has constructed all the score-tables, and it then uses whichever table is guaranteed to yield the most parsimonious description.

The program performs at a superior level to previous procedures for minimizing Boolean expressions. This set of models, for example:

```
 a      b     c     d
 a      b     c    ¬d
¬a      b     c     d
 a      b    ¬c    ¬d
¬a      b     c    ¬d
¬a     ¬b     c     d
¬a     ¬b    ¬c     d
```

yields the following description using the Quine-McCluskey method:

b and c ori,, a and, b and not d ori, not a and, not b and d.

Our program yields a maximally parsimonious description, which contains one less atomic proposition, and several fewer connectives:

ifi, b and, ifi a then d then c and, ifi, ifi d then a then b.

The program is a generalization of the model theory of propositional deductions. In principle, it will find a member of the set of maximally parsimonious descriptions for any set of models, whether they are input directly or else from a set of Boolean premises. It therefore solves the problem of finding a member of the simplest possible switching circuits equivalent to a given circuit. But, as we have mentioned, the task is computationally intractable: as the number of atoms increases so it takes increasingly longer to evaluate all the possible score-tables.

What about conclusions from quantified premises? It should be straightforward to develop a procedure for formulating conclusions that takes as its input one or more models, and that looks for the appropriate quantifiers to characterize the relation between a pair of terms that are not explicitly related in any premise. Given a relevant pair of terms, A and C, and a model, the procedure will establish whether the relation between them is affirmative or negative. It will then work down through the hierarchy of possible interrelations in terms of their semantic strength. With two quantifiers, for example, the strongest possible affirmative relation is:

1. $(\forall A)(\forall B)$ ARB: All A are in relation, R, to all B.

Two slightly weaker ones are:

2. $(\exists A)(\forall B)$ ARB: Some A are in relation, R, to all B.
3. $(\exists B)(\forall A)$ BRA: Some B are in relation, R, to all A.

Still weaker, respectively, are the following:

4. $(\forall B)(\exists A)$ BRA: All B are in relation, R, to some A.
5. $(\forall A)(\exists B)$ ARB: All A are in relation, R, to some B.

And, finally, the weakest possible relation is:

6. $(\exists A)(\exists B)$ ARB: Some A are in relation, R, to some B.

There is a similar hierarchy for negative interrelationships. It would be useful to generalize this procedure so that the description describes all the items in a set of models. We have not yet solved this problem.

CONCLUSIONS

A program for reasoning on the basis of models calls for three principal components. First, it must be able to interpret premises expressed in a subset of natural language and to construct an appropriate set of models for them. Reasoning can be based on other sorts of information, such as vision, but we have considered only verbal reasoning here. Second, the program must be able to use these models to formulate a conclusion—a parsimonious conclusion that makes explicit information that was not expressed in the premises. Third, the program must be able to search for alternative models of the premises.

We have shown how all three components work. The first stage in constructing a model of a premise consists in a compositional interpretation of its meaning (i.e. intension). This calls for a grammar and a lexicon, which both contain grammatical and semantic information. Their provision is straightforward in the cases that we have considered, but what about the use of abstract terminology, e.g. inferences about possession? If the task of specifying a full semantics is too difficult, then it can be finessed: it is necessary only to deal with that part of the meaning of a word that yields valid deductions. This information can, if necessary, be treated, not as part of a lexical entry, but as an additional premise (a meaning postulate), which will be realized in all relevant models. The guiding principle is that models need to represent only those aspects of the situation that pertain to inference.

The meaning of a premise is used to determine which of the following procedures should be used:

Starting a model *ab initio*.
Adding information to a model.
Combining models in terms of a common referent.
Verifying the premise.

The meaning is also used in carrying out the selected procedure, and the resulting model represents the situation referred to by the premise (its extension).

The formulation of parsimonious conclusions is an intricate and intractable process, but its general nature is clear—at least for propositional connectives. The set of models has to be recursively divided into partitions that each contain no more than two items to be described.

The descriptions of these partitions can than be assembled in a way that is guaranteed to yield a parsimonious description.

When a program searches for an alternative model, it is at liberty to undo two sorts of information: arbitrary decisions and default values, and to insert instead some other, perhaps specified, value. This possibility confers on a model-based reasoning system the power both to make valid deductions from a finite set of models and to make non-monotonic inferences. As in a geometric proof, the program maintains a model until, and unless, it conflicts with an assertion. At this point, the model is revised so as to satisfy all the assertions in the discourse. If the attempt fails for good reason, then the current assertion genuinely conflicts with the earlier information built into the model. This process is complementary to deduction. Non-monotonic reasoning calls for a search for potentially verifying models; deduction calls for a search for potentially falsifying models. Hence, a model is a representative sample because it can always be revised so as to satisfy any truly consistent discourse. The moral is that an excellent method for maintaining consistency, whether in a program or a brain, is to work directly with models.

CHAPTER 10

Beyond Deduction: Thinking, Rationality, and Models

The puzzle of how people reason deductively may seem parochial for anyone not embroiled in it. We can imagine such a reader thinking: *Deduction is a small and perhaps artificial domain, and so does it matter whether people reason by manipulating formal rules, rules with a specific content, or mental models? They probably use all three.* What we want to do in this final chapter is to explain why the puzzle matters to cognitive science, and why we think that we have solved it. The whole of our book has been one long argument, and so we begin by recapitulating its principal points. We then go beyond deduction to examine some consequences of the model theory for cognitive science. These consequences bring us back to the issues that we raised at the beginning of the book: deductive competence and its aquisition, the nature of other forms of thought, and whether human beings are rational. By returning to these problems, and to the short-comings of the model theory, we can round off our account with a better picture of deduction.

A RECAPITULATION OF THE ARGUMENT OF THE BOOK

The Three Theories of Performance

In the opening chapter, we distinguished five main families of thought: calculation, deduction, induction, creation, and association. Granted that calculation depends on procedures that have been taught, it does not seem too mysterious. Deduction, however, is not taught to children.

They are seldom instructed in the art by parents, pedagogues, or peers, and so it develops with little guidance from others. It appears to develop as part of the natural make-up of all human beings, underlying many cognitive abilities from the formulation of plans to the pursuit of arguments. Induction and creation may be more important, but they are much harder to unravel. Computer programs model them only to a limited degree (see e.g. Holland, Holyoak, Nisbett and Thagard, 1986; Keane, 1985, 1987, 1988, 1990), but they routinely model deduction, and there is even a *Journal of Automated Reasoning*.

What is computed when people who have not been taught logic make a deduction? They start, according to our theory of competence, with information—either evidence of the senses or a verbal description. They can assess whether a given conclusion follows validly from this information, but in real life there is often no given conclusion. That is why we prefer to use open-ended reasoning tasks in which subjects draw their own conclusions: logic alone is insufficient to characterize intelligent reasoning in this case. A natural or artificial system needs to draw a conclusion that is not merely valid, but also useful. To this end, human reasoners tend to generate a conclusion that maintains the information conveyed by the premises, that re-expresses it more parsimoniously, and that establishes something not originally explicit. If nothing meets these constraints, they declare that there is no valid conclusion.

How are the computations carried out? This question lies at the heart of the puzzle, and has received three contrasting answers—formal rules, content-specific rules, mental models. None appeals to unanalyzable or mystical processes; all are sufficiently articulated to be modelled computationally. Abundant data have been gathered since the turn of the century (e.g. Störring, 1908), and if they do not decide amongst the three approaches, then the consequences are more serious than the failure to settle a border dispute among warring theories of deduction. Controversies in cognitive science may be beyond the scope of empirical resolution.

No amount of data, of course, can pick out one theory against all comers. Infinitely many theories are compatible with any finite set of observations. But, our problem is simpler: it is to decide amongst three possibilities. One of them, however, is not a fully independent option. A rule such as:

If x is a psychologist then x is an experimenter.

or a pragmatic reasoning schema such as:

If the action is to be taken, then the precondition must be
satisfied.

can be only part of a general inferential system. Like their logical
cousins, meaning postulates, these content-specific rules require
additional inferential machinery if the theory is to account for
deductions that do not depend on factual knowledge. Hence, the general
theoretical possibilities reduce to two: formal rules or mental models.

Theories based on formal rules assume that verbal premises are
translated into an internal representation of their logical form, i.e., an
abstract syntactic structure. In fact, as Evans (1989, p. 67) has observed,
many theories are seriously incomplete because they offer no account of
this process of encoding, or of the translation of conclusions back into
natural language. Deduction itself consists in an attempt to derive a
conclusion from the premises using formal rules of inference (e.g.
Osherson, 1975; Braine, 1978; Braine and O'Brien, 1989; Rips, 1983,
1989; Macnamara, 1986; Sperber and Wilson, 1986; Pollock, 1989). If no
derivation of the conclusion can be found, then reasoners will respond
that the inference is invalid. According to rule theories, the difficulty of
a deduction depends on two factors: the number of steps in the
derivation, and the relative availability, or ease of use, of the rules used
in the derivation. Modus ponens, for instance, is easy because there is
a corresponding rule in mental logic:

If p then q
p
∴ q

Modus tollens is harder because it calls for a longer derivation:

If p then q
not-q

p
   (by hypothesis)
∴ q
   (by modus ponens)
∴ q and not-q
   (by conjunction)
∴ not-p
   (by *reductio ad absurdum*)

In contrast, the model theory assumes that people reason from their understanding of a situation, and that their starting point is accordingly a set of models—a single model for a single situation—that is constructed from perceiving the world or from understanding discourse, or both. As we have illustrated for a variety of domains, models follow the principle of structural identity (Johnson-Laird, 1983, p. 419): their structures are identical to the structures of the states of affairs, whether perceived or conceived, that the models represent. They can represent disjunctive alternatives and they can represent negation directly. Otherwise, they correspond to Levesque's (1986) concept of a vivid representation and Inder's (1987) concept of a physical model. After the construction of models of the premises, the next step is to formulate a putative conclusion. Because the process is based on models of the premises, it naturally maintains their semantic information. No conclusion can be drawn in some cases unless an implicit model has been "fleshed out" explicitly. If there is a conclusion, the final step is to search for alternative models that might refute it. The conclusion is valid if there are no such counterexamples. According to this theory, the difficulty of a deduction depends on two principal factors: whether implicit information has to be made explicit, and whether the deduction depends on the construction of more than one model. We have examined these predictions in all of the major domains of deduction.

Propositional Reasoning

In the domain of propositional reasoning, the model theory explains all the replicable phenomena (see Chapter 3). Modus ponens is easier than modus tollens because of the explicit information in initial models of conditionals. The conditional:

If there is a circle then there is a triangle.

elicits one explicit model and one implicit model:

[o]   Δ
  . . .

The premise for modus ponens:

There is a circle.

eliminates the implicit model, and so the conclusion is immediately forthcoming:

There is a triangle.

But, the modus tollens premise:

There is not a triangle.

eliminates the explicit model to leave only the implicit model, from which nothing seems to follow. The deduction can be made only by fleshing out the models of the conditional, e.g.:

[o]   [Δ]
[¬o]   [Δ]
[¬o]   [¬Δ]

The modus tollens premise now eliminates the first two models to yield the conclusion:

There is not a circle.

The difference in difficulty between the two deductions, according to rule theories, arises from the lengths of their derivations. This hypothesis fails to explain why the difference disappears when the conditional premise is expressed using "only if":

There is a circle only if there is a triangle.

If people used the rule for modus ponens, then the difference in difficulty should swap round—granted, as formal theorists assume, that the premise is equivalent to:

If there is not a triangle then there is not a circle.

In contrast, the model theory postulates that the "only if" premise leads to the construction of explicit models of both the antecedent and the negated consequent:

[o]   Δ
¬o   [¬Δ]
. . .

Hence, both deductions are of the same difficulty. The rule theory can be altered *post hoc* to accommodate this phenomenon, but as we showed in Chapter 3, there are a number of other results that presently defy explanation in terms of rules, e.g. the greater ease of deductions based on exclusive disjunction (two models) than those based on inclusive disjunction (three models).

The model theory led to novel predictions of its own. It correctly anticipated, for example, that modus tollens would be easier for bi-conditional premises. It also predicted the striking difficulty of "double disjunctions" and the sorts of error that occur with these problems. Given such premises as:

Linda is in Cannes or Mary is in Tripoli.
Mary is in Havana or Cathy is in Sofia.

a typical conclusion is:

Linda is in Cannes and Cathy is in Sofia and Mary may be in Tripoli.

It is based on only some of the possible models of the premises, and it is invalid because other models falsify it. Rule theories, however, have yet to lead to the discovery of novel phenomena: adherents have fitted their theories to the proportions of correct evaluations of variegated sets of deductions, typically using one parameter for each rule of inference (see e.g. Braine et al, 1984).

Conditionals

Although attempts have been made to develop rule theories for connectives that do not occur in formal logic (see e.g. Rips's, 1983, remarks about causation), a major problem for these accounts is the lack of uniform logical properties for many connectives. Some indicative conditionals, for example, are truth-functional, i.e. they have meanings equivalent to a truth-table definition, whereas others are not. The model theory accommodates both sorts. Those with "defective" truth tables have only an implicit model of the state in which the antecedent is false. Such implicit models account for the failure of subjects to select potential counterexamples in Wason's selection task. The knowledge elicited by certain conditionals can lead subjects to flesh out their models, and so modus tollens and the selection task are then reliably easier.

Counterfactual conditionals, such as:

If tigers had no teeth, they would gum you to death.

cannot be truth-functional because antecedent and consequent are both false. Theories based on formal rules therefore have little to say about them, but in Chapter 4 we showed how their meanings can be mentally represented by models of actual and counterfactual states.

Models can be interrelated by a common referent or by general knowledge. These relations in turn can block both modus ponens and modus tollens. Hence, the model theory predicts that a pair of conditionals, such as:

If Lisa goes fishing, then she has a fish supper.
If Lisa catches some fish, then she has a fish supper.

can block modus ponens (Byrne, 1989a). When subjects are told:

Lisa goes fishing.

they tend not to conclude:

Lisa has a fish supper.

because they have been reminded by the second conditional that Lisa also needs to catch some fish. The suppression of the deduction shows that people do not have a secure intuition that modus ponens applies equally to any content. Yet, this intuition is a criterion (see Chapter 4) for the existence of formal rules in the mind. The model theory also predicted the sorts of sentences that are likely to be paraphrased by conditionals—those that describe an outcome as a possibility, because a possibility tallies with the implicit model in the set for a conditional.

Relational reasoning

In a rule theory, the logical properties of a relation have to be stated in postulates or content-specific rules. The model theory does not need such postulates. Their work is done by a representation of the meaning of the relation, i.e. its contribution to truth conditions. One advantage is that the logical properties of relations emerge from their meanings. It is then easy to see why certain relations have properties that are affected by the situation under discussion. Thus, "to the right of" calls for an indefinite number of different degrees of transitivity (Johnson-Laird, 1983, Chapter 11). The premises:

Matthew is to the right of Mark.
Mark is to the right of John.

lead naturally to a transitive conclusion:

∴ Matthew is to the right of John.

provided that the seating arrangement resembles Leonardo Da Vinci's painting of *The Last Supper*. The conclusion may be blocked, however, if the individuals are seated at a round table. The degree of transitivity then depends on the radius of the table and the proximity of the seats. The logical properties of the relation require an indefinite number of different meaning postulates—one for each degree of transitivity. Yet, if the meaning of such expressions relates to a reference individual:

$$
\begin{array}{c}
\text{to the front of X} \\
\uparrow \\
\text{to the left of X} \leftarrow \quad \text{X} \quad \rightarrow \text{to the right of X} \\
\downarrow \\
\text{to the back of X}
\end{array}
$$

then the degree of transitivity is an automatic consequence of the seating arrangement.

This account led to an unexpected difference between models and rules. Certain spatial deductions require just one model yet call for complex derivations based on rules (see Ohlsson, 1981; and Hagert, 1983). The difference arises because objects interrelated in a single model may not have occurred in the same premise, and so a formal procedure needs to derive the relation between them. In contrast, objects may be interrelated in a single premise and so a rule can be immediately applied to them, and yet the description as a whole may be compatible with more than one possible model. Hence, the two sorts of theory make opposing predictions. The results reported in Chapter 5 corroborated models, not rules.

Reasoning with Quantifiers

Most theorists agree that people reason from singly-quantified premises, i.e. syllogisms, by constructing a semantic representation of them. No rule theory has accounted for the phenomena of syllogistic reasoning. Indeed, it is remarkable that the derivation of the following very easy deduction:

Some of the athletes are bakers.
All of the bakers are canoeists.
∴ Some of the athletes are canoeists.

calls for exactly the same sequence of rules in the predicate calculus as the following very hard deduction:

Some of the bakers are athletes.
None of the bakers is a canoeist.
∴ Some of the athletes are not canoeists.

Given this identity (see Table 6.3), such derivations cannot be used by ordinary reasoners. In fact, the errors that they make correspond to conclusions based on a subset of the models of the premises—typically just one of the models (as in the case of propositional reasoning). Our study of the ability of subjects to remember their conclusions bore out the hypothesis that they search for alternative models. Even when they correctly refrained from drawing a conclusion, if they later thought that they had drawn one, it was invariably the one which the theory predicts that they had initially constructed, only to reject because it was refuted by an alternative model. The main controversy about syllogisms is thus not between rules and models, but about the nature of models: are they Euler circles, Venn diagrams, strings of symbols, or what?

We argued in Chapter 6 that models represent finite sets of entities by finite sets of mental tokens rather than by circles inscribed in Euclidean space. This hypothesis leads to the correct predictions about the difficulty of syllogisms. For example, the easy syllogism in the pair above calls for only one model whereas the hard syllogism calls for three. With Euler circles, however, the easy syllogism calls for 16 representations and the hard syllogism calls for 15 representations. Our studies of the quantifier, "only", further implied that models can represent negation explicitly (*pace* Inder, 1987), presumably by a specific annotation.

These proposals generalize to the representation of multiply-quantified assertions. Suppose, for example:

Some of the infantry in front of the tanks were in corn fields.
All the tanks were further from the town than any of the corn
    fields in front of them were.

You should be able to deduce:

∴ Some of the infantry were nearer to the town than any of the
    tanks were.

A formal derivation of the conclusion takes many steps in the predicate calculus. And the premises cannot be represented by Euler circles or

Venn diagrams, which can cope only with singly-quantified assertions. Yet they can be represented by a model. In Chapter 7, we examined reasoning with multiple quantifiers and, once again, the results confirmed the predictions of the model theory. We can reject the theories based on formal rules.

Or can we?

In making predictions from rule theories, we were forced to extend them into a new domain. This tactic may have been misguided. It might have been more prudent to point out the inability of current theories to deal with quantifiers. In fact, critics have argued that we may have constructed the wrong rule theories. The criticism puts us in an interesting dilemma. On the one hand, there was no rule theory of multiply-quantified reasoning, and so, the critics said, we could not claim that our experiments ruled out such theories, because there was none to be ruled out. On the other hand, when our various proposals failed to square with the experimental evidence, they said that our rule theories were the wrong ones. If we offered a theory, *it* was wrong; if we did not offer a theory, *we* were wrong. In tho cvenl, we could not restrain our curiosity about how well rule theories might fare. Moreover, the main body of any such theory—the part dealing with connectives—does exist (e.g. Braine, 1978; Rips, 1983), and so extensions for dealing with quantifiers might have accounted for our results. We constructed various rule theories, spurred on by critics' comments, but we never came close to one that could cope with the phenomena.

Meta-deduction

People have a tacit grasp of the need to search for counterexamples, but they also have the capacity for self-reflective thought. They can introspect and evaluate their own reasoning. In this way, some subjects are even able to discover rudimentary rules during an experiment, e.g. nothing follows from two syllogistic premises that both contain "some" (Galotti, Baron, and Sabini, 1986). Exceptional individuals may be prompted to seek more reliable aids to deduction. That, we believe, is why Aristotle was led to invent logic. And, most importantly, the reflective ability can be used by cognitive scientists to construct theories about itself. Meta-deduction enables reasoners to reason about reasoning.

In Chapter 8, we accepted a challenge from Rips (1989) and showed how higher-level strategies for solving meta-logical problems could be implemented in a computer program that reasons with models. The resulting theory accounted for certain experimental results that Rips's own formal theory left unexplained. Moreover, the following Gödelian argument counts against any formal theory of meta-deduction:

Suppose that someone, say Rips, devises an allegedly comprehensive system of meta-logical reasoning based only on formal rules. We will call this system, FR (for Formal Rules). Now consider the following meta-logical proposition:

Assertion A asserts that A is not derivable in FR.

This claim is either true or false. If it is true, then there is a true meta-logical assertion that cannot be captured within FR. Hence, FR is incomplete. If the claim is false, then FR allows one to derive an assertion that asserts of itself that it is not derivable in FR. Hence, FR is inconsistent. A purely formal account of meta-logical reasoning is bound to be either incomplete or inconsistent.

Models in Programs for Reasoning

Our final report concerned the development of model-based programs for deduction. When a program searches for an alternative model that will accommodate some recalcitrant piece of information, it is at liberty to undo two sorts of information: arbitrary decisions and default values, and to insert instead some other, perhaps specified, value. This possibility, as we showed in Chapter 9, confers on a deductive program the power to make both non-monotonic inferences and valid deductions. We also showed how models underlie an algorithm that is guaranteed to find a maximally parsimonious conclusion equivalent to any set of premises in the propositional calculus. This task is equivalent to simplifying circuits made up from Boolean units.

THE IMPLICATIONS OF
THE MODEL THEORY

Suppose that the essentials of the model theory are correct, and that people make deductions by building models and searching for counterexamples. What, then? The main implications for cognitive science are threefold: for the development of deductive competence, for thinking in general, and for the concept of rationality. We will examine each of these topics in turn.

The Acquisition of Deductive Competence

The acquisition of deductive competence is profoundly puzzling for theories based on formal rules. Given some existing deductive ability children might learn other rules of inference by generalization (Falmagne, 1980), but how could they learn formal rules in the first place? Piaget's answer, to echo the words of Braine and Rumain (1983), is a logic that cannot develop at adolescence, or at any time: "it is too problematic to stand as a psychological model of anything". So intractable is the problem for formal rules that many theorists suppose that deductive ability is not learned at all. It is innate. Fodor (1980) has even argued that, in principle, logic could not be learned. The difficulty with this argument is not that it is wrong, although it may be, but that it is too strong. It is hard to construct a case against the learning of logic that is not also a case against its evolution. If it could not be acquired by trial-and-error and reinforcement, then how could it be acquired by neo-Darwinian mechanisms? Trial-and-error is analogous to the random shuffling of genes; reinforcement is analogous to natural selection. The boundary between evolution and learnability must therefore be drawn in terms of computational tractability. What is intractable for an individual to acquire in a lifetime may be tractable for natural selection, which carries out millions of experiments over millions of years. The philosophical arguments for inborn logic, however, have yet to get to grips with this consideration.

The acquisition of deductive competence is much less problematical if what has to be acquired is a capacity to build models of the world, either directly by perception or indirectly by understanding language, and a capacity to search for alternative models. The unfolding of these abilities under the control of innate constraints seems quite feasible. What develops in childhood is the ability to understand language, the processing capacity of working memory (Hitch and Halliday, 1983; Case, 1985), and the meta-ability to reflect on one's own performance. Seven year-olds cannot cope with syllogisms because they do not understand quantifiers correctly (see Inhelder and Piaget, 1964). Nine year-olds can cope with one-model syllogisms, but not with more than one model (Johnson-Laird, Oakhill, and Bull, 1986; Acredolo and Horobin, 1987). Their working memory appears to lack sufficient capacity to retain alternative models of the premises. And even adults have difficulty, as we have seen, when a deduction depends on multiple models.

Mental Models and Other Modes of Thought

In real life, people often lack sufficient information to make valid deductions. They are forced to make plausible inductive inferences like those of Sherlock Holmes, which go beyond the semantic information in the premises (see Galotti, 1989, for a review). Consider the following example from Johnson-Laird and Anderson (1989):

> The old man was bitten by a poisonous snake. There was no
> known antidote available.

When subjects are asked what happened, they reply that the old man died. But, when asked whether there are any other possibilities, they can envisage alternatives. People differ in this imaginative ability, but if the experimenter tells them that their conclusion is not in fact true, then this meta-knowledge—even though it is not "reinforcing" in the standard operant way—helps them to envisage different scenarios. The order in which they are generated is fairly consistent. Thus, the conclusions to the present problem were produced in roughly the following order:

1. The old man died.
2. The poison was successfully removed, e.g. by sucking it out.
3. The old man was immune to the poison.
4. The poison was weak, and not deadly.
5. The poison was blocked from entering the circulatory system, e.g. by the man's thick clothing.

The final conclusion is almost a denial of one of the premises—a phenomenon that has been observed in other studies (Perkins, Allen, and Hafner, 1983).

Everyday inferences are plainly not deductively closed: reasoners can continue to produce ever more baroque possibilities *ad nauseam*, e.g. the old man was kept alive long enough for someone to invent an antidote. At no point can a stage be reached in which all the alternative possibilities have definitely been eliminated. Hence, one can never validly deduce that the old man died. Inferences of this sort, which lie outside deduction, cannot be accounted for by deductive formal rules. If they are to be explained in terms of rules, then these rules have to capture plausible inferences (Collins and Michalski, 1989). Yet, as our colleague Bruno Bara and his collaborators at the University of Milan have shown, the same general machinery of constructing models and searching for alternatives readily extends to them (Bara, Carassa, and Geminiani, 1984, 1985).

An analogous extension of the theory may explain how people construct arguments in favour of, or against, particular propositions. In collaboration with Mark Keane, of the University of Dublin, Trinity College, we have confirmed the intuition (common to many logicians) that logic is not the primary guide to this process. When you are asked to advance an argument in favour of, say, the following proposition:

The Government should subsidize ballet.

the real task is to find a relevant fact. You may argue that:

Without subsidy, the ballet would be too expensive for anyone to attend apart from the very rich.

The mysterious feature of the process is how the relevant information comes to mind. The process is inductive or, more accurately, abductive (see Peirce, 1931), and obviously driven by the content of the problem. No theory based on formal rules can elucidate it. What is needed is a semantic theory in which the construction of a model of the initial proposition triggers the recall of pertinent facts (cf. Gentner, 1989; Holyoak and Thagard, 1989; Keane, Byrne, and Johnson-Laird, 1990).

Everyday reasoners are often "motivated", that is, they may want to reach a particular conclusion, an accurate one perhaps, or one that is self-serving (see e.g. Nisbett and Ross, 1980; and for a different view, Kunda, in press). They may reach the desired conclusion only if they can find evidence to support it (Darley and Gross, 1983), and so motivation can clearly affect the evidence that comes to mind. Unlike rules theories, however, the model theory allows that the inferential process itself can be influenced by motives: the search for alternatives that refute a putative conclusion can be thorough or cursory depending on motivational factors (see Chapter 5 for our studies of such effects).

A similar picture emerges from studies of reasoning based on uncertain or probabilistic information. Tversky and Kahneman have demonstrated many departures from rationality, particularly from the syntax and semantics of the probability calculus (see e.g. Kahneman, Slovic, and Tversky, 1982). They have even sketched a mechanism that dovetails with the model theory (Tversky and Kahneman, 1973, p.229):

Some events are perceived as so unique that past history does not seem relevant to the evaluation of their likelihood. In thinking of such events we often construct *scenarios*, i.e. stories that lead from the present situation to the target event. The plausibility of the scenarios that come to mind, or the difficulty of producing them, then serve as a clue to the likelihood of the event. If no reasonable scenario comes to mind, the event is deemed impossible or highly unlikely. If many scenarios come to mind, or if the one scenario that is constructed is particularly compelling, the event in question appears probable.

In our view, such an approach is preferable to one that attempts to exploit "fuzzy" sets or other sophisticated formal apparatus. Everyday inferences from uncertain premises seem no harder psychologically than those based on precise knowledge. Yet, fuzzy sets and their cognates call for much more complicated rules than classical sets.

In short, as Craik (1943) proposed long ago, thinking is the manipulation of models. Our research corroborates the claim, but deduction is not special in its demand for models. One consequence is that other modes of thought—induction, analogy, creative problem-solving, and the generation of new ideas—are likely to be based on models. A model, as we have argued, has a structure that is remote from verbal assertions, but close to the structure of the world as humans conceive it. Hence, it may be an egregious error to assume that the representations underlying these other modes of thought take the form of propositional representations or semantic networks, which have structures that do not correspond to human conceptions of the world.

Rationality versus Relativism

Rationality is the source of an interminable debate amongst philosophers, anthropologists, and sociologists. A famous episode in anthropology poses the question (Evans-Pritchard, 1937). A certain African tribe, the Azande, use a ritual called the "poison oracle" to determine whether an accused individual is a witch. The decision hangs on whether a poisoned fowl lives or dies, and the answer is checked by poisoning another fowl and framing the query in different words. The Azande also believe, however, that witchcraft is inherited, that it is therefore common to all members of a clan, and that a post-mortem examination of the intestines yields decisive information about whether an individual was a witch. Evans-Pritchard suggested to his informants that a few systematically chosen post-mortems would settle once and for all which clans were guilty, and there would then be no need for the poison oracle. The Azande did not see matters in this light, and continued to regard the guilt of an individual as an open question. When he charged them with inconsistency, they demurred and avoided his challenge. The fundamental question is: were they irrational? That is, do our criteria of rationality—whatever they may be—apply in other cultures, or are the criteria themselves *relative* to a culture?

This question has perplexed all those who have thought about it, and it has split them into two opposing camps: rationalists, who argue for a core of rational cognitive principles common to all human societies; and relativists, who argue for purely "local" criteria of rationality, for the incommensurability of the beliefs of different groups—even those of scientists of different theoretical persuasions, and for the radical intranslatability of such beliefs from one language to another. Relativism is advocated for many concepts, but our concern is solely with rationality.

If relativism is right, then the principles of deduction differ from one society to another, and perhaps from one epoch to another—as certain historians have argued (see Burke, 1986). Hence, psychological studies of deduction are at best of parochial interest. Most of the debate, as evinced by such sources as Wilson (1970), Finnegan and Horton (1973), and Hollis and Lukes (1982), has indeed been conducted with scant regard for psychological evidence. We will argue, however, that the model theory provides a way to resolve the controversy.

To concentrate our minds, we state two strong but contrasting views. Hollis (1970) asserts that certain simple forms of deduction, such as modus ponens, are universally compelling. Barnes and Bloor (1982) disagree and demand evidence for universality. None is forthcoming, and so they make a deeper claim. If modus ponens were truly compelling in all societies, then its universal validity would call for explanation. No such account, they argue, could be constructed without circularity. Their argument derives from Lewis Carroll's (1895) classic paper, "What the tortoise said to Achilles".

In this neat logical fable, Achilles presents the tortoise with the premises of a modus ponens deduction and presses him to accept the conclusion. The tortoise refuses unless Achilles justifies this form of deduction. His attempt to do so, however, hinges on modus ponens. Hence, the justification of the deduction appears to presuppose its own validity. Barnes and Bloor are convinced by the tortoise, and they conclude that no account of deductive competence justifies a unique system of logical conventions. They write:

> Logic, as it is systematized in textbooks, monographs or research papers, is a learned body of scholarly lore, growing and varying over time. It is a mass of conventional routines, decisions, expedient restrictions, dicta, maxims, and *ad hoc* rules. The sheer lack of necessity in granting its assumptions or adopting its strange and elaborate definitions is the

point that should strike any candid observer. Why should anyone adopt a notion of "implication" whereby a contradiction "implies" any proposition? What is compelling about systems of logic which require massive and systematic deviation from our everyday use of crucial words like "if", "then", and "and"?

(Barnes and Bloor, 1982, p. 45)

To which we might add that there are infinitely many different modal logics, i.e. logics for "possibly" and "necessarily", and the question of which, if any, corresponds to ordinary modal reasoning is probably answered in a word: none.

Yet, is relativism right? In our view, there *is* a central core of rationality, which appears to be common to all human societies. It is the semantic principle of validity: an argument is valid only if there is no way in which its premises could be true and its conclusion false. A corollary of the principle is that certain *forms* of argument are valid, and these forms can be specified by formal rules of inference. It is a gross mistake, however, to suppose that these rules are *per se* cognitive universals. Rationality is problematical if it is supposed to be founded on rules. This foundation makes relativism attractive because systematic error is hard to explain, unless one abandons rationality in favour of alternative, and perhaps illicit, rules of inference (cf. Levy-Bruhl, 1910; von Domarus, 1944; Jackendoff, 1988). Moreover, logical reasoning in situations divorced from practical contexts, that is, reasoning of the sort made possible by formal rules, appears to depend on literacy and schooling (Cole and Scribner, 1974; Luria, 1976; Orasanu and Scribner, 1982). The common denominator of rationality is the search for counterexamples: anything else is logical icing on everyday competence.

Our defence of universal rationality should not be confused with the claim that human beings never err deductively (see Chapter 2). On the one hand, if they were perfectly rational, they would not have invented logic. They would have had no need for it. On the other hand, if they were completely irrational, they could not have invented logic. In fact, human beings are rational in principle, but err in practice. On Evans-Pritchard's account, the Azande erred—just as, for example, so many scientists erred in accepting that Uri Geller could bend spoons, or that polywater could exist. Not only are errors easy to explain when reasoning is founded on models, but the theory does not need to sacrifice rational competence in explaining irrational performance. Humans need logic, but they can invent it.

THE CRITIQUE OF MENTAL MODELS

Criticisms of the Original Theory

Adherents of formal rules have, not surprisingly, made many swingeing criticisms of the model theory. We have already answered the charge that the theory is empirically inadequate—that it does not apply to propositional reasoning, or to Wason's selection task (see Chapters 3 and 4). Now is the time to reply to the other objections, which we will divide into the metaphysical, the methodological, and the logical.

The metaphysical criticisms of mental models:

1. The theory violates the tenet that "cognitive psychology has to do without semantic notions like truth and reference that depend on the relationship between mental representations and the world" (Rips, 1986; see also Oden, 1987). We do not accept the tenet. Without truth and semantics, there is no notion of validity, meta-logic disappears, and little of mental life is left (for a similar response, see e.g. Hofstadter and Dennett, 1981; Haugeland, 1985, Russell, 1987; Barwise, 1989). We note that Rips (1989) himself abandons the tenet by arguing that the following proposition:

> If I am telling the truth, then the natural deduction theory is
>   correct.

appears to be logically true, and so it seems to support his account of meta-deduction. The tenet's adherents tend to think of the brain as disembodied, but it should not be isolated from the causal chain in which energy triggers nerve impulses, from which it constructs an internal model of the external world. Analogous systems enable robots to construct representations of the world. When humans or robots construct a model from a verbal description, and evaluate it in relation to a perceptual model, it is hard to deny them semantic notions such as truth and reference. The assumption can be challenged, of course, but the argument is metaphysical.

2. Mental models are unnecessary. Various authors, including Pylyshyn (1973, 1981) and Rips (1986) have argued that everything can be represented by *propositional representations*, i.e. syntactically structured strings of symbols in a mental language. Because any mental representation ultimately depends on neural events, more stringent reductionists have argued that talk of a mental language is in turn

THE CRITIQUE OF MENTAL MODELS

unnecessary if it is supposed to refer to anything other than neural events (Churchland, 1986). The issue is not yet open to empirical study. In our view, however, mental models are no more problematical than, say, the use of arrays in high-level computer programming languages. Mental computations can rely on high-level structures, too.

The methodological criticisms of mental models:

3. The theory is not clear (Rips, 1984, 1986; Goldman, 1986), and unfairly capitalizes on a visual metaphor (Ford, 1985). In fact, the theory is sufficiently explicit to have been implemented in computer programs, which cannot capitalize on metaphors (see Chapter 9). It has also been criticized on many grounds that would be obviated by obscurity, e.g. it has been accused of being false.

4. The theory is unworkable. The use of models to simulate real phenomena requires too much knowledge, and too many possibilities to be taken into account, for it to be a realistic theory of human reasoning (Rips, 1986). Rips continues:

> The moral is that unless you know a great deal about a system, even qualitative simulations are off limits, given the normal memory and processing limits that human beings have to contend with. For any system that is the least complex, we're thrown back on crude rules of thumb that are far from literal simulation.

This criticism attacks a position that we have never defended. We argue that when people make deductions, such as those of the sort that Rips (1983) himself has studied, they do so by constructing models of the premises. The models can be radically incomplete. If a deduction required the construction of, say, a complete model of the workings of a television set, the task would certainly exceed ordinary human competence.

5. The theory is untestable: mental models are too flexible, and no possible results could refute the theory. But, if the results of our experiments had turned out differently, they could have vindicated rule theories, and the present book along with the model theory would not exist.

The logical criticisms of mental models:

6. **Mental models are irrational.** Theories based on formal rules of logic account for human rationality, but, according to the source of this criticism, any theory that abandons logic abnegates reason. In fact, the model theory is in no way inconsistent with logic: it merely gives up the formal approach (rules of inference) for a semantic approach (search for counterexamples). A parallel division occurs in logic itself between proof-theoretic methods and model-theoretic methods (see Chapter 1). The formal view is so inbred, alas, that some theorists, such as Cherniak (1986, p. 78) have supposed that any nonformal means of making deductions verges on the mystical.

7. **There is little or no difference between mental models and formal rules of inference:**

> Procedures are necessary to specify how the models should be used ... So manipulation of mental models is not fundamentally different from manipulation of mental propositions. It seems then the rules that operate on the models must *be* inference rules. If so, the contrast Johnson-Laird sets up between mental logic and mental models collapses.

> (Goldman, 1986, p.292; see also Rips, 1986)

This misapprehension is akin to the mistaken assumption that the semantic method of truth tables is not fundamentally different from the syntactic method of proof in the propositional calculus (see Chapter 1). In fact, there is a profound difference between the two sorts of psychological theories. They postulate different sorts of mental representation, and different sorts of procedures: rule theories employ representations that are language-like and that contain variables, whereas mental models are remote from the structure of sentences and do not contain variables. At the heart of deduction for rule theories is the application of formal rules of inference, such as modus ponens, to representations of the logical forms of sentences. At the heart of deduction for model theories is a search for alternative models of the premises. The search makes no use of modus ponens or any other formal rules of inference.

8. **Mental models are nothing more than the first-order predicate calculus.** If the claim were true, then it might not count as a criticism. But, in any case, it is false. The predicate calculus applies to expressions that can have an infinite set of models. There is no decision procedure for the predicate calculus, and there is no way of proving theorems

within it using models directly (see Chapter 1). The model theory applies only to finite sets of models; it has a decision procedure; and works directly with finite models. A more sensible worry, in fact, is how people could reason about infinite sets if their models are finite (Barwise and Etchemendy, 1989). Our guess is that they have to understand certain models of processes, such as the procedure that generates the successor of an integer, before they can reason about infinite sets (Johnson-Laird, 1983, p. 444-5). We note, however, that ordinary reasoners and even some extraordinary reasoners, such as Galileo, are notoriously bad at reasoning about infinities.

9. Mental models and formal rules both depend on syntactic procedures (Martin Braine, personal communication). This claim is true for the computer programs modelling both sorts of theory: existing computer programs operate in a syntactic way, i.e., they are unable to make genuine semantic interpretations of the symbols they employ. Nevertheless, the programs for manipulating models make no use of any formal rule such as modus ponens; and the programs for manipulating formal rules make no use of models. Moreover, unlike existing programs, human beings do have access to the meanings of expressions: their models can be real because of the causal links between models and the world (see Johnson-Laird, 1983, p. 399 *et seq*). Mental models do not supplement inference rules, but are a distinct algorithm for reasoning that renders formal rules superfluous. Indeed, as we have shown, the two sorts of theory lead to different empirical predictions. That must surely be the decisive rebuttal to the thesis that the difference between them collapses.

Shortcomings of the Current Theory

The model theory is, of course, incomplete. We have implemented it in programs for propositional reasoning, spatial reasoning, quantificational reasoning, and meta-deduction. Yet there remain topics that we have not fully elucidated, such as modal reasoning, and many points of uncertainty. We know how a mental process might be carried out, but we do not know for certain how it is carried out. Consider, for example, the search for alternative models. Reasoners appear to formulate an initial conclusion, which they often abandon in the light of an alternative model. We see signs of the process in the pattern of their errors, in the revisions they make when they are allowed to re-evaluate their conclusions (Johnson-Laird and Bara, 1984), and in their erroneous memories for conclusions they have drawn (see Chapter 6). But, how are the alternatives generated, and how is the search for them terminated? We do not know. The search could be conducted at random, or it might be based on a simple deterministic procedure. It could be terminated whenever a certain number of alternatives have been examined. We suspect that none of these approaches is right, and that people try to negate putative conclusions (see Chapter 9), and that the capacity of working memory is the main factor in terminating searches.

Ultimately, cognitive science needs an account of the underlying *components* out of which deduction and other cognitive abilities are assembled. Sternberg (1988) has argued along these lines, and postulated components for deductive performance, for the acquisition of knowledge, and even meta-components for assembling new procedures out of old. But the components of thought need to be specified in a computable way. They should be formulated as the constituents of a high-level programming language that embodies a unified theory of mental architecture. One such mental architecture is provided by parallel distributed processing (Rumelhart and McClelland, 1986) in which analogues of models have also been proposed (Rumelhart, 1989). Newell (1990) has outlined an alternative theory, SOAR; and he and his colleagues have been successful in re-constructing model theories of deduction within its architecture (Polk and Newell, 1988). They envisage the search for alternative models as taking place in a problem-space in which each state corresponds to a model (see Newell and Simon, 1972). Our only misgiving is the claim that the system moves from one model to another as a result of a single mental operation. In vision, a model is constructed by parallel operations; the same principle may well apply to the construction of models in deduction.

Our work yields two morals for establishing such explanatory frameworks. First, meta-deduction calls for mental symbols with an explicit structure, i.e. the assessment of the truth-preserving properties of a particular form of argument requires an explicit representation of that form. Other components of deductive processing may depend on low-level processes that use distributed representations. Second, mental models are a form of data-structure that plays a central role in the computational architecture of the mind, entering not only into thinking in general, but also perception (Marr, 1982), the comprehension and production of discourse (Johnson-Laird, 1983), and the representation of beliefs and other intentional contents (McGinn, 1989).

EPILOGUE

We began this book with two main questions: how to characterize the nature of human deductive competence, and how to describe the underlying deductive mechanism. We have now answered both questions. If formal rules of inference were in the mind, then the development of logic as an intellectual discipline would be largely a matter of externalizing these principles. And if "psychologism" were correct, then logic would be merely the systematization of the natural principles of thought. We repudiate both these doctrines. No formal logic exists in the heads of anyone other than logicians. The principles of thought are not based on formal rules of inference.

Why then have so many theorists in so many disciplines accepted the rule theory? One reason is the weight of tradition; another is the greater accessibility of formal accounts of logic. We have tried to show that deduction can be carried out by other means, and that these means are more plausible psychologically. Let us sum up the case for the model theory. Although the mechanism that enables individuals to make deductions is not available to introspection, experimental evidence shows that the *content* of premises with the same logical form can have a decisive effect on what conclusions people draw (see Chapter 4). Even Piaget discovered this effect, and introduced a clause in small print —the "horizontal décalage", essentially a re-description of the phenomenon—to try to sweep it away. Yet the phenomenon is inimical to formal theories of inference. The evidence also shows that when people reason they are concerned about meaning and truth. They are influenced by what they believe to be true, which affects both the conclusions that they formulate for themselves and their evaluation of given conclusions. When they draw their own conclusions, they maintain the semantic information from the premises, and treat conclusions that throw it away as improper. Finally, without exception, the results of our experiments corroborated the model theory's predictions about propositional, relational, quantificational, and meta-logical reasoning. Easy deductions call for one explicit model only; difficult deductions call for more than one explicit model; and erroneous conclusions correspond to a subset of models of the premises.

There are many uncertainties, gaps, and perhaps downright flaws, in the theory of mental models. But, we are convinced of the truth of the broad view given in this volume—at least to the degree that anyone should be committed to a theory. The search for counterexamples can be carried out directly by constructing alternative models. The method makes an excellent system for computer reasoning. The evidence suggests that it is the mainspring of human reasoning.

References

Acredolo, C. and Horobin, K. (1987). Development of relational reasoning and avoidance of premature closure. *Developmental Psychology, 23,* 13-21. (10)

Adams, E.W. (1975). *The logic of conditionals.* Dordrecht: Reidel. (4)

Adams, M.J. (1984). Aristotle's logic. *The Psychology of Learning and Motivation* (Vol. 18). New York: Academic Press. (6)

Anderson, J.R. (1983). *The architecture of cognition.* Hillsdale, NJ: Lawrence Erlbaum Associates. (2)

Anno, M. and Nozaki, A. (1984). *Anno's hat tricks.* London: Bodley Head. (8)

Appiah, A. (1985). *Assertion and conditionals.* Cambridge: Cambridge University Press. (4)

Arevalo, Z. and Bredeson, J.G. (1978). A method to simplify a Boolean function into a new minimal sum-of-products for programmable logic arrays, *IEEE transactions on computing,* C-27, 1028-1030. (9)

Austin, J.L. (1970). Truth. In J.O. Urmson and J.G. Warnock (Eds.), *Philosophical papers of J.L Austin,* 2nd Edition. Oxford: Oxford University Press. (8)

Baddeley, A.D. (1986). *Working memory.* Oxford: Clarendon Press. (2)

Bara, B.G., Carassa, A.G., and Geminiani, G.C. (1984). Inference processes in everyday reasoning. In D. Plander (Ed.), *Artificial intelligence and information-control systems of robots.* Amsterdam: Elsevier. (10)

Bara, B.G., Carassa, A.G., and Geminiani, G.C. (1985). Mental models in everyday reasoning. *Cognitiva 85.* Paris. (10)

Note: Where a citation occurs with two dates, e.g. Spinoza, B. (1677/1949), the first is the date of original publication, and the second is the date of the work that is referenced. The numbers in parentheses refer to the chapters of the present book in which the works are cited.

217

Barclay, J.R. (1973). The role of comprehension in remembering sentences. *Cognitive Psychology,* 4, 229-254. (5)

Bar-Hillel, Y. and Carnap, R. (1964). An outline of a theory of semantic information. In Y. Bar-Hillel (Ed.), *Language and information.* Reading, MA: Addison-Wesley. (1)

Bar-Hillel, Y. (1967). Dictionaries and meaning rules. *Foundations of Language, 3,* 409-414. (5)

Barnes, B. and Bloor, D. (1982). Relativism, rationalism, and the sociology of knowledge. In M. Hollis and S. Lukes (Eds.), Rationality and relativism. Oxford: Basil Blackwell. (10)

Barwise, J. (1989). *The situation in logic.* Stanford: Center for the Study of Language and Information. (2, 4, 10)

Barwise, J. and Cooper, R. (1981). Generalized quantifiers and natural language. *Linguistics and Philosophy,* 4, 159-219. (1)

Barwise, J. and Etchemendy, J. (1987). *The liar: An essay in truth and circularity.* New York: Oxford University Press. (8)

Barwise, J. and Etchemendy, J. (1989a). *A situation-theoretic account of reasoning with Hyperproof.* Unpublished paper. Center for the Study of Language and Information. Stanford University. (2)

Barwise, J. and Etchemendy, J. (1989b). Model-theoretic semantics. In M. Posner (Ed.), *Foundations of cognitive science.* Cambridge, MA: Bradford Books, MIT Press. (2, 7, 10)

Begg, I. and Denny, J. (1969). Empirical reconciliation of atmosphere and conversion interpretations of syllogistic reasoning. *Journal of Experimental Psychology, 81,* 351-354. (6, 7)

Berry, D.C. (1983). Metacognitive experiences and transfer of logical reasoning. *Quarterly Journal of Experimental Psychology, 35A,* 39-49. (4)

Beth, E.W. (1955/1969). Semantic entailment and formal derivability. In J. Hintikka (Ed.), *The philosophy of mathematics.* Oxford: Oxford University Press. (1)

Beth, E.W. (1971). *Aspects of modern logic.* New York: Humanities Press. Dordrecht: Reidel. (9)

Beth, E.W. and Piaget, J. (1966). *Mathematical epistemology and psychology.* Dordrecht: Reidel. (4)

Bledsoe, W.W. (1977). Non-resolution theorem proving. *Artificial Intelligence, 9,* 1-35. (2, 9)

Boole, G. (1847/1948). *The mathematical analysis of logic, being an essay towards a calculus of deductive reasoning.* Oxford: Basil Blackwell. (2)

Boole, G. (1854). *An investigation of the laws of thought on which are founded the mathematical theories of logic and probabilities.* London: Macmillan. (2)

Braine, M.D.S. (1978). On the relation between the natural logic of reasoning and standard logic. *Psychological Review, 85,* 1-21(1, 2, 3, 10)

Braine, M.D.S. (1979). On some claims about if-then. *Linguistics and Philosophy, 3,* 35-47. (4)

Braine, M.D.S. and O'Brien, D.P. (1984). Categorical syllogisms: a reconciliation of mental models and inference schemas. Unpublished manuscript. (6)

Braine, M.D.S. and O'Brien, D.P. (1989). A theory of If: A lexical entry, reasoning program, and pragmatic principles. Mimeo, New York University. (4, 10)

Braine, M.D.S., Reiser, B.J., and Rumain, B. (1984). Some empirical justification for a theory of natural propositional logic. *The psychology of learning and motivation* (Vol. 18). New York: Academic Press. (2, 3)

Braine, M.D.S. and Rumain, B. (1983). Logical reasoning. In J.H. Flavell and E.M. Markman (Eds.), *Carmichael's handbook of child psychology. Vol. III: Cognitive development* (4th Edn.). New York: Wiley. (2, 3, 7, 6)

Broadbent, D.E. (1958). *Perception and communication.* London: Pergamon. (6)

Brown, A. (1987). Metacognition, executive control, self-regulation, and other more mysterious mechanisms. In F.E. Weinert and R. Kluwe (Eds.), *Metacognition, motivation, and understanding.* Hillsdale, N.J.: Lawrence Erlbaum Associates. (2)

Bundy, A. (1983). *The computer modelling of mathematical reasoning.* London: Academic Press. (2)

Burke, P. (1986). Strengths and weaknesses in the history of mentalities, *History of European ideas,* 7. (10)

Byrne, R.M.J. (1986). *The contextual nature of conditional reasoning.* Ph.d thesis, University of Dublin, Trinity College, Republic of Ireland. (4)

Byrne, R.M.J. (1989a). Suppressing valid inferences with conditionals. *Cognition, 31,* 61-83. (4, 10)

Byrne, R.M.J. (1989b). Everyday reasoning with conditional sequences. *Quarterly Journal of Experimental Psychology, 41A,* 141-166. (5)

Byrne, R.M.J. and Johnson-Laird, P.N. (1989a). Models of conditional sequences. Unpublished manuscript. University of Wales College of Cardiff. (4)

Byrne, R.M.J. and Johnson-Laird, P.N. (1989b). Spatial reasoning. *Journal of Memory and Language, 28,* 564-575. (5)

Byrne, R.M.J. and Johnson-Laird, P.N. (1989c). Re-constructing inferences. Unpublished manuscript. University of Wales College of Cardiff. (6)

Byrne, R.M.J. and Johnson-Laird, P.N. (1990a). The use of propositional connectives. Manuscript submitted for publication. University of Wales College of Cardiff. (4)

Byrne, R.M.J. and Johnson-Laird, P.N. (1990b). Models and deduction. In K. Gilhooly, M.T.G. Keane, R. Logie, and G. Erdos (Eds.), *Lines of thought: Reflections on the psychology of thinking* (Vol. 1). London: Wiley. (4)

Byrne, R.M.J. and Johnson-Laird, P.N. (in press). Remembering conclusions we have inferred: what biases reveal. In J-P. Caverni (Ed.), *Cognitive biases.* Amsterdam: North Holland. (6)

Carroll, L. (1895). What the tortoise said to Achilles. *Mind, 4,* 278-280. (10)

Case, R. (1985). A developmentally based approach to the problem of instructional design. In S.F. Chipman, J.W. Segal, and R, Glaser (Eds.), Thinking and learning skills. Vol. 2: Research and open questions. Hillsdale, NJ: Lawrence Erlbaum Associates. (10)

Ceraso, J. and Provitera, A. (1971). Sources of error in syllogistic reasoning. *Cognitive Psychology, 2,* 400-410. (6)

Chapman, L.J. and Chapman, A.P. (1959). Atmosphere effect re-examined. *Journal of Experimental Psychology, 58,* 220-226. (6)

Charniak, E. and McDermott, D. (1985). *Introduction to artificial intelligence.* Reading, MA: Addison-Wesley. (2)

Cheng, P.W. and Holyoak, K.J. (1985). Pragmatic reasoning schemas. *Cognitive Psychology, 17,* 391-416. (2, 4)

Cheng, P.W. and Holyoak, K.J. (1989). On the natural selection of reasoning theories. *Cognition, 33,* 285-313. (4)

Cheng, P.W., Holyoak, K.J., Nisbett, R.E., and Oliver, L.M. (1986). Pragmatic versus syntactic approaches to training deductive reasoning. *Cognitive Psychology, 18,* 293-328. (4)

Cherniak, C. (1986). *Minimal rationality.* Cambridge, MA: MIT Press. (10)

Chomsky, N. (1959). On certain formal properties of grammars. *Information and Control, 2,* 137-167. (9)

Chomsky, N. (1965). *Aspects of the theory of syntax,* Cambridge, MA: MIT Press. (2)

Chomsky, N. (1981). *Lectures on government and binding.* Dordrecht: Foris. (2)

Chrostowski, J.J. and Griggs, R.A. (1985). The effects of problem content, instructions, and verbalization procedure on Wason's selection task. *Current Psychological Research and Reviews, 4*, 99-107. (4)

Churchland, P.S. (1986). *Neurophilosophy.* Cambridge, MA: MIT Press. (10)

Clark, H.H. (1969). Linguistic processes in deductive reasoning. *Psychological Review, 76*, 387-404. (5)

Clark, H.H. and Clark, E.V. (1977). *Psychology and language: An introduction to psycholinguistics.* New York: Harcourt Brace Jovanovich. (3, 6)

Clocksin, W. and Mellish, C. (1981). *Programming in Prolog.* New York: Springer-Verlag. (2)

Cohen, L.J. (1981). Can human irrationality be experimentally demonstrated? *Behavioral and Brain Sciences, 4*, 317-370. (2)

Cole, M. and Scribner, S. (1974). *Culture and thought: a psychological introduction.* New York: Wiley. (10)

Collins, A. and Michalski, R. (1989). The logic of plausible reasoning: A core theory. *Cognitive Science, 13*, 1-49. (10)

Conan Doyle, A. (1892). *A study in scarlet.* London: Harper. (1)

Cooper, R. (1983). *Quantification and syntactic theory.* Dordrecht: Reidel. (2)

Cosmides, L. (1989). The logic of social exchange: Has natural selection shaped how humans reason? Studies with the Wason selection task. Cognition, 31, 187-276. (4)

Craik, K. (1943). *The nature of explanation.* Cambridge: Cambridge University Press. (10)

Darley, J.M. and Gross, P.H. (1983). A hypothesis-confirming bias in labeling effects. *Journal of Personality and Social Psychology, 44*, 20-33. (10)

DeSoto, L.B., London, M., and Handel, L.S. (1965). Social reasoning and spatial paralogic. *Journal of Personality and Social Psychology, 2*, 513-521. (5)

Dewdney, A.K. (1989). People puzzles: theme and variations. *Scientific American, 260*, 1 (January), 88-91. (2, 8)

Dickstein, L.S. (1975). Effects of instructions and premise order in errors in syllogistic reasoning. *Journal of Experimental Psychology: Human Learning and Memory, 104*, 376-384. (5)

Dickstein, L.S. (1978). The effects of figure on syllogistic reasoning. *Memory and Cognition, 6*, 76-83. (6)

Domarus, von E. (1944). The specific laws of logic in schizophrenia. In J.S. Kasinin (Ed.), *Language and thought in schizophrenia.* Berkeley: University of California Press. (3, 10)

Doyle, J. (1979). A truth maintenance system. *Artificial Intelligence, 12*, 231-272. (1, 10)

Doyle, J. (1982). Automatic deduction: E. Non-monotonic logics. In P.R. Cohen and E.A. Feigenbaum (Eds.), *The handbook of artificial intelligence* (Vol. 3). Los Altos, CA: William Kaufmann, pp. 114-119. (10)

Duda, R., Gaschnig, J., and Hart, P. (1979). Model design in the Prospector consultant system for mineral exploration. In D. Michie (Ed.), *Expert systems in the micro-electronic age.* Edinburgh: Edinburgh University Press. (2)

Dudman, V. H. (1988). Indicative and subjunctive conditionals. *Analysis, 48*, 113-122. (4)

Dunne, P.E. (1988). *The complexity of Boolean networks.* London: Academic Press. (9)

Egan, D.E. and Grimes-Farrow, D.D. (1982). Differences in mental representations spontaneously adopted for reasoning. *Memory and Cognition, 10*, 297-307. (5)

Ehrlich, K. and Johnson-Laird, P.N. (1982). Spatial descriptions and referential continuity. *Journal of Verbal Learning and Verbal Behavior, 21*, 296-306. (5)

Ennis, R.H. (1975). Children's ability to handle Piaget's propositional logic. *Review of Educational Research, 45*, 1-41.

Erickson, J.R. (1974). A set analysis theory of behavior in formal syllogistic reasoning tasks. In R. Solso (Ed.), *Loyola symposium on cognition* (Vol. 2). Hillsdale, NJ: Lawrence Erlbaum Associates. (1, 2, 6)

Etherington, D.W., Borgida, A., Brachman, R.J., and Kautz, H. (1989). Vivid knowledge and tractable reasoning: Preliminary Report. Mimeo, Murray Hill, NJ: AT&T Bell Laboratories. (2)

Evans, J.St.B.T (1972). Interpretation and "matching bias" in a reasoning task. *Quarterly Journal of Experimental Psychology, 24*, 193-199. (4)

Evans, J.St.B.T. (1977a). Toward a statistical theory of reasoning. *Quarterly Journal of Experimental Psychology, 29A*, 297-306. (2)

Evans, J.St.B.T. (1977b). Linguistic factors in reasoning. *Quarterly Journal of Experimental Psychology, 29*, 297-306. (3)

Evans, J.St.B.T. (1982). *The psychology of deductive reasoning.* London: Routledge & Kegan Paul. (1, 2, 3)

Evans, J.St.B.T. (1984). Heuristic and analytic processes in reasoning. *British Journal of Psychology, 75*, 451-468. (2)

Evans, J.St.B.T. (1987). Reasoning. In H. Beloff and A.M. Colman, A.M. (Eds.), *Psychological Survey, 6*, 74-93. (2, 3, 4)

Evans, J.St.B.T. (1989). *Bias in human reasoning: Causes and consequences.* Hove, UK: Lawrence Erlbaum Associates. (4)

Evans, J.St.B.T., Barston, J.L., and Pollard, P. (1983). On the conflict between logic and belief in syllogistic reasoning. *Memory and Cognition, 11*, 295-306. (6)

Evans, J.St.B.T. and Beck, M.A. (1981). Directionality and temporal factors in conditional reasoning. *Current Psychological Research, 1*, 111-120. (3)

Evans, J.St.B.T, and Lynch, J.S. (1973). Matching bias in the selection task. *British Journal of Psychology, 64*, 391-397. (4)

Evans, J.St.B.T. and Newstead, S.E. (1980). A study of disjunctive reasoning. *Psychological Research, 41*, 373-388. (3)

Evans-Pritchard, E.E. (1937). *Witchcraft: Oracles and magic among the Azande.* Oxford: Oxford University Press. (10)

Falmagne, R.J. (1980). The development of logical competence. In R.H. Kluwe and M. Spada (Eds.), *Developmental models of thinking.* New York: Academic Press. (10)

Feigenbaum, E.A., Buchanan, B.G., and Lederberg, J. (1979). On generality and problem solving: a case study using the DENDRAL program. In D. Michie (Ed.), *Expert systems in the micro-electronic age.* Edinburgh: Edinburgh University Press. (2)

Feigenbaum, E.A. and McCorduck, P. (1984). *The fifth generation: Artificial intelligence and Japan's computer challenge to the world.* London: Pan Books. (2)

Fillenbaum, S. (1977). Mind your p's and q's: The role of content and context in some uses of *and, or,* and *if.* In G.H. Bower (Ed.), *Psychology of learning and motivation* (Vol. 11). New York: Academic Press. (1)

Finnegan, R. and Horton, R. (1973). *Modes of thought: Essays on thinking in Western and Non-Western societies.* London: Faber and Faber. (10)

Flavell, J.H. (1979). Metacognition and cognitive monitoring: A new area of cognitive-developmental inquiry. *American Psychologist, 34*, 906-911. (2)

Fodor, J.A. (1980). Fixation of belief and concept acquisition. In M. Piattelli-Palmarini (Ed.), *Language and learning: The debate between Jean Piaget and Noam Chomsky.* London: Routledge & Kegan Paul. (2, 10)

Fodor, J.D. (1982). The mental representation of quantifiers. In S. Peters and E. Saarinen (Eds.), *Processes, beliefs, and questions.* Dordrecht: Reidel. (7)

Ford, M. (1985). Review of "Mental models". *Language, 61*, 897-903. (2, 6)

Frege, G. (1884/1959). *The foundations of arithmetic.* Oxford: Basil Blackwell. (2)

Fujimura, K. (1913/1978). *The Tokyo puzzles*. New York: Scribner. (8)

Galotti, K.M. (1989). Approaches to studying formal and everyday reasoning. *Psychological Bulletin, 105*, 331-351. *(10)*

Galotti, K.M., Baron, J., and Sabini, J.P. (1986). Individual differences in syllogistic reasoning: deduction rules or mental models? *Journal of Experiment Psychology: General, 115*, 16-25. (10)

Gazdar, G., Klein, E., Pullum, G., and Sag, I. (1985). *Generalized phrase structure grammar*. Cambridge, MA: Harvard University Press. Oxford: Basil Blackwell. (9)

Gelernter, H. (1963). Realization of a geometry theorem-proving machine. In E.A. Feigenbaum and J. Feldman (Eds.), *Computers and thought*. New York: McGraw-Hill. (2)

Gentner, D. (1989). The mechanisms of analogical learning. In S. Vosniadou and A. Ortony (Eds.), *Similarity and analogical reasoning*. Cambridge: Cambridge University Press. (10)

Gentzen, G. (1935/1969). Investigations into logical deduction. In M.E. Szabo (Ed. and trans.), *The collected papers of Gerhard Gentzen*. Amsterdam: North-Holland. (1)

Gimpel, J.F., (1965). A method of producing a Boolean function having an arbitrarily described prime implicant table, *IEEE Transactions on Computing, 14*, 484-488. (9)

Girotto, V. and Legrenzi, P. (1989). Mental representation and hypothetico-deductive reasoning: The case of the THOG problem. *Psychological Research, 51*, 129-135. (3)

Goffman, E. (1959). *The presentation of self in everyday life*. N.Y. Doubleday. (8)

Goldman, A.I. (1986). *Epistemology and cognition*. Cambridge, MA: Harvard University Press. (2)

Goodman, N. (1947). The problem of counterfactual conditionals. *Journal of Philosophy, 44*, 113-128. (4)

Grice, H.P. (1975). Logic and conversation. In P. Cole and J.L. Morgan (Eds.), *Syntax and semantics. Vol. 3: Speech acts*. New York: Seminar Press. (1, 2, 4)

Griggs, R.A. (1983). The role of problem content in the selection task and in the THOG problem. In J.St.B.T. Evans (Ed.), *Thinking and reasoning: Psychological approaches*. London: Routledge & Kegan Paul. (4)

Griggs, R.A. (1984). Memory cueing and instructional effects on Wason's selectional task. *Current Psychological Research and Reviews, 3*, 3-10. (4)

Griggs, R.A. and Cox, J.R. (1982). The elusive thematic-materials effect in Wason's selection task. *British Journal of Psychology, 73*, 407-420. (4)

Griggs, R.A. and Newstead, S.E. (1982). The role of problem structure in a deductive reasoning task. *Journal of Experimental Psychology: Language, Memory, and Cognition, 8*, 297-307. (3)

Guyote, M.J. and Sternberg, R.J. (1981). A transitive-chain theory of syllogistic reasoning. *Cognitive Psychology, 13*, 461-525. (2, 6)

Hagert, G. (1983). *Report of the Uppsala Programming methodology and artificial intelligence laboratory*. (5, 10)

Hagert, G. (1984). Modeling mental models: Experiments in cognitive modeling of spatial reasoning. In T. O'Shea (Ed.), *Advances in artificial intelligence*. Amsterdam: North-Holland. (5)

Harman, G. (1972). Deep structure as logical form. In D. Davidson and G. Harman (Eds.), *Semantics of natural language*. Dordrecht: Reidel. (2)

Harman, G. (1986). *Change in view: Principles of reasoning*. Cambridge, MA: Bradford Books, MIT Press. (10)

Harper, W.L., Stalnaker, R., and Pearce, G. (Eds.) (1981). *Ifs: Conditionals, belief, decision, chance, and time*. Dordrecht: Reidel. (4)

Haugeland, J. (1985). *Artificial intelligence: The very idea.* Cambridge, MA: MIT Press. (2)

Hayes, P. (1977). In defense of logic. *Proceedings of the Fifth International Joint Conference on Artificial Intelligence,* 559-565. (2)

Henle, M. (1962). The relation between logic and thinking. *Psychological Review, 69,* 366-378. (2)

Henle, M. (1978). Foreword to Revlin, R. and Mayer, R.E. (Eds.), *Human reasoning.* Washington, DC: Winston. (2)

Henle, M. and Michael, M. (1956). The influence of atitudes on syllogistic reasoning. *Journal of Social Psychology, 44,* 115-127. (6)

Hewitt, C. (1971). PLANNER: a language for proving theorems in robots. *Proceedings of the Second Joint Conference on Artificial Intelligence.* (2)

Hintikka, J. (1955). Form and content in quantification theory. *Acta Philosophica Fennica, VIII,* 7-55. (1)

Hitch, G.J. and Halliday, M.S. (1983). Working memory in children. *Philosophical Transactions of the Royal Society of London, Series B, 302,* 325-340. (10)

Hobbes, T. (1651/1968). *Leviathan.* London: Penguin Books. (1)

Hofstadter, D.R. (1985). *Metamagical themas: Questing for the essence of mind and pattern.* New York: Basic Books. (4)

Hofstadter, D.R. & Dennett, D.C. (1981). *The mind's I: Fantasies and reflection on self and soul.* London: Harvester. (2)

Holland, J., Holyoak, K.J., Nisbett, R.E., and Thagard, P. (1986). *Induction: Processes of inference, learning, and discovery.* Cambridge, MA: Bradford Books, MIT Press. (10)

Hollis, M. (1970). Reason and ritual. In B.R. Wilson (Ed.), *Rationality.* Oxford: Basil Blackwell. pp. 221-239. (10)

Hollis, M. and Lukes, S. (1982). *Rationality and relativism.* Oxford: Basil Blackwell. (10)

Holyoak, K.J. and Thagard, P. (1989). Analogical mapping by constraint satisfaction. *Cognitive Science, 13,* 295-355. (10)

Hornstein, N. (1984). *Logic as grammar: An approach to meaning in language.* Cambridge, MA: Bradford Books, MIT Press. (2)

Hunter, I.M.L. (1957). The solving of three-term series problems. *British Journal of Psychology, 48,* 286-298. (5, 6)

Huttenlocher, J. (1968). Constructing spatial images: a strategy in reasoning. *Psychological Review, 75,* 286-298. (5)

Inder, R. (1987). *Computer simulation of syllogism solving using restricted mental models.* PhD. Thesis, Cognitive Studies, Edinburgh University. (2, 6, 10)

Inhelder, B. and Piaget, J. (1958). *The growth of logical thinking from childhood to adolescence.* London: Routledge & Kegan Paul. (2)

Inhelder, B. and Piaget, J. (1964). *The early growth of logic in the child: Classification and seriation.* New York: Harper and Row. (10)

Jackendoff, R. (1972). *Semantic interpretation in generative grammar.* Cambridge, MA: MIT Press. (2)

Jackendoff, R. (1988). Exploring the form of information in the dynamic unconscious. In M.J. Horowitz (Ed.), *Psychodynamics and cognition.* Chicago: University of Chicago Press. (3, 10)

Jackson, F. (1987). *Conditionals.* Oxford: Basil Blackwell. (4)

Jackson, S.L. and Griggs, R.A. (1990). The elusive pragmatic reasoning schemas effect. *Quarterly Journal of Experimental Psychology, 42A,* 353-373. (4)

James, W. (1890). *The principles of psychology* (Vol. 2). New York: Holt. (5, 6)

Janis, I. and Frick, P. (1943). The relationship between attitudes towards conclusions and errors of judging logical validity of syllogisms. *Journal of Experimental Psychology, 33,* 73-77. (6)

Jeffrey, R. (1981). *Formal logic: Its scope and limits.* (2nd Ed.). New York: McGraw-Hill. (1)

Johnson-Laird, P.N. (1970). The interpretation of quantified sentences. In G.B. Flores d'Arcais and W.J.M. Levelt (Eds.), *Advances in psycholinguistics.* Amsterdam: North-Holland. (2)

Johnson-Laird, P.N. (1972). The three-term series problem. *Cognition, 1,* 57-82. (5)

Johnson-Laird, P.N. (1975). Models of deduction. In R.J. Falmagne (Ed.), *Reasoning: Representation and process in children and adults.* Hillsdale, NJ: Lawrence Erlbaum Associates. (2, 6)

Johnson-Laird, P.N. (1978). The meaning of modality. *Cognitive Science, 2,* 17-26. (4)

Johnson-Laird, P.N. (1983). *Mental models: Towards a cognitive science of language, inference and consciousness.* Cambridge: Cambridge University Press. (1, 2, 4, 5, 6, 7, 10)

Johnson-Laird, P.N. (1986). Conditionals and mental models. In E.C. Traugott, A. ter Meulen, J.S. Reilly, and C.A. Ferguson (Eds.), *On conditionals.* Cambridge: Cambridge University Press. (4)

Johnson-Laird, P.N. (1988a). A taxonomy of thinking. In R.J. Sternberg and E.E. Smith (Eds.), *The psychology of human thought.* New York: Cambridge University Press. (1)

Johnson-Laird, P.N. (1988b). *The computer and the mind: An introduction to cognitive science.* London: Fontana. (2)

Johnson-Laird, P.N. (1988c). Freedom and constraint in creativity. In R.J. Sternberg (Ed.), *The nature of creativity: Contemporary psychological perspectives.* Cambridge: Cambridge University Press. (10)

Johnson-Laird, P.N. (1989). *Propositional reasoning: An algorithm for deriving parsimonious conclusions.* Manuscript submitted for publication. Princeton University, New Jersey. (9)

Johnson-Laird, P.N. (in press). The development of reasoning. In P. Bryant and G. Butterworth (Eds.), *Causes of development.* Hemel Hempstead, Herts.: Harvester-Wheatsheaf. (10)

Johnson-Laird, P.N. and Anderson, T. (1989). *Common-sense inference.* Unpublished manuscript, Princeton University, New Jersey. (10)

Johnson-Laird, P.N. and Bara, B. (1984). Syllogistic inference. *Cognition, 16,* 1-61. (2, 6, 10)

Johnson-Laird, P.N. and Byrne, R.M.J. (1989). *Only* reasoning. *Journal of Memory and Language, 28,* 313-330. (6)

Johnson-Laird, P.N. and Byrne, R.M.J. (1990). Meta-logical puzzles: Knights, knaves and Rips. *Cognition, 36,* 69-84. (8)

Johnson-Laird, P.N., Byrne, R.M.J., and Schaeken, W. (1990). *Reasoning by model: The case of propositional inference.* Unpublished manuscript.Princeton University, New Jersey. (3)

Johnson-Laird, P.N., Byrne, R.M.J., and Tabossi, P. (1989). Reasoning by model: The case of multiple quantification. *Psychological Review, 96,* 658-673. (7)

Johnson-Laird, P.N., Legrenzi, P., and Legrenzi, Sonino, M.S. (1972). Reasoning and a sense of reality. *British Journal of Psychology, 63,* 395-400. (4)

Johnson-Laird, P.N., Oakhill, J.V., and Bull, D. (1986). Children's syllogistic reasoning. *Quaterly Journal of Experimental Psychology, 38A,* 35-58. (10)

Johnson-Laird, P.N. and Steedman, M. (1978). The psychology of syllogisms. *Cognitive Psychology, 10,* 64-99. (6)

Johnson-Laird, P.N. and Tagart, J. (1969). How implication is understood. *American Journal of Psychology, 82,* 367-373. (4)

Johnson-Laird, P.N. and Wason, P.C. (1970). Insight into a logical relation. *Quarterly Journal of Experimental Psychology, 22*, 49-61. (4)

Kahneman, D. and Miller, D. (1986). Norm theory: Comparing reality to its alternatives. *Psychological Review, 93*, 136-153. (4)

Kahneman, D., Slovic, P., and Tversky, A. (Eds.) (1982). *Judgement under uncertainty: Heuristics and biases*. Cambridge: Cambridge University Press. (10)

Kamp, J.A.W. (1981). A theory of truth and semantic representation. In J. Groenendijk, T. Janssen, and M. Stokhof, (Eds.), *Formal methods in the study of language*. Amsterdam: Mathematical Centre Tracts. (2)

Kant, I. (1800/1974). *Logic*. Trans. R.S. Hartman and W. Schwarz. New York: Bobbs-Merrill. (2)

Karnaugh, M., (1953). The map method for synthesis of combinatorial logic circuits, *Transactions of AIEE, 72*, 593-598. (9)

Kaufmann, H. and Goldstein, S. (1967). The effects of emotional value of conclusions upon distortions in syllogistic reasoning. *Psychonomic Science, 7*, 367-368. (6)

Keane, M.T.G. (1985). On drawing analogies when solving problems: A theory and test of solution generation in an anolgical problem solving task. *British Journal of Psychology. 76*, 449-458.

Keane, M.T.G. (1987). On retrieving analogues when solving problems. *Quarterly Journal of Experimental Psychology, 39A*, 28-41. (10)

Keane, M.T.G. (1988). *Analogical problem solving*. Chichester: Ellis Horwood. New York: Wiley. (10)

Keane, M.T.G. (in press). *Analogical thinking*. Manuscript in preparation. Hove, UK: Lawrence Erlbaum Associates. (10)

Keane, M.T.G., Byrne, R.M.J., and Johnson-Laird, P.N. (1990). *On the nature of arguments*. Manuscript in preparation. University of Dublin, Trinity College. (10)

Keenan, E.L. (1971). Quantifier structures in English. *Foundations of Language, 7*, 255-284. (2, 3, 6)

Kempson, R.M. (1988). Logical form: the grammar cognition interface. *Journal of Linguistics, 24*, 393-431. (2)

Klaczynski, P.A., Gelfand, H., and Reese, H.W. (1989). Transfer of conditional reasoning: Effects of explanations and initial problem types. *Memory and Cognition, 17*, 208-220. (4)

Klayman, J. and Ha, Y-W. (1987). Confirmation, disconfirmation and information in hypothesis testing. *Psychological Review, 94*, 211-228. (4)

Kneale, W. and Kneale, M. (1962). *The development of logic*. Oxford: Clarendon Press. (1, 8)

Kotovsky, K. and Simon, H.A. (1989). What makes some problems really hard: Explorations in the problem space of difficulty. *Cognitive Psychology. 22*, 143-183. (8)

Kowalski, R.A. (1979). *A logic for problem solving*. Amsterdam: Elsevier. (2)

Kunda, Z. (in press). The case for motivated reasoning. *Psychological Bulletin*. (10)

Lakoff, G. (1970). Linguistics and natural logic. *Synthese, 22*, 151-271. (2)

Leech, G.N. (1969). *Towards a semantic description of English*. London: Longmans. (2)

Legrenzi, P. (1970). Relations between language and reasoning about deductive rules. In G.B. Flores D'Arcais and W.J.M. Levelt (Eds.), *Advances in psycholinguistics*. Amsterdam: North-Holland. (3)

Leibniz, G. (1666/1966). Dissertation on the Combinatorial Art. In G.H.R. Parkinson (Ed. and trans.), *Logical papers: A selection*. Oxford: Clarendon Press (1)

Leibniz, G. (1765/1949). *New essays concerning human understanding*. Trans. A.G. Langley. LaSalle, IL: Open Court. (2)

Levesque, H.J. (1986). Making believers out of computers. *Artificial Intelligence, 30*, 81-108. (2, 3, 6, 10)

Levy-Bruhl, L. (1910/1966). *How natives think.* New York: Washington Square Press. (3, 10)

Lewis, D.K. (1973). *Counterfactuals.* Oxford: Basil Blackwell. (4)

Lewis, D.K. (1976). Probabilities of conditionals and conditional probabilities II. *Philosophical Review, 95,* 581-589. (4)

Lindsay, R., Buchanan, B.G., Feigenbaum, E.A., and Lederberg, J. (1980). *Applications of artificial intelligence for chemical inference: The DENDRAL project.* New York: McGraw-Hill. (2)

Luria, A.R. (1976). *Cognitive development: Its cultural and social foundations.* Cambridge, MA: Harvard University Press. (10)

Macnamara, J. (1986). *A border dispute: The place of logic in psychology.* Cambridge, MA: Bradford Books, MIT Press. (2, 10)

Madruga, J. A. G. (1984). Procesos de error en el razonamiento silogistico: doble procesamiento y estrategia de verificacion por. In M. Carretero and J.A.G Madruga (Eds.), *Lecturas de psicologia del pensamiento.* Madrid: Alianza. (6)

Mani, K. and Johnson-Laird, P.N. (1982). The mental representation of spatial descriptions. *Memory and Cognition, 10,* 181-187.(5)

Manktelow, K.I. and Evans, J.St. B.T. (1979). Facilitation of reasoning by realism: Effect or non-effect? *British Journal of Psychology, 70,* 477-488. (4)

Manktelow, K.I. and Over, D.E. (1987). Reasoning and rationality. *Mind and Language, 2,* 199-219. (4)

Markovits, H. (1984). Awareness of the "possible" as a mediator of formal thinking in conditional reasoning problems. *British Journal of Psychology, 75,* 367-376. (4)

Markovits, H. (1985). Incorrect conditional reasoning among adults: Competence or performance? *British Journal of Psychology, 76,* 241-247. (4)

Markovits, H. and Nantel, G. (1989). The belief-bias effect in the production and evaluation of logical conclusions. *Memory and Cognition, 17,* 11-17. (6)

Marr, D. (1982). *Vision: A computational investigation into the human representation and processing of visual information.* San Francisco: W.H. Freeman. (2, 10)

May, R. (1985). *Logical form: Its structure and derivation.* Cambridge, MA: MIT Press. (2)

McCarthy, J. (1980). Circumscription—a form of non-monotonic reasoning. *Artificial Intelligence, 13,* 27-39. (10)

McCarthy, J. (1986). Applications of circumscription to formalizing common-sense knowledge. *Artifical Intelligence, 28,* 89-116. (10)

McCluskey, E.J. (1956). Minimization of Boolean functions, *Bell System Technical Journal, 35,* 1417-1444. (9)

McDermott, D. (1987). A critique of pure reason. *Computational Intelligence, 3,* 151-160. (1)

McDermott, D. and Doyle, J. (1980). Non-monotonic logic. I. *Artificial Intelligence, 13,* 41-72. (2, 10)

McGinn, C. (1989). *Mental content.* Oxford: Basil Blackwell.

Michie, D. (Ed.) (1979). *Expert systems in the micro-electronic age.* Edinburgh: Edinburgh University Press. (2)

Mill, J.S. (1843). *A system of logic.* London: Longman. (2)

Miller, G.A. and Johnson-Laird, P.N. (1976). *Language and perception.* Cambridge: Cambridge University Press. Cambridge, MA: Harvard University Press. (4, 5)

Minsky, M. (1975). Frame-system theory. In R.C. Schank and B.L. Webber (Eds.), *Theoretical issues in natural language processing.* Pre-prints of a conference at MIT.

Rep. in P.N. Johnson-Laird and P.C. Wason (Eds.), *Thinking: Readings in cognitive science*. Cambridge: Cambridge University Press. (10)

Moore, R.C. (1982). Automatic deduction: A. Overview. In P.R. Cohen and E.A. Feigenbaum (Eds.), *The handbook of artificial intelligence* (Vol. 3). Los Altos, CA: William Kaufmann. (9)

Moore, R.C. (1985). Semantical considerations on nonmonotonic logic. *Artificial Intelligence, 25*, 75-94. (10)

Newell, A. (1981). Reasoning, problem solving and decision processes: The problem space as a fundamental category. In R. Nickerson (Ed.), *Attention and performance* (Vol. 8). Hillsdale, NJ: Lawrence Erlbaum Associates. (2, 6)

Newell, A. (1990). *Unified theories in cognition.* Cambridge, MA: Harvard University Press. (2, 10)

Newell, A., Shaw, J.C., and Simon, H.A. (1963). Empirical explorations with the Logic Theory Machine. In E.A. Feigenbaum, and J. Feldman (Eds.), *Computers and thought*. New York: Mcgraw-Hill. (2)

Newell, A. and Simon, H.A. (1972). *Human problem solving*. Englewood Cliffs, NJ: Prentice-Hall. (2)

Newstead, S.E. (1990). Conversion in syllogistic reasoning. In K. Gilhooly, M.T.G. Keane, R. Logie, and G. Erdos (Eds.), *Lines of thought: Reflections on the psychology of thinking* (Vol. 1). London: Wiley. (6)

Newstead, S.E. and Griggs, R.A. (1983). The language and thought of disjunction. In J.St.B.T. Evans (Ed.), *Thinking and reasoning: Psychological approaches*. London: Routledge & Kegan Paul. (3)

Newstead, S.E., Manktelow, K.I., and Evans, J.St.B.T. (1982). The role of imagery in the representation of linear orderings. *Current Psychological Research, 2*, 21-32. (5)

Newstead, S.E., Pollard, P., and Griggs, R.A. (1986). Response bias in relational reasoning. *Bulletin of the Psychonomic Society, 24*, 95-98. (5)

Niemalä, I. (1988). Decision procedures for autoepistemic logic. In E. Lusk and R. Overbeek (Eds.), *Ninth international conference on automated deduction.* Berlin: Springer-Verlag. pp. 675-684. (9)

Nisbett, R.E. and Ross, L. (1980). *Human inference: strategies and shortcomings of social judgement.* Englewood Cliffs NJ.: Prentice Hall. (10)

Oakhill, J.V. and Johnson-Laird, P.N. (1985a). Rationality, memory and the search for counterexamples. *Cognition, 20*, 79-94. (4)

Oakhill, J.V. and Johnson-Laird, P.N. (1985b). The effects of belief on the spontaneous production of syllogistic conclusions. *Quarterly Journal of Experimental Psychology, 37A*, 553-569. (6)

Oakhill, J.V., Johnson-Laird, P.N., and Garnham, A. (1989). Believability and syllogistic reasoning. *Cognition, 31*, 117-140. (6)

O'Brien, F. (1939/1967). *At swim-two-birds*. Harmondsworth, Middx.: Penguin Books. (Book dedication.)

Oden, G.C. (1987). Concept knowledge and thought. *Annual Review of Psychology, 38*, 203-227. (2)

Ohlsson, S. (1981). *Model-based vs. propositional inference in a spatial reasoning task*. Mimeo, Department of Psychology, University of Stockholm. (5, 10)

Ohlsson, S. (1984). Induced strategy shifts in spatial reasoning. *Acta Psychologica, 57*, 46-67. (5)

Olson, D. R. and Bialystok, E. (1983). *Spatial cognition: The structure and development of mental representations of spatial relations*. Hillsdale, N.J.: Lawrence Erlbaum Associates. (5)

Oppacher, F. and Suen, E. (1985). Controlling deduction with proof condensation and heuristics. In J.H. Siekman (Ed.), *Eighth international conference on automated deduction.* New York: Springer-Verlag. (1)

Orasanu, J. and Scribner, S. (1982). The development of verbal reasoning: pragmatic, schematic, and operational aspects. In W. Frawley (Ed.), *Linguistics and literacy.* New York: Plenum. (10)

Osherson, D. (1975). Logic and models of logical thinking. In R.J. Falmagne (Ed.), *Reasoning: Representation and process in children and adults.* Hillsdale, NJ: Lawrence Erlbaum Associates. (2, 3, 10)

Parsons, C. (1960). Inhelder and Piaget's "The growth of logical thinking" II: A logician's viewpoint. *British Journal of Psychology, 51,* 75-84.

Partee, B.H. (1975). Montague grammar and transformational grammar. *Linguistic Inquiry, 6,* 203-300. (7)

Partee, B.H. (1979). Semantics—mathematics or psychology? In Bäuerle, R., Egli, U., and von Stechow, A. (Eds.), *Semantics from different points of view.* Berlin: Springer-Verlag. (2)

Peirce, C.S. (1931-1958). *Collected papers* (8 Vols.). Edited by C. Hartshorne, P. Weiss, and A. Burks (Eds.). Cambridge, MA: Harvard University Press. (10)

Pelletier, F.J. (1986). Seventy-five problems for testing automatic theorem provers. *Journal of Automated Reasoning, 2,* 191-216. (9)

Perkins, D.N., Allen, R., and Hafner, J. (1983). Difficulties in everyday reasoning. In W. Maxwell (Ed.), *Thinking: An interdisciplinary report.* Philadelphia: The Franklin Institute Press. (10)

Piaget, J. (1953). *Logic and psychology.* Manchester: Manchester University Press. (2)

Polk, T.A. and Newell, A. (1988). Modeling human syllogistic reasoning in Soar. In *Tenth annual conference of the Cognitive Science Society,* 181-187. Hillsdale, NJ: Lawrence Erlbaum Associates. (2, 6, 10)

Pollock, J. (1989). *How to build a person: A prolegomenon.* Cambridge, MA: MIT Bradford Books. (10)

Polya, G. (1957). *How to solve it* (2nd Edn.). New York: Doubleday. (2)

Potts, G.R. (1978). The role of inference in memory for real and artificial information. In R. Revlin and R.E. Mayer (Eds.), *Human reasoning.* New York: Wiley. (5)

Prawitz, D. (1965). *Natural deduction: A proof-theoretical study.* Stockholm: Almqvist & Wiksell. (1)

Pylyshyn, Z.W. (1973). What the mind's eye tells the mind's brain: A critique of mental imagery. *Psychological Bulletin, 80,* 1-24. (2)

Pylyshyn, Z.W. (1981). The imagery debate: Analogue media versus tacit knowledge. In N. Block (Ed.), *Imagery.* Cambridge MA: M.I.T. Press. (2)

Quine, W.V.O. (1952). *Methods of logic.* London: Routledge & Kegan Paul. (4)

Quine, W.V.O. (1955). A way to simplify truth functions. *American Mathematical Monthly, 59,* 521-531. (9)

Reiter, R. (1973). A semantically guided deductive system for automatic theorem-proving. *Proceedings of the third international joint conference on artificial intelligence.* Pp. 41-46. (1, 2, 9)

Reiter, R. (1980). A logic for default reasoning. *Artificial Intelligence, 13,* 81-132. (10)

Revlin, R. and Leirer, Von O. (1978). The effects of personal biases on syllogistic reasoning. In R. Revlin and R.E. Mayer (Eds.), *Human reasoning.* New York: Wiley. (6)

Revlis, R. (1975). Two models of syllogistic reasoning: feature selection and conversion. *Journal of Verbal Learning and Verbal Behavior, 14,* 180-195. (2, 6)

Richardson, J.T.E. (1987). The role of mental imagery in models of transitive inference. *British Journal of Psychology, 78,* 189-203. (5)

Riesbeck, C.K. and Schank, R.C. (1989). *Inside case-based reasoning.* Hillsdale, NJ: Lawrence Erlbaum Associates. (2, 4)

Rips, L.J. (1983). Cognitive processes in propositional reasoning. *Psychological Review,* *90*, 38-71. (2, 3, 10)

Rips, L.J. (1984). Reasoning as a central intellectual ability. In R.J. Sternberg (Ed.), *Advances in the study of human intelligence.* Hillsdale NJ: Lawrence Erlbaum Associates. (2)

Rips, L.J. (1986). Mental muddles. In M. Brand and R.M. Harnish, (Eds.), *Problems in the representation of knowledge and belief.* Tucson: University of Arizona Press. (2, 3, 8)

Rips, L.J. (1989). The psychology of knights and knaves. *Cognition, 31,* 85-116. (8, 10)

Rips, L.J. and Marcus, S.L. (1977). Suppositions and the analysis of conditional sentences. In M.A. Just and P.A. Carpenter (Eds.), *Cognitive processes in comprehension.* Hillsdale, NJ: Lawrence Erlbaum Associates. (4)

Roberge, J.J. (1978). Linguistic and psychometric factors in propositional reasoning. *Quarterly Journal of Experimental Psychology, 30,* 705-716. (3)

Robinson, J.A. (1965). A machine-oriented logic based on the resolution principle. *Journal of the Association for Computing Machinery, 12,* 23-41. (2)

Robinson, J.A. (1979). *Logic: Form and function, the mechanization of deductive reasoning.* Edinburgh: Edinburgh University Press. (1, 9)

Rogers, H. (1967). *Theory of recursive functions and effective computability.* New York: McGraw-Hill. (5)

Rumain, B., Connell, J., and Braine, M.D.S. (1983). Conversational comprehension processes are responsible for reasoning fallacies in children as well as adults: IF is not the Biconditional. *Developmental Psychology, 19,* 471-81. (4)

Rumelhart, D.E. (1989). Towards a microstructural account of human reasoning. In S. Vosniadou and A. Ortony (Eds.), *Similarity and analogical reasoning.* Cambridge: Cambridge University Press. (10)

Rumelhart, D.E. and Norman, D.A. (1981). Analogical processes in learning. In J.R. Anderson (Ed.), *Cognitive skills and their acquisition.* Hillsdale, NJ: Lawrence Erlbaum Associates. (4)

Rumelhart, D.E. and McClelland, J.L. (1986). *Parallel distributed processing: Explorations in the microstructure of cognition, Vol. 1: Foundations.* Cambridge, MA: Bradford Books, MIT. (10)

Russell, J. (1987). Rule-following, mental models, and the developmental view. In M. Chapman and R.A. Dixon (Eds.), *Meaning and the growth of understanding: Wittgenstein's significance for developmental psychology.* New York: Springer-Verlag. (2)

Ryle, G. (1949). *The concept of mind.* London: Hutchinson. (4)

Seuren, P.A.M. (1969). *Operators and nucleus: A contribution to the theory of grammar.* Cambridge: Cambridge University Press. (2)

Shortliffe, E. (1976). *MYCIN: Computer-based medical consultations.* New York: Elsevier. (2)

Simon, H.A. (1982). *Models of bounded rationality* (Vols. 1 and 2). Cambridge, MA: MIT Press. (2)

Smullyan, R.M. (1968). *First-order logic.* New York: Springer-Verlag. (1)

Smullyan, R.M. (1978). *What is the name of this book? The riddle of Dracula and other logical puzzles.* Englewood Cliffs, NJ: Prentice-Hall. (2, 8)

Sperber, D. and Wilson, D. (1986). *Relevance: Communication and cognition.* Oxford: Basil Blackwell. (2, 10)

Spinoza, B. (1677/1949). *Ethics.* Trans. W.H. White and Ed. by J. Gutmann. New York: Hafner. (2)

Stalnaker, R.C. (1968). A theory of conditionals. In N. Rescher (Ed.), *Studies in logical theory.* Oxford: Basil Blackwell. (4)

Stalnaker, R.C. (1981). A defence of conditional excluded middle. In W.L. Harper, R. Stalnaker, and G. Pearce (Eds.), *Ifs: Conditionals, belief, decision, chance, and time.* Dordrecht: Reidel. (4)

Stanfill, C. and Waltz, D. (1986). Toward memory-based reasoning. *Communications of the Association for Computing Machinery, 29,* 1213-1228. (2)

Staudenmayer, H. (1975). Understanding conditional reasoning with meaningful propositions. In R.J. Falmagne (Ed.), *Reasoning: Representation and process in children and adults.* Hillsdale, NJ: Lawrence Erlbaum. (3)

Staudenmayer, H. and Bourne, L.E. (1978). The nature of denied propositions in the conditional reasoning task: Interpretation and learning. In R. Revlin and R.E. Mayer (Eds.), *Human reasoning.* New York: Wiley. (3)

Sternberg, R.J. (1985). *Beyond I.Q.: A triarchic theory of human intelligence.* Cambridge: Cambridge University Press. (5)

Sternberg, R.J. (1988). *The triarchic mind: A new theory of human intelligence.* NY: Viking. (10)

Sternberg, R.J. and Weil, E.M. (1980). An aptitude-strategy interaction in linear syllogistic reasoning. *Journal of Educational Psychology, 72,* 226-239. (5)

Störring, G. (1908). Experimentelle Untersuchungen über einfache Schlussprozesse. *Archiv für die gesamte Psychologie, 11,* 1-27. (10)

Strawson, P.F. (1950). On referring. *Mind, 59,* 320-344. (1)

Tarski, A. (1956). The concept of truth in formalized languages. In A. Tarski *Logic, semantics, metamathematics: Papers from 1923 to 1938.* Oxford: Oxford University Press. (1)

Thagard, P. (1988). *Computational philosophy of science.* Cambridge, MA: M.I.T. Press. (10)

Traugott, E.C., ter Meulen, A. , Reilly, J.S., and Ferguson, C.A. (1986). *On conditionals.* Cambridge: Cambridge University Press. (4)

Tversky, A. and Kahneman, D. (1973). Availability: A heuristic for judging frequency and probability. *Cognitive Psychology, 5,* 207-232. (10)

Valentine, E.R. (1985). The effect of instructions on performance in the Wason selection task. *Current Psychological Research and Reviews, 4,* 214-223. (4)

Wason, P.C. (1959). The processing of positive and negative information. *Quarterly Journal of Experimental Psychology, 11,* 92-107. (3, 6)

Wason, P.C. (1965). The context of plausible denial. *Journal of Verbal Learning and Verbal Behavior, 4,* 7-11. (4)

Wason, P.C. (1966). Reasoning. In B.M. Foss (Ed.), *New horizons in psychology.* Harmondsworth, Middx.: Penguin. (4)

Wason, P.C. (1977). Self-contradictions. In P.N. Johnson-Laird and P.C. Wason (Eds.), *Thinking: Readings in cognitive science.* Cambridge: Cambridge University Press. (3)

Wason, P.C. (1983). Realism and rationality in the selection task. In J.St.B.T. Evans (Ed.), *Thinking and reasoning: Psychological approaches.* London: Routledge & Kegan Paul. (4)

Wason, P.C. and Green, D.W. (1984). Reasoning and mental representation. *Quarterly Journal of Experimental Psychology, 36A,* 597-610. (4)

Wason, P.C. and Johnson-Laird, P.N. (1969). Proving a disjunctive rule. *Quarterly Journal of Experimental Psychology, 21,* 14-20. (4)

Wason, P.C. and Johnson-Laird, P.N. (1972). *Psychology of reasoning: Structure and content.* London: Batsford. Cambridge, MA: Harvard University Press. (1, 2, 3, 4)

Waterman, D.A. and Hayes-Roth, F. (Eds.) (1978). *Pattern directed inference systems*. New York: Academic Press. (2)

Wetherick, N. and Gilhooly, K. (1990). The figural effect in syllogistic reasoning. In K. Gilhooly, M.T.G. Keane, R. Logie, and G. Erdos (Eds.), *Lines of thought: Reflections on the psychology of thinking, Vol. 1*. London: Wiley. (6)

Wilkins, M.C. (1928). The effect of changed material on the ability to do formal syllogistic reasoning. *Archives of Psychology, 16*, 102. (6)

Wilson, B. R., (Ed.) (1970). *Rationality*. Oxford: Basil Blackwell. (10)

Wilson, D. (1975). *Presuppositions and non-truth-functional semantics*. London: Academic Press. (4)

Winston, P.H. (1984). *Artificial intelligence* (2nd Edn.). Massachusetts: Addison-Wesley. (2)

Wittgenstein, L. (1953). *Philosophical investigations*. Trans. by G.E.M. Anscombe. New York: Macmillan. (10)

Woodworth, R.S. and Sells, S.B. (1935). An atmosphere effect in formal syllogistic reasoning. *Journal of Experimental Psychology, 18*, 451-460. (6, 7)

Wos, L. (1988). *Automated reasoning: 33 basic research problems*. Englewood Cliffs, NJ: Prentice-Hall. (9)

Author Index

233

Subject Index